Free Thoughts

on

Religion,

the

Church,

and

National Happiness.

By *B. M.*

The Second Edition.

Revised, corrected, and enlarged, with many Additions by the Author.

L O N D O N:

Printed for Jonh Brotherton, at the
Bible in *Cornhill*. M.DCC.XXIX.

Printing Statement:

Due to the very old age and scarcity of this book, many of the pages may be hard to read due to the blurring of the original text, possible missing pages, missing text and other issues beyond our control.

Because this is such an important and rare work, we believe it is best to reproduce this book regardless of its original condition.

Thank you for your understanding.

THE
PREFACE.

*E*VIL *Custom often fastens an odious signification on words that do not deserve it, and which in justice of speech cannot be used but in a good sense : so bigots, and the* enemies of truth, *would insinuate that* Free Thoughts *must be impious and atheistical, in the same manner as lewd debauchees by the words* good-natur'd lady *would have you understand a whore. That this bugbear has not frighten'd me, Reader, you see ; but that it likewise may not deter you from perusing the following sheets, I shall keep you in no*

A 2 *suspence,*

*sufpence, but in as few words, and as fast
as I can, acquaint you with the design and
argument of them. The whole you will find
divided into twelve chapters.*

*IN the first, I treat of religion in gene-
ral, of deifm and atheifm, both fpeculative
and practical; of chriftians, and to whom we
ought not to deny that name. I demonftrate,
that what is commonly underftood by faith and
believing, is the eafieft part of chriftianity,
in which very few are defective; but that
the moft difficult part of our religion confifts in fubduing our paffions to the love of
GOD, and in obedience to his commands. I
touch upon the wrong notions the vulgar have
concerning thefe matters, as well as the degrees of offences committed to GOD. I fpeak
of fin, and what makes an action fuch. Laftly, I prove from the main doctrine of the gofpel, that chriftians, who are obferving of their
duty, cannot hate others upon any religious
account whatever, and from thence draw a
conclufion conducing to peace and mutual concord.*

IN

IN the second, I urge still further, that the worst of sinners seldom offend for want of faith, and endeavour to prove, that most christians are convinced of their trespasses, and a future state; and that the wishes even of very wicked men are generally virtuous; but that the difficulty they meet with in the real amendment of the heart, being almost unsurmountable, they seek out for an equivalent to rid them of their fears; that this they find in the observance of some of the branches of outward piety and devotion in appearance, altogether foreign to real virtue; that men have all along been encouraged in this delusion by priestcraft; and lastly, that by relying too much on the efficacy of such outward forms, they learn to remove those terrible apprehensions, which wickedness is ever accompany'd with, till they have deceived their consciences into a perfect ignorance of themselves. To render this important truth the more useful and conspicuous to every reader, I have illustrated what I have said in three very different characters, with which I conclude that chapter.

A 3

IN

IN the third, rites and ceremonies are treated of, relating to publick worship, and some differences touch'd upon between our national church, and those who diffent from it. Throughout the whole, my aim is peace and union, and my only endeavour, if not to reconcile them, at least to remove the ill opinion which the clergy on both fides have taught them to entertain of one another, and which I demonstrate to them, is much worse than either of them deserve. The reader will observe, that in my addresses to both parties, as I speak to either, I am rather leaning on the fide of their adversaries, which I have done for no other reason, but that I thought it the duty of a man, who hopes for success in a mediation between two enemies. I end with setting forth the benefit that will accrue to both parties from making use of the healing maxims I propose.

IN the fourth, I speak of religious mysteries in general, and more particularly of the Trinity, shew the difference between knowledge and belief, and touch on the divinity of JESUS CHRIST, and the HOLY GHOST.

I deny

I deny nothing of what our church asserts concerning this mystery, nor yet judge uncharitably of others for refusing to comply with every syllable of the Athanasian creed. I touch on the credulity of the ignorant, I dissuade from dogmatising in matters of faith, and the inhumanity of imposing upon one another creeds of human invention: Since the holy scripture must be the sole rule of faith, and every one at last must judge for himself. These sentiments I confirm with quotations from two eminent prelates of our church. I wind up all with a plain distinction between what is above reason, and what is against it ; to convince of their errors, first, the vain and arrogant philosopher, who, puff'd up with his own sufficiency, has too narrow a thought of GOD's omnipotence, and rejects mysteries for no other reason, than that they surpass his understanding ; secondly, the priest-ridden superstitious bigot, who shuts his eyes to common sense, and stupidly imagines, that he can believe plain contradictions.

THE fifth, I open with a discourse on the will, and examine into the freedom of it : I touch upon predestination, and the grand ob-

A 4.   *jection*

jection that lies against it : I set down the system of the two principles, dip into the controversies concerning the origin of evil, and make remarks on several answers of the fathers to the Manichees, and the argument of Epicurus against Providence. I shew on the one hand, that a supposition of the most absolute free-will, such as the Socinians hold, cannot solve the difficulty it should remove; and on the other, how hard it is for a predestinarian, who has only natural reason to assist him, to avoid making GOD the author of sin : from thence I conclude, that in the affair of free-will and predestination, one of the greatest mysteries of the christian religion is invelop'd, and therefore is a fitter subject for the exercise of humility and toleration, than it is for disputes and animosities. To corroborate this opinion I refer to St. Paul, who seems to assert predestination in the plainest, and states the objection against it in the harshest, manner, without so much as endeavouring to answer it, or solving the difficulty any other way than by his humble resignation to the unsearchable depth of the divine wisdom. I exhort men to follow the example of the apostle, and cease to contend

for

for what neither party can demonstrate, and leave off with a bright example of moderation, which I recommend to all clergymen.

IN the sixth, I enquire into the cause of the affection and esteem the vulgar have for temples abstract from religion. I prove, that as their incapacity hinders them from being affected with true holiness and spirituality, they are forc'd to transfer the respectful awe which their superstition fills them with, on things visible, and such as fall under the senses, and that consequently churches must be the chief object of their adoration. I speak of the use that has been made of this frailty of the vulgar in all religions: I take notice of the various significations of the word Church, and the benefit of knowing them. I touch on the miraculous manner after which the gospel was propagated in the time of the apostles, and the different methods their successors have made use of since. I illustrate the heroism of the clergy with several examples from history, that evidence the vast prowess that has been express'd, and the great hazards that have been run for the advancement of the temporal grandeur and authority

thority of the church ; and lasty, I demonstrate that the protestant clergy have not discover'd less fondness for power and dominion,
since the reformation, than the Roman priests,
whom they separated from chiefly upon that
account.

IN the seventh, I observe, that to get
wealth, and raise the worldly greatness of
the church, the policy of the clergy has not
been inferiour to their courage. I speak of
the wrong and impious use to which they
perverted, for their own gain, what the gospel teaches concerning the soul's immortality,
their zeal and inveteracy against human learning, in order to breed ignorance and superstition ; their anger and indignation against
those of their own profession, who at any
time attempted to undeceive the people.   I
give examples of the church's strict adherence to her friends, and her inviolable esteem to those who promote her temporal interest ; and her resentment, and the violence
of her hatred against all, even the best of
men, who question her authority, or touch
upon the . failings of the clergy. I relate
what popes are requir'd to be, and give
                                                      some

some instances to prove, that the cause of religion at Rome is postpon'd to the temporal interest of the church; I mention other branches of priestcraft, pious frauds, calumnies and downright falsities, which the fathers, to promote the worldly grandeur of the church, have made use of in refuting the heathens, and conclude with a remarkable instance of insincerity, which protestants have been guilty of in their controversies against the papists.

IN the eighth, I treat of schism, and the cause of it, and relate several extravagancies of ancient hereticks, and others, since the reformation: I hint at the nuisances that were removed from the church by the reformation, and particularly the celibacy of the clergy, and I speak of the ridiculous pretensions to chastity that have been made by the church of Rome. I assert, that these very nuisances were the tools, by the help of which the church of Rome had triumph'd over all the schisms and heresies till the reformation, and that the protestant clergy, as soon as schisms arose among themselves, perceiv'd what they had parted with, were sorry ry for it, and have been labouring ever since to find out equivalents for what they lost. I speak of the diffenters, and the quarrels of the proteſtant clergy with one another, and their averſion to a re-union, and thoſe who have endeavour'd to procure it; and I prove, from their own teſtimonies, how unfairly they have dealt with one another: I point at an eaſy remedy to prevent ſchiſms, or at leaſt the miſchiefs that are occaſioned by them, and end with the imputations and ſlander, which the orthodox and diſſenters in England fling at each other.

IN the ninth, I prove from the temper of the clergy, ſhewn in the 'foregoing chapter, that a ſchiſm once broach'd, is not to be cur'd but by death, baniſhment, and an utter extirpation of the ſchiſmaticks, and therefore plead for toleration, but aſſert, that the national church in every country is for perſecution. This I prove to be true by examples and quotations not only of the great ſticklers to the papal authority, and other Roman catholicks, but likewiſe of the Lutherans and Calviniſts, and all clergymen, when oppos'd and in power. I prove, that national churches

allow

allow no schismaticks to be sincere in their opinions, whatever they suffer for it: That those who have been persecuted, as soon as their sect is uppermost, and they are able, treat others who differ from them, just as they had been treated before themselves; that the reasons and arguments for persecution, alledg'd by the protestants against the dissenters, are not only the same as papists made use of against the reformers, and the orthodox above a thousand years ago against the hereticks, but likewise the same which the pagans used against the primitive church; and I give an instance, where a defender of the heathen faith, after a cruel persecution, treated the christians, and their religion, with as much pity and contempt, as the most haughty rigorist of the orthodox could the silliest enthusiast. I shew the insignificancy of persecuting by halves: I hint at the barbarity with which the gospel has been propagated in America, and the East-Indies, and orthodoxy maintain'd in other places. All these I offer as arguments against persecution, and point at a remedy to prevent the evils apprehended from an excessive toleration. I speak of civil wars from religious quarrels,

draw

*draw a veil over our own misfortunes ; and
from the examples of calamities which others
have suffer'd, I endeavour to deter the reader from the first approaches of what might
lead to such fatal times.*

*I N the tenth, I assert, that pre-emi-
nence is due to the ministry of the gospel a-
bove all other callings : that in the foregoing
chapters I have said nothing against the clergy to render them odious to the laity, and
that the most eminent in other professions
are guilty of gross failings, as destructive to
their functions as those I have charged the
clergy with ; that all things have a wrong
side, and that we ought to distinguish between
the intent of a calling, and what it may be
perverted to.   I prove, that in all professions
men make the most of their business for their
own ends ; that from our infancy we are
taught to mind and take care of ourselves ;
that if men are more encroaching in one
profession, than they are in another, it proceeds from nothing but their having a greater
opportunity ; and that men of all professions
would lord it over others if they could.   I
prove, that men in all employments boast of*
                                        their

their original, if it be to their advantage, though they are vaftly degenerated, and act from quite contrary principles. I prove at large, that after the time of the apoftles, as foon as the miniftry of the gofpel became a profeffion that men were brought up to for a livelihood, the clergy have not been lefs guilty of frailties and vices, or poffefs'd with more real worth or real goodnefs than the laity. From thence I infer, that the clergy ought not to be more independent on the government than the laity, or enjoy any privilege or power to injure others with impunity, more than is allow'd to men of other profeffions; and I endeavour to refute what is generally alledg'd againft this affertion. I infift upon it, that this maxim of keeping clergymen in due bounds of obedience, interferes not with the veneration due to their order, or their enjoyment of worldly comforts equally with the laity, and give an inftance of good harmony and commendable behaviour between the clergy and the laity. I fpeak of preaching, and the feveral ways it is made deftructive to the peace of the fociety. I give cautions to prevent the mifchiefs that may be occafioned by it. I detect

tect the infincerity of feveral pretences and evafions often made ufe of by feditious preachers. I give an inftance of a pious man, and one of the greateft reformers, who, led away by zeal or paffion, preach'd a fermon that tended to fedition. I demonftrate, that to fow difcord is a more heinous crime in a clergyman, than it is in any other, and remove the fcruples that are made againft punifhing them. I conclude, with infifting upon it, that the two points I have chiefly urg'd in this chapter, are not inconfiftent together, and illuftrate my fentiments concerning our behaviour to the clergy, in a comparifon which no reafonable man will be offended at.

IN the eleventh, I fpeak of government in general, and our conftitution in particular. I affert, that no government can fubfift, to which a paffive obedience is not paid, and examine into the caufe of our quarrels concerning that doctrine. I enquire into the fupreme power, and whole foveraignty of the nation, and prove that our unlimited obedience is only due to commands given by the three eftates jointly. I demonftrate, that
the

the power to make laws must include a power of preserving them from being violated with impunity; that a great share of the soveraignty remains virtually in the people, and that the high prerogatives of the king interfere not with their liberties. I prove, that it is easy to know when the king breaks his contract with his people, and give reasons, why a contract ratify'd between them ought to be no less binding to the one than it is to the other. I touch upon the succession, and the divine right of kings, and shew the absurdity of maintaining, that GOD enjoyns us obedience to monarchy only with exclusion of all other forms of government. I state two objections, the one against that share of soveraignty which belongs to the people, the other against the validity of those laws that have made an alteration in the succession. To solve these, I take notice of the difference between later and former times, as to the situation of power among the three estates, which furnishes me with arguments to answer the objections. I prove that the enemies to the present establishment, are inconsistent in their complaints, and speak of oaths, and swearing with mental

a   reser-

reservation. I enquire into the legitimacy of the Pretender, *and prove it to be doubtful at last: I set forth the conjuncture of time he was born in, and end with a character of king* William *the third, to whom we owe the succession in the illustrious house of* Hanover.

IN the last chapter, I enumerate the native blessings of Great Britain, *especially the southern part of it, and reckon our laws and liberties to be the greatest. I enquire into the reason of our discontents, and compare our murmurs and uneasiness to the complaints of those who are afflicted with the spleen. I exhort to wisdom, and define it. I speak of courts, and the persons they are generally compos'd of. I explode our partiality concerning ministries and statesmen. I dissuade men from relying too much on their honesty on the one hand, and from misconstruing their actions on the other. I demonstrate, that many of our complaints are unreasonable, and that in some real grievances the evil is much inferior to our apprehensions of it; that the expedient our malecontents wish for to redress them, is impracticable.*

practicable, without the ruin of half the nation, and that the very attempt to compass it must be attended with greater calamities, than can befall us under the present establishment. I touch on the Peerage-bill, the war with Spain, and the keeping of Gibraltar. I set forth, what is required, as to religious matters, to procure peace and felicity to a nation. I hint at several sets of people, whose murmurings are not to be regarded, and conclude, that it is our own faults if we are not happy.

THOSE who are vers'd in books will soon discover, that I have made great use of Monsieur Baile, without mentioning him. I confess he is the learned man I speak of in Page 102. The citations likewise which I have borrow'd from that author, without naming him, are many. Particularly in the fifth chapter many arguments are in a manner transcribed from him. As he has taken more pains, and used more arts, than any other in these latter ages, in shewing what might be plausibly said for many heterodox opinions, I have in representing the difficulties which lie on both sides of the controver-

sies,

fies, consulted my own ease so much, as to take many of the reasonings as I find them in him, without giving myself the trouble to examine the solidity of them; and therefore, as I claim no credit from such of them as are good, I desire the reader not to look upon the other as mine, or that I adopt them or make myself responsible for them; tho' they are set down in the same manner as if they had been my own, many of them I think wrong; but it is enough to my purpose that so great a man thought them at least plausible; and I thought they would read better in the manner they now stand, than if I had stated them only as his opinions, which would have occasioned many breaks in the discourse. Had this been done out of vanity to compliment myself, or disregard to the honour of that great man, I would have been wise enough not to have spoke of it now. The reasons I had for doing as I have done, are more than one : In the first place, Monsieur Baile's dictionary is not common, but among men who have great libraries, and quoting it would have signify'd little to the greatest part of my readers. As to the truth of facts, which is the most material, the

au-

authors and evidences I quote, are the same as are in the dictionary, which, if I had referr'd to, the reader could have learn'd no more by searching after the authors there quoted, than what now he may do by looking before him, without any further trouble. Besides, I imagin'd, that it would be unpleasant, if not disgustful, to see the same name so often repeated in the notes, especially to those who are unacquainted with the vastness of that work.

I shall make no further apology for any part of the performance. I can see a great many faults in it, more than I know how to mend. Was it equal with the design, there would be but few better books in the world: as it is impossible I could have had any other aim but the common good, and the publick tranquillity, methinks I hear the candid reader say; What pity it is, a man with so good a design, should not be better qualilify'd! This will never displease me, and I envy not the men of brighter parts, and greater genius, their uncommon capacities, whilst they are labouring to fasten calumnies on their adversaries, conceal the evil actions and

worse

worse designs of their own party, and neglect no artifice to be gracefully disingenuous.

WHAT I would vindicate, is not the strength of my understanding, but the rectitude of my will. Had interest or vain glory influenc'd my labours, my pains might have been better bestow'd than to rush between two enemies that hate every body who strives to part them.

I well know the common fate of moderation; it neither procures you friends, nor appeases your enemies, and fixes a man as a mark to the two factions, that place themselves in the opposite extream: but I have *still worse to fear, considering the bold truths I have spoke; and many will wonder at my temerity, and ask,* Who is it ? Has he a great estate ? What calling, or employment does he follow ? Does he ever intend to thrive, or indeed to live ? Is he pistol-proof, and does he imagine, there are no daggers, nor no poison in the world ? *I am not ignorant of the hazards I run; but what lessens my apprehensions is, that I can never suffer but from the unjust*

resent-

resentment of those, great part of whose duty consists in teaching others to have none.

AT all events I have performed a good action; for when a man endeavours to promote the interest and temporal felicity of the nation he lives in, without detriment to any other, or deviating from the path of virtue, to find out ways to heal our divisions, and the unhappy breaches of parties, without injuring any, by Remedies both easy and pleasant, that shall not only cost nothing, but moreover be a visible security to every man's possession, and heighten all manner of satisfaction a good man can wish for in the enjoyment of them.

WHEN a man writes in defence of truth and liberty, without offending GOD, the least injury to the civil power, or ill manners to superiours : when he speaks up for, and exhorts to true piety, with plainness and sincerity, without fiction or enthusiasm, without slandering, or misrepresenting even the worst or the least shadow of flattery to any mortal : when by strengthening the authority of sovereigns, he strives to banish

nish discord and animosities from the society, and recommend peace and union to all communions, as well as charity to all mankind: when a man is conscious of all this, he may, without any prejudice to his modesty, pronounce his work a good action, though it had no other good quality besides. This is a thought he may reflect upon; he may pause, he may ruminate, and, after all, have the solid satisfaction, without flattering his performance, or entertaining romantick notions, to imagine and assure himself, that whilst he is employ'd in the pursuit of such ends, and dies in such a cause, time cannot be better spent, nor life better lost.

N. B. Tho' the additions and alterations of this second edition are many and considerable, yet what is said of *Gibraltar*, agrees exactly with the first that was printed in 1720.

TITLES

TITLES

OF THE

CHAPTERS.

b

Chap.

ERRATA.

PAGE 122. line 17. after *Thomists*, add *or*. p. 145. l. 14. for *such*, r. *inch*. p. 208. l. 2. for *injur'd*, r. *abjur'd*. p. 231. l. 8. r. *against*. p. 242. l. 2. dele *of*. p. 303. l. 9. for *private*, r. *publick*. p. 306. l. 6. dele the last *no* p. 320. l. 7. r *conjunctures*. p. ib. l. 18. r. *least*. p. 323. l. 6. after *all*, add *these*. p. 325. l. 23. after *takes* add *no*. p. 378. l. 22. r. *kings*. p. 395. l 14. r. *have*.

Free-Thoughts, &c.

CHAP. I.

Of RELIGION.

ELIGION in general confifts in an acknowledgment of an immortal power, that, fuperior to all earthly dominion, invifibly governs the world, and a refpectful endeavour to difcharge fuch duties, as every one fhall apprehend to be requir'd of him by that immortal power. This definition comprehends whatever *Mahometans* or *Pagans*, as well

B as

as *Jews* or *Christians*, understand by the word *Religion*. I shall only address my self to the last of these, and say nothing, at least in this chapter, than what shall be short and plain, not less adapted to one part of the universal church than to any other, and no more than what the meanest christian ought to be acquainted with. In the whole, I shall study to promote, what we stand most in need of, peace and charity; and by the way take notice of some truths, which, tho' uncontested, yet few divines, of any sect or persuasion, seem fond of informing us of.

OUR religion requires of us faith and good works: that is, the duties of a christian are to believe the mysterious as well as the historical truths of the gospel, and, by the assistance of GOD's spirit, to live up to the rules of it. I know very well, that that strong confidence, entire trust, and reliance, which a christian ought to repose in the certainty of the sacred oracles, are not comprehended in the idea, which the vulgar have, when they make use of the word faith or belief: it is by many look'd upon as a thing of choice, as if men could believe

what

what they pleas'd, and feveral are perfuaded, that they believe what, on better examination will be found, they believe not, and this only for want of knowing what it really is *to believe*.

HE who believes, in the common acceptation, that there is a GOD, and that the world is rul'd by providence, but has no faith in any thing reveal'd to us, is a deift; and he, who believes neither the one nor the other, is an atheift. Of thefe I don't believe there are many, and I would have no man fo uncharitable as to think any man guilty of atheifm, who does not openly profefs it. Were we to judge of a man's belief, by ftrictly examining into his actions, faith would be fcarcer than can be eafily imagin'd.

WHOEVER allows of the Old and New Teftament, how differently foever from others he may conftrue fome paffages of either, fo he but believes the whole to be the word of GOD, ought to be call'd a chriftian, even before he is baptized. We have many people in a year executed for enormous crimes, yet they are all deem'd chriftians, tho' but bad ones, who by their e-

duca-

ducation were once look'd upon as such, and profess not to disbelieve the things I mention'd; and therefore none should be call'd atheists, unless by speaking or writing they contradict or deny them. Atheists are either speculative or practical; speculative atheists are those unhappy people, who, being too fond of knowledge or reasoning, are first deluded into scepticism, till, unable to extricate themselves from the mazes of philosophy, they are at last betray'd into a disbelief of every thing they cannot comprehend, and become the most convincing evidences of the shallowness of human understanding. The number of these has always been very small; and, as they are commonly studious, peaceable men, the hurt they do to the publick is inconsiderable. To make this not appear a paradox, we are but to reflect on what it is men are govern'd by in the conduct of their lives, and we shall find, that very few act from the principles they profess, whilst all the rest are sway'd by their passions and inclinations; and therefore it ought not to appear more strange to us, that an atheist
should

should be a quiet moral man, than that a christian should lead a very wicked life.

PRACTICAL atheists are generally libertines, who first have been guilty of all manner of vice and profaneness, and afterwards, not daring to reflect on the enormity of their sins, or the punishment they deserve from the vengeance of heaven, lay hold on atheistical arguments, to skreen themselves from their own fears, and only deny a GOD, because they wish there was none. Practical atheists, as they commonly spend their lives in riot, and ridiculing every thing that is holy, generally dye (unless they happen to repent) in uncommon agonies and despair. These detestable creatures, which no opulent nation ever was free from, will stop at no mischief, and are generally produced from sprightly youth, too carelesly look'd after in a liberal education, and it seldom happens, that any of the meaner ignorant people are tainted with this impiety.

THE christian world abounds with persons wicked and prophane; but of real atheists there are fewer by much than is commonly imagin'd. The multitude in all

countries of the world, let their religion be
what it will, are so generally and so pow-
erfully influenced by fear and superstition,
that atheism can never affect the bulk of
the people. The belief of spirits, a devil,
witchcraft, fortune, or any power above us,
must always, if men will reason at all, include the belief of a first cause and supreme
being.

T o those who were brought up *Jews*,
Mahometans or *Pagans*, it may not be an
easy matter to lay down their prejudice, and
come over to our religion; and it is possible,
that they may make a thousand scruples
before they can heartily embrace it, whilst
they are unassisted with the divine grace;
but a christian by education finds no hard
task in believing every thing contain'd in
the gospel, and what more has been taught
him by tradition from his infancy. I
would have it observ'd, that here the word
believing is to be understood in the large
sense it is commonly receiv'd in; and then
we shall find, that throughout the nation
the christian faith, according to the common acceptation, is that part of our religion, in which the generality of the people
                                                    are

are the leaſt defective: if we enquire of thoſe, who attend the greateſt profligates in the laſt moments of life, even the *Ordinaries* of priſons, we ſhall hear but few complaints as to this point.

NOTHING is eaſier than *to believe*; men may be ſincere in their faith, and even zealous for the religion they profeſs, and at the ſame time lead wicked lives, and act quite contrary to their belief. Thoſe who chearfully ſuffer perſecution for their faith, ought not to be ſuſpected of inſincerity; yet in all ages there have been many inſtances of people, who, for their religion, left their country, their eſtates, employments, friends, and relations, but could never bring themſelves to renounce their ſenſual pleaſures.

Jovian the emperor, who ſucceeded *Julian*, was a chriſtian: the proofs he gave of his zeal to the goſpel, before he aſcended the throne, are indiſputable. In the firſt place, * he ſhewed himſelf very ready to renounce his poſt rather than his religion, when *Julian* commanded the officers of his troops to embrace paganiſm,

* Socrat. *lib.* 3. c. 22.

B 4 or

or refign their employment.   * In the fecond place, he would not accept of the empire, till having declared, that he was a
chriftian, and that he would not command
heathens,   the foldiers had likewife declared, that they were chriftians; † yet *Jovian* was a glutton, and fhamefully addicted
to wine and women.   Behold a ftanch
chriftian, who on the one hand was capable of preferring his religion to the *Roman*
empire, and on the other immers'd in fin
and voluptuoufnefs !

THE greateft difficulty of our religion
is to live up to the rules of chriftianity.
To conquer our paffions, and mortify our
darling lufts, is, what few of us fet about
in earneft ;   and as to higher and heroick
virtues, they are very fcarce to be met
with. Who loves his enemies, or does good
to them that hate him ? how miferable are
the common notions of religious duties a-
mong us ! The vulgar hardly know any
heinous fins,   befides murder,   theft and
adultery, and either finging, gaming, or

---

* Socrat. *lib.* 3. *c.* 22.
† Ammian. Marcellin. *lib* 25.

working

working on a funday; and he, who is not guilty of any of them, and moreover abſtains from ſwearing, drunkenneſs, and Fornication, is counted virtuous; and, if he frequents any publick worſhip, ſhall be call'd a very ſober man and a good chriſtian; let him envy and back-bite his neighbours, be proud, uncharitable, covetous, and revengeful, as much as he pleaſes, and not be poſſeſs'd of one grain of real religion; whereas every body, that can but read and will examine the ſcriptures, may, without any other learning, or ſpiritual guide, be fully convinc'd, not from one or ten places in the goſpel, but the whole aim, drift and meaning of it, that all the rules of morality, and other duties incumbent on a chriſtian, are not to be perform'd for any worldly conſideration, or other reaſon, but the love of GOD and holineſs; and conſequently, that to judge from our actions, we ought to enquire into the motives that ſet us to work.

A young lady ſhall juſtly be call'd virtuous, whilſt ſhe expreſſes no immodeſty in her diſcourſe or behaviour, and withſtanding all the temptations of man, and the

moſt

moſt powerful inclinations from within, keeps her honour and reputation unſpotted. But the ſame may be done by a heathen; and, unleſs we disbelieve all hiſtory, old *Pagan Rome* has had more women of try'd honour, and exalted virtue to boaſt of, than any country, ſince the coming of CHRIST. The fear of children, and the ſcandal of being counted a whore, often prove ſufficient guards to the moſt wicked and laſcivious women, and even ſuch, as without thoſe dangers would have hardly ſtay'd till the queſtion was ask'd them.

THOSE likewiſe of more refin'd notions, the women of education, rank and good ſenſe, even when by marriage they are ſhelter'd from ſome of the fears I mention'd, may often obſtinately defend their honour without being religious; when they conſider, that it is the richeſt Jewel they are poſſeſs'd of, a treaſure, with which, in the opinion of all men whoſe eſteem is valuable, no beauty, wit or fortune can come in competition; and that thoſe who are known to have loſt it, are deſpis'd by all the world, and ſeldom regarded, even by thoſe who have robb'd them of it.

BUT

BUT there is a vaſt difference between not committing an immorality from a principle of pride and prudence, and the avoiding of ſin for the love of GOD.

WHEN a woman poyſons her husband, and at the ſame time refuſes to proſtitute her ſelf, it will be difficult perhaps to dive into the principle ſhe is guided by; but it is very certain, that the love of GOD is not the motive of her continence; for had that any power over her, ſhe could not be guilty of ſo execrable a fact.

TO detect the frailties and evil diſpoſition of man's heart in general, never was counted to be cenſorious; and to give the leſt handle to perſons to judge uncharitably of one another, is what I deteſt the moſt. My aim is to make men penetrate into their own conſciences, and by ſearching without flattery into the true motives of their actions, learn to know themſelves.

A ſingle man, we'll ſay, in the prime of his youth and ſtrength, when luſt is moſt raging, wholly abſtains from fornication. Would he know the motive of his forbearance, let him examine himſelf; and, if he finds that he curbs his inclinations, and

mor-

mortifies his flesh to avoid sin, and be-cause he is afraid of offending GOD, he may be satisfied that he acts from a good principle: but if he avoids lewd women, because they are expensive, and himself is covetous, or if he is with-held by the dread he has for some diseases, or the loss of his reputation, he has no reason to flatter him-self, that his continence proceeds from any religious concern. This is not conquering the passions, but bartering one for another, and perhaps for two or three; for what he loses in the pleasures he might receive from lust, is repaid to him in pride, world-ly interest, and the insurance of his health from that quarter.

A covetous man, who is made a sheriff, is obliged to be at greater expences, at least that year, than he has been used to, or else be laugh'd at or despis'd by every body; but this way of living proves him not more generous, or a better man. He only sacrifices a little of his avarice to a great deal of pride.

THE worldly interest of the whole socie-ty often interferes with the eternal wel-fare of every particular Member of it.

We

We daily fee men rous'd from floth and idlenefs, and fpurr'd on to emulation and ufeful labour, by no better principle than envy; and it is generally taken for granted, that covetoufnefs and pride are the chief promoters of trade and induftry: but can it on the other hand be denied, that thefe vices, againft which the gofpel fo juftly cautions us, contain the feeds of almoft all the iniquities and diforders that are committed?

LYING, flander, and revenge, as long as they produce no vifible mifchief to others, are generally look'd upon as peccadillos, and trefpaffes of little moment; and yet it is certain, that there is no revelation nor folid reafon, that can affure us, that they are always lefs heinous in the fight of GOD than murder or adultery.

How often do we hear people own to us, in relating fome of the paffages of life, that they were forc'd to tell a lye; yet nothing is more evident from fcripture, than that lying is a mortal fin. How whimfical are our notions! it is hardly denied, but that every body is guilty of lying at one time or other, and yet to be

up-

upbraided with it, is counted ſo ſcandalous, that whoever bears it with patience,
is immediately by all the world condemned for a coward, without any further proceſs.

SLANDER and back-biting are made
a jeſt of: among the faſhionable part
of mankind this vice is treated as a piece
of gallantry to ſhew one's wit, daily practi-
ſed for the entertainment of both ſexes.
The generality of the world looks upon it
as an amuſement for idle people, ſo in-
offenſive, that ſcandal and tea with equal
indifference are ſpoke of as inſeparable com-
panions.

WHEN a man threatens revenge on
thoſe who have offended him, he is hardly blamed, if we are perſuaded that he
has been highly injured. But how ſhocking would it be to hear him ſay, that he
would venture eternal damnation for the
pleaſure of his reſentment? and where's
the difference? the meaning of the laſt expreſſion is included in the firſt.

THE great view of all governments in
the adminiſtration of juſtice, is to ſecure
every one's property and the publick peace,
and

and to prevent any thing being tranfacted againft the intereft of the nation or country under their care. For this reafon, the various punifhments which human laws inflict on different crimes, are in moft cafes proportioned to the prejudice they are of to the civil fociety, or the vifible damage any of its members did or might fuftain by them. It is not the fame with offences done to Almighty GOD; the leaft of them, if we believe the gofpel, wilfully committed, makes us liable to eternal damnation, if we do not repent of it before we dye.

HOW trifling, or at leaft how venial to human capacities would feem the fin of *Adam*, fhould we only confider the act it felf, by which it was committed? yet how great has been the punifhment, and how terrible the confequences to himfelf and all his pofterity! nothing could be more innocent than the eating of an apple: there was no prejudice in it to human fociety, or any of the creation; and the whole enormity of *Adam*'s crime was deriv'd from the bare prohibition.

WHAT

WHAT is a sin therefore is such, not as a mischief upon earth, but an affront to heaven.

The chief duty then of real religion among christians, consists in the sacrifice of the heart, and is a task of self-denial to be perform'd with the utmost severity against nature.

THE use I would make of what has been said, is to put my reader in mind, that without this inward sense of religion no outward worship, nor any act of seeming devotion or charity, can be of the least service to us, as to eternal salvation. That, as the doctrine of CHRIST plainly forbids malice, hatred and revenge, and every where exhorts us to meekness, patience, humility, peace and charity to all men, so a christian, who is really such, can never hate others upon any religious account, tho' they were *Mahometans* or *Pagans*.

THAT if we examine our selves, we shall find, that the generality of us are not possess'd with any great share of this inward religion, and that, if we had more

of

of it, we fhould love one another better than we do.

FROM all which we may eafily conclude, that religion is not the caufe of the unhappy breaches, that divide *Great Britain*; and that therefore all divines of what perfuafion foever, who would infinuate the contrary to us, and perverting the word of GOD, make a handle of it to breed quarrels and animofities, or any way difturb the publick peace, are evil teachers and feducers of the people.

C   C H A P.

CHAP. II.

Of Outward Signs of DEVOTION.

AS most men are worse than they would seem to be, so again they are better, than from their actions, if we were acquainted with all, we would judge them to be; for, tho' the neglect of those duties, which interfere with their passions, be almost general, yet it proceeds not, as some imagine, from want of faith, an aversion to religion, or an unwillingness to be good; but the unsurmountable difficulty they meet with, in striving against nature, and conquering their inclinations, of which I have spoke in the aforegoing chapter. There are not many among us, who are not convinc'd that they daily do amiss, and offend GOD, and who, when they have time to think and be serious, are not sorry for it.

THERE

THERE is no chriſtian, ſome few profligate wretches excepted, but what will own to you, and really believes, that he is indebted to GOD, not only for his Being, but likewiſe for every good thing that happens to him, and all the benefits he enjoys in this life. Many, tho' otherwiſe wicked people, are really thankful for them in their hearts, whenever they have leiſure to reflect upon them, and moreover, are often looking out for commodious ways of ſhewing their gratitude; but as they can ſeldom find any that ſuit their conveniency, they content themſelves with hoping that they ſhall meet with them at one time or other.

MOST people believe ſincerely, that they ought to obey GOD's commands, and have often an apprehenſion, that they ſhall be puniſhed for the neglect of it. But then, if they are in health, a future ſtate is counted a great way off, and every body hopes to repent before he dies: beſides the aſſurance men have from the goſpel, that GOD is as merciful as he is juſt, is not always made uſe of the right way. Another proof, that men generally are perſuaded of the truth of the goſpel, is, that the duties

C 2 and

and severities of the christian religion seem so reasonable to them, that they would abominate any one who should preach up loose morals; and there is hardly a drunkard, a whore-master, or any loose jilt in town, if ever they go to any publick worship, but what would be ready to throw stones at a minister, who should tell them, that their actions were commendable, and GOD approv'd of the life they led. The worst of sinners have their fits of devotion, and many of them will not only be very angry at a prophane jest, or hearing any thing ridicul'd they have a religious veneration for; but would likewise be desirous to make an atonement to GOD for their crimes at any rate, except parting with their darling lust.

CHRISTIANS then are not bad for want of faith, or of wishing to be good; but because they are not able to overcome their appetites, and curb their passions, or rather have not resolution enough to set about and persevere in the attempt of it, whilst they are unassisted with the divine grace.

WHILST

WHILST this incapacity on the one hand makes them look on their real duty as an impoſſibility, and their faith on the other repreſents to them the risk they run of eternal damnation, they endeavour to find out ſome equivalent, which may rid them of their fears: like lazy ſchool-boys they'll do any thing to avoid the rod, but their task. This has been the ſource of all the bigotry and ſuperſtition of *Rome:* hence have been derived all ridiculous penances, prayers for the dead, indulgences for the living, powers to releaſe ſouls from purgatory, and whatever could be impos'd on ignorance and credulity, by the craft and avarice of a deſigning clergy, who, in removing the terrors of deluded conſciences for money, have acted the part of knaviſh uſhers, when they take bribes for conniving at the neglects of the ſcholars.

THOSE of them who have been the moſt artful, and dived the furtheſt into our nature, have been always moſt remiſs in promoting an inward ſenſe of religion, and ſhewing us our real duty, but left no ſtone unturned to encreaſe our faith, and en-

encourage ſhews of outward devotion. Firſt, they made people believe, that all their neglects, all their ſins and offences proceeded only from want of faith; whereas believing too much was one of their greateſt failings. After that, all the demonſtration they required of their faith conſiſted in acts of outward devotion, and they always proportioned the ſeverity of diſcipline to the capacity and humour of their devotees. A preciſe bigot ſhall be forced with fifty laſhes to expiate a ſin, which a wild debauchee ſhall atone for with three *Pater-noſters*, or half a dozen *Ave-maries.* The jeſuits are, of all prieſts, the eaſieſt caſuiſts; for which reaſon the confeſſors of princes, and people of the higheſt quality, who refuſe to be teazed with troubleſome penances, are all fathers of that order.

By what has been ſaid, I have endeavoured to lay open the firſt cauſe of the diſregard, the generality of chriſtians have always had for the amendment of the heart, and of the mighty ſtreſs they have laid at the ſame time on acts of outward devotion, beyond what they deſerved. My

next

next bufinefs fhall be to demonftrate, that this perverfenefs of judgment ftill continues among us, even thofe who pretend to be the greateft enemies to fuperftition; which to perform, I fhall find fufficient proof from one act of outward devotion I fhall inftance in.

CHRISTIANS are commanded to meet and join together in divine worfhip: therefore going to church is a neceffary duty; but it can make no atonement for the neglect of other duties equally neceffary, even when performed from a principle of piety and devotion, much lefs when comply'd with out of cuftom, or when made ferviceable to a worfe intention. There are abundance of idle people of both fexes, who are daily puzzled in contriving how to fpend their time: of thefe fome go conftantly to Prayers both forenoon and afternoon. They do very well, no body blames them for it, but why fhould they make a merit of it, when they are confcious, that were they not to go, it would be more troublefome, and they would not know what to do with that hour?

THOSE

THOSE who go to church as they should do, go with an intent to amend their lives, and become more perfect in all christian virtues, otherwise the action it self is indifferent, and all the good to be done at church depends on the motive of coming thither, and the use that is made of it. He who goes to church every day for twenty years together, and persists in a wicked course of life, or any one habitual sin he is hardened in, is not a better christian than the man who never goes there at all.

GREAT numbers of young people, of both sexes, are constantly to be seen at church, whose chief end in going thither is to display their finery, and indulge their pride, and perhaps the hopes of raising a more shameful passion in others. To the vainest and most lascivious of these the church is often the place they take the greatest delight in, because they can no where have a better opportunity of setting themselves off, to each other, to the best advantage, and thousands of them go to see and be seen. Would you discover the truth of this, have but patience till by the

ne-

neglect of the fempftrefs, the mantua-maker, or the taylor, or fome other accident or misfortune they are difappointed in any of their accoutrements, and are obliged either to ftay at home, or appear in a drefs, by which their vanity might fuffer, or at leaft not be fufficiently flatter'd, and you fhall find, that rather than go to church, they'll ftay at home for a fortnight.

THE worft and moft profligate of the mob, and fuch as are wholly deftitute of all goodnefs and morality, may likewife be drawn to church by the unchriftian zeal and licentioufnefs of divines. Thefe are the trufty fatellites that follow in fhoals, and furround the firebrands of each party. To hear others rail'd at, and their betters revil'd, is the height of their pleafure; and therefore, when men are loaded with curfes, and worried with invectives by a favourite minifter, and damnations are with clamours denounc'd from the pulpit, why fhould a bull-baiting, where men are often expos'd to danger themfelves, be more approv'd of than a Sermon, of which they are fure all the mifchief will fall on their adverfaries only; or the church,

D where

where they are sheltered from the weather, not be preferr'd to a bear-garden, where they can but have the same diversion, and must stand in the rain, or be choak'd with the dust?

A man need not be very censorious, who will allow no great merit in the going to church of these wretches; yet it is remarkable, that often, when they are transported with joy at the violence of voice and gesture, by which they are inspired with a mortal hatred against those of a different opinion, many of them are so stupidly ignorant of their own condition, as to imagine that they are discharging a christian duty, whilst they are wholly employed in gratifying the malice and rancour of their hearts.

It would be endless to give all the instances, by which one might prove, that most men relying too much on forms and outward devotion, place a merit in things that have none. For this reason, I shall say nothing of keeping the sabbath, almsgiving, and other duties, that might be referr'd to this head; but in the remainder of this chapter, present the reader with two or three chara&ers, which I believe will help to confirm what hitherto I have af-ferted. As to the rites and ceremonies of outward worfhip, too rigidly infifted on by fome, and too peevifhly reje&ed by o-thers; they are one of the chief caufes of our inteftine quarrels, and for that rea-fon fhall be fpoke of by themfelves at large hereafter.

HORATIO was apprentice to a credi-table tradefman, and but nineteen years old, when he was married to a young beau-tiful creature, with a tolerable fortune, who was a neighbour's daughter fal'n in love with him. He had always been a diligent youth, and the beft fervant his mafter ever had; who pardoning this fault, gave him up his indentures, and *Horatio* was fet up for himfelf before he was twenty. He had not been married much above three years, when his wife died of a confumption; having often mifcarried, but never had a child born alive. In lefs than half a year after, *Horatio* took another, who was a hale country lafs, juft turn'd of fifteen, and brought him a very good portion. This had no children before fhe was three and

D 2   twenty,

twenty, but since that, they have had one almost every year, and two or three times twins. She is now with child, and lay in about seven months ago. He has a sincere love for her, and she is a very prudent woman. The small-pox has veen very fatal to their children; and of twenty they had born alive, but nine are left, six sons and three daughters. *Horatio*, who is now fifty one, has always been an industrious thriving man, and maintain'd his family in plenty. He has never been drunk, always kept orderly hours; he is belov'd by his neighbours, and has the character of a very good humour'd man. He is a strict church-man, keeps all the fasts in the year, and never eats meat on a *friday*. All last *Lent* he abstain'd from flesh and wine, and kept the *holy week* with still a more extraordinary Rigour.

HORATIO never had receiv'd the least blemish in his reputation, when, on *Easter-sunday*, whilst he was gone to church with his family, all in new cloaths, the impertinent curiosity of a servant, that was left at home, made a discovery very much to his disadvantage. As *Horatio* was always

ways

ways very mindful when he chang'd his cloaths, to remember his letter-case, his money, and whatever he had about him; so now in dressing himself, he had taken every thing out of the coat and breeches he pull'd off the night before, and had, to the best of his thinking, very carefully examin'd every where; but, as ill-luck would have it, forgot to feel in, what he very seldom made use of, the left pocket of the waste-coat, where he had put two letters to keep them safe, and not mix them with other papers. In the one was a bill from a farmer in *Surrey*, who had the care of two bastard children of *Horatio*'s; the other was a scrawl of a mistress that was ready to lye in. These were found out by his cook-maid, as she was rummaging in his bed-chamber. The maid had malice e-nough to shew them her mistress, who, having read about a third part of one of them, and asked her, how she came by them, folded it up again; and without look-ing in the other, put them both into the same pocket they had been taken out of. The next day she turn'd away the cook, but with abundance of good humour; and,

D 3 having

having paid what was due to her, made her a prefent of three guineas, on a promife of fecrecy, which fhe earneftly required of her. The wife has never fince open'd her lips, nor fhew'd the leaft chagrin about the letter; but the wench has broke her word, and the thing is known, tho' not pub-lickly.

NOT long ago a worthy divine, who is a particular friend of *Horatio*'s, and has a great value for him, hinted it to him with all the caution and good manners imaginable. *Horatio* own'd all, and pre-vented the reproofs he expected, by go-ing on thus. The frailty of the flefh is one, I have hitherto not been able to con-quer; but never was guilty of taking un-lawful pleafures, but when my wife was in child-bed, or otherwife out of order, and no man has more love or friendfhip for a woman, than I have for her. I have examin'd my felf on this head, continued he, very feverely, and am well affured, that if it be a fin, it will be forgiven me; but on our friendfhip let me hear no more of it.

HO-

HORATIO is a man of senſe, and has been an impartial arbitrator in fifty diſputes of other people: is it not ſtrange, that a ſtrong inclination ſhould ſo violently over-power a man's reaſon, as at laſt, againſt his will, to corrupt his judgment? For, let *Horatio* have his ſurety from what part ſoever he pleaſes, I am ſtill more ſure, he has it not from the goſpel; and that himſelf is a notorious ſinner, and has not one chriſtian virtue to boaſt of.

IT is wrong always to judge of man's inclinations from the ſins he is guilty of. Princes may neither be cruel nor covetous in their temper, even when they are the cauſe of war, of rapine, and devaſtation; their ambition blinds them, or makes them overlook the ſteps, on which it mounts. Private perſons are betray'd into wickedneſs after the ſame manner, and men often commit ſins with reluctancy, and conſent with regret, to what their darling vice forces them to ſubmit.

EMILIA had a great ſhare of wit and beauty, but pride enough to outweigh both: ſhe was every way well accompliſh'd, and her diſcretion hid the greateſt part of

D 4   her

her frailty : she hated all female acquaintance, and yet shew'd no fondness to man : she was a pattern of modesty, and remain'd virtuous till she was five and twenty; at which time, her father, who was a merchant, dying insolvent, *Emilia* was left destitute to the wide world. Two months after she grants the last favour to a *Jew*, and gets five hundred pounds by the bargain. She soon discards him, admits another, and abates of her price. She had six gallants in less than a month; and in half a year's time, *Emilia* became a common miss of the town. As she was a well-bred woman, that never drank to excess, and guilty of no other crimes besides prostitution, she had a very good income, and no rakish customers ; being expensive in nothing but cloaths and furniture, she hoarded up money. All the women of her profession hated her, and she them more inveterately. At three and thirty she had a fit of sickness, which alter'd her much for the worse ; upon which, finding her trade to fall off, she left it, and retir'd with five thousand pounds in her pocket. She went a hundred miles off, changed her name,

and

and was married to an old knight, who had little or nothing, and spent her above half of what she had.

HER husband has been dead these two years, and *Emilia* is now turn'd of fifty. She is grave in her dress, and solemn in her gate : She has left off house-keeping, lives within compass, and, with her woman and foot-boy, boards in a very sober family. She appears very devout, is never absent from prayers, and has for some years read nothing but divinity; she delights in controversy, and is well versed in ecclesiastical history, and so good a disputant, that, all around her, there is no body able to cope with her. Since she left her first employ, she has not been guilty of one act of incontinence; but as she commits no fault her self that way, she is resolved not to connive at the least shadow of it in others. She talks very well, and passes not a day without telling lies, either of her birth and family, or else the virtues of her youth. She never had a child; and the hatred to her sex, especially those of merit, continues. She is the most censorious woman in the world; and, in the seventeen years

she

she had been in the country, she has broke off above twenty matches, that, in all probability, would have been happy ones, and ruin'd above fifty reputations, that never deserved it; yet she is so circumspect, as well as sly in her insinuations, and manages her slander with so much dexterity, that she has never been openly detected.

Emilia is fam'd both for wisdom and piety; the parson of the parish extols her to the skies, but is afraid of her in his heart; every body admires and stands in awe of her, and no woman in the county has more respect paid her. Half a year ago she made her will, and left every farthing she has to rebuild the front of a little alms-house, that has a very little income, and stands about a mile off from where she lives. Over the porch is to be her effigy in stone, with an inscription of her own indicting underneath it. Since she has had this design, she often visits the poor inhabitants, to whom she gives what charity she can spare, and who, in return, take her to be a saint, and trumpet her praise all over the country.

WHAT

WHAT *Emilia* thinks of her self is worth any man's notice. Her proſtitution ſhe is ſure never proeeeded from luſt, but neceſſity, *ergo* no ſin. The miſchief ſhe does with her ſlander, ſhe aſcribes to the averſion ſhe has to vice. When ſhe reflects on the hours ſhe ſpends at church, and in reading, and then thinks on the will ſhe has made, ſhe flatters her ſelf with having perform'd every chriſtian duty, and her conſcience is entirely clear. Is it not ſtrange, that *Emilia*, with all her cunning, never ſuſpected her ſelf to be an ill woman, and knows not to this hour, that envy and vanity are her darling vices?

HYPOCRISY every body knows is a fair outſide, put on to hide deformities within, deſignedly to cheat and circumvent others: but when men are as good, as unaſſiſted with the divine grace it is in their power to be, and not bad in any thing, but what interferes with their leading paſſion; what muſt we ſay of them, when outwardly they appear upright, and yet their hearts are very corrupt from that one ſin, which, in ſpight of all their fears and wiſhes, over-rules them? for it is un-

unjuft to call people hypocrites, when they fet out with no ill defign, and by their fair appearance deceive themfelves more, ten to one, than they can do others of any tolerable experience. What I fay will be better illuftrated by the following example.

CRATO is a rich mifer, who has no real value for any thing but money: he is humble in his drefs, and frugal in his diet; he rails at the vices of the age, and the luxury of the times. He thinks no virtue more commendable than induftry, and is a mortal enemy to beggars. Ufury and extortion he knows very well to be great fins in a chriftian, neither does he affirm, that he is not guilty of them fome-times, but he hopes GOD will forgive him, and wifhes he could withdraw his heart from this wicked world more than he does. He never drinks wine, or any thing that is ftrong; and no hermit ever practis'd grea-ter aufterity. If you talk to him of reli-gion, he lifts up his eyes, and owns to you that he is a great finner: what is moft wonderful, he does it with fincerity, with tears in his eyes, and a bitter Sigh at al-

most

moſt every word. In the mean time he is
peeviſh to his wife, ill-natur'd to his children, a ſharper in his dealings, a litigious
neighbour, and has never a friend in the
world. Cathedral worſhip he calls popery,
and the ſurplice is the garment of the
whore of *Babylon :* he turns pale at the
ſound of an organ, and no *Roman Catho-*
lick can have more ſuperſtition in keeping
of holy-days, than he diſcovers in affecting
to neglect them.

HE is a rigid öbferver of the ſabbath,
never fails of hearing two long ſermons
every *ſunday*, and hardly eats any thing
before ſupper. He never takes nor ſuf-
fers any of his family to take the leaſt,
even the moſt harmleſs recreation that
day. What time he has upon his hands
is ſpent in reading the ſcripture, or ſome
other book of devotion, or elfe ſitting ſtill
without any other exerciſe, but looking pi-
tifully, and yawning at firſt, and towards
the evening, nodding and ſtarting by turns,
without ſpeaking a word. After ſupper he
ſings a pſalm, ſays his prayers, and goes to
bed the moſt contented man alive, and, by
his own conceit, often throws himſelf into

an

an enthufiafm of joy, which the filly wretch believes to be an infallible token of heavenly favour, and mifconftrues as a reward to his foul for the good life he leads. This keeping of the fabbath, he imagines, atones for all; for tho' no man is more afraid of hellfire than himfelf, and all the week long he deceives and over-reaches as much as he can, without incurring any penalty of the law; yet he flatters himfelf, that the outward devotion of one day in feven, and his abftinence from every thing his avarice will not let him enjoy, will balance all accounts.

SOME time ago having pafs'd the *funday*, as ufually, came to him the next morning a petty tradefman for ten pounds, that had been due feveral months; his wife was ready to lye in, and he knew not where to get a farthing any where elfe. *Crato* anfwers him very calmly, that he could never have come in a worfe time; that he had not half that fum in the houfe; that he fhould be forc'd to borrow money himfelf that very day, to pay in at the bank, and that all the directors were rogues. The poor man begs and prays, and tells him,

him, that he never was in greater neceffity in his life; but all in vain. *Crato*, who has no compaffion, but upon his own cafh, and knew the other valued his cuftom, and would not dare to difoblige him, puts off his dun for a fortnight longer, and in lefs than two hours after, lets an extravagant rake have five hundred pounds at twenty *per cent*.

HE never was heard to fwear an oath, but has more than once hir'd knights of the poft, and brib'd a lawyer to ruin an orphan. He is confcious of his tranfgreffions, but fays they are human frailties, and that no man is free from fin: after that he knowingly and wilfully repeats the fame over again, and fo has done for near forty years, without ever having endeavoured, or fo much as refolved to amend; yet *Crato* is generally counted a very religious man, and every ftep his avarice makes, is by many attributed to the feverity of his morals.

C H A P.

CHAP. III.

Of Rites and Ceremonies in DIVINE WORSHIP.

THAT the difficulty there is in conquering our paſſions, is the greateſt obſtacle to chriſtian virtue, has been ſufficiently proved in the two foregoing chapters. Another reaſon, why the generality of men are ſo little affected with inward religion, is, that the vulgar, and all people of mean capacities, can find nothing in it that ſuits them. It is wholly ſpiritual, and there is nothing ſtrikes the ſenſes. In the time of our Saviour and his diſciples, the wonders that were daily wrought to the aſtoniſhment of all who beheld them, were ſufficient to awaken the attention even of careleſsneſs and ſtupidity it ſelf; but when miracles were ceaſed, the influences of the holy Spirit, which had been ſo openly manifeſted

ɪ   in

in the actions as well as doctrine of the
apostles, and render'd the divinity of their
miffion almoft indifputable, were never after fo eminently vifible in their fucceffors;
which was the reafon that the charms of
the gofpel did not work fo irrefiftibly on
the minds of the fenfual, the illiterate, and
men of grofs underftanding, as they had
done before; and the fervent zeal of pro-
felytes began to cool in many after the firft
century.

THE chriftians before *Conftantine the
Great,* throughout the empire, were every
where furrounded with the gawdy fhew
and pompous ceremonies of triumphant
paganifm. The wealth and skill laid out
in their idols and temples; the mirth and
luxury of their feafts; the folemnity of
their facrifice, and ftatelinefs of their pro-
ceffions, were very attractive to vulgar eyes.
If to thefe we add the rich and fpotlefs
garments, as well as venerable afpects of
their priefts, their fubordination and variety, and the awfulnefs of their office, we
fhall conclude, that the pagan idolatry
muft have had a great influence over the
weak minds of poor and ignorant people,

E   when

when they saw it submitted to by princes
and emperors themselves.

THE heathen priests at first despised
and ridicul'd the christian religion, and
for some time after contented themselves
with crushing it by the secular power;
but when they found that in spight of all
persecutions, it still got more ground, and
began to be embraced by many senators,
and people of great quality, they thought
their temples in danger, and had recourse
to reasonings and remonstrances; but not
being able to maintain their own theology,
they drew in philosophers and orators to
defend it, as their country's cause.

THUS christianity came to be attacked
in form, its doctrine censur'd, and the
whole oppos'd by popular arguments, which
the *Roman* catholicks have since made
use of in the disputes with the protestants,
and have not been forgot by the church
of *England* against dissenters, and have still
receiv'd the same answer from the adversaries of the national church, which some
of the primitive christians made to them
at first.

As

As many learned men had embraced chriſtianity, and their cauſe was far the better, the pagans were generally defeated by them; yet their claſhings together were of a long continuance. And it is likely, that whilſt the pagan prieſts left no ſtone unturned to maintain their own, the government being likewiſe on their ſide, the pious churchmen of thoſe times, who were not willing, that the ſpreading of the name of CHRIST ſhould be retarded by any neglect of theirs, were of opinion, that faith and piety might be aſſiſted by outward circumſtances of devotion, and therefore introduced ſeveral comely ceremonies and decorations into their worſhip, which they had no precept for from the goſpel; thinking themſelves obliged, in behalf of the vulgar, to join ſome outward ſhew to their good reaſoning; as the heathens, who had always truſted to the pomp and ſplendour of their religion, and never been uſed to ſpeak in defence of their theology, now condeſcended to enter into debate with them, and join reaſoning to their outward ſhew.

ON

E 2

ON this mean foundation of some few inoffensive rites and ornaments the pride and avarice of the succeeding clergy, as they encreased in power, and emperors became christians, have built all the luxurious machinery of the Roman-catholick superstition. How soon christians began to deviate from the primitive simplicity of their worship, is not easily determin'd; but we have reason to think, that it was very early; because it is evident from *Prudentius*, that they had already images in some of their churches in the beginning of the fourth century, or before.

WHATEVER *has an outward appearance of piety*, says a learned man, *and may be observed without having any virtue in the soul, was always easily entertain'd among ignorant nations, who on the contrary did always neglect whatever requires some virtue to be practiced.* This truth has been always profoundly understood by the priests of most countries, and the use to be made of it to their benefit been so eminently improved among the christians, that their clergy in the city of *Rome* has in lux, and religious pageantry, at least equalled

their

their heathen predeceſſors, but far exceeded them in their arrogant (not to call them worſe) pretenſions to holineſs, power, and authority.

Long in the moſt haughty manner had the *Roman* clergy, the empire of the eaſt being deſtroyed, maintain'd an abſolute ſway over the conſciences of ſovereigns, as well as ſubjects in all the chriſtian world; till their own flagrant vices and the contentions among themſelves were the occaſion, that many of the better ſort of them proteſted againſt the tyranny of *Rome*, and at laſt, by the help of ſecular powers, brought to paſs what we call the reformation; by which ſeveral kingdoms, of which *England* was the chief, and other ſtates and principalities in *Germany, Switzerland,* and the *Low Countries,* withdrew themſelves from the uſurpation of the *Roman* high-prieſt.

The great deſign then in hand, or at leaſt the chief pretence was to remove all objects of idolatry from churches, and other publick places, to aboliſh all ſuperſtitious ceremonies, and other abuſes that were crept into the church. This was executed in every country with more or leſs rigour,

rigour, according to the heat or moderation of the guides and leaders they fol-
lowed.

I fhall take no notice of what was done
abroad, or of our own relapfe in the reign
of queen *Mary*, but defire every body to
take a view of what lies before, him, and
impartially to confider the rites and ceremonies in general, that cannot be proved
to be of apoftolick inftitution, and which
yet the *Englifh* divines, together with the
government, have retain'd, or alter'd into
fuch, as are made ufe of in our church, as
by law eftablifhed.

I beg the reader's pardon for leading
him fo far about; but I could not better,
to my mind, fet in a true light the innocent original, prodigious increafe, and reafonable curtailing of ceremonies, and the
changing _nem into thofe we have now,
than the way I have done it in. And as
my great aim is national concord and the
publick tranquillity, the ufe I would make
of fuch a view is this,

I would on one hand fhew the diffenters, that the motive of inventing fome
rites and ceremonies may be pious and laudable;

dable; and that the end of the reformation was not to deftroy ufeful order and
decency, but idolatry and fuperftition, and
whatever, by a covetous and ambitious
clergy, had been calculated to exhauft and
enflave the laity. From hence I would
take an opportunity of obferving to them,
that no rites or ceremonies infifted on by
the church of *England* could be excepted
againft on thofe heads. And fhould they
ask me why other proteftant countries made
not ufe of the fame, I would anfwer what
I have partly hinted at already, that the
zeal and violence with which the *Roman*
catholick religion was proceeded againft in
all countries, that are now proteftant, chiefly depended on the temper and infinuations of the firft reformers they hearken'd
to; and that it is evident that feveral of
them, tho' otherwife men of learning and
great qualifications, were too much led a-
way by human paffion, and that many of
their actions had not fo much difcovered
the influence of the Holy Ghoft, as that
of a reftlefs and vindictive fpirit.

I would tell them likewife, that at the
time of the reformation, the known method,

thod, commonly ufed to make a crooked ftick ftrait, had been over-ftrain'd, and practis'd with too general an application: and that in thofe days the zeal of proteftants had been fo blind, as in many cafes to take away not only their charity, but likewife their underftanding. To prove which, and not fpend too much time in running through particulars, it will be fufficient to take into confideration only one inftance of the anti-zeal, and extravagance of the reformers.

CHRIST died on a crofs; with this, jews and infidels, in the firft ages, have often upbraided his followers; who on the contrary glory'd in it, and no good chriftian ever yet was afham'd to own the ignominious death of his Lord and Mafter. In tract of time the crofs became the banner and enfign of chriftianity. Of this veneration, which was juftly given to the fign of the crofs, in remembrance of our Saviour's fufferings, definging priefts made an ill ufe. By virtue of it, they pretended to cure difeafes, exorcife and perform feveral other miracles. This foon made that every thing had the fign of the crofs
upon

upon it, or was made in that ſhape; and few things were wore, or made uſe of, that had not the figure of it expreſſed, either in painting, ſculpture, or embroidery. Several eccleſiaſticks pretended to have parts of the real croſs which our Saviour ſuffer'd upon, and ſold in ſmall and bigger pieces more of it, than would fill half a dozen firſt rate men of war. They openly paid adoration to it, wherever they ſaw it, and made others do the ſame. In ſhort, they made it the chief engine of idolatry and ſuperſtition, in all their trade.

THIS was a ſad and wicked abuſe of a thing otherwiſe indifferent; but was this a juſt cauſe of the horror and deteſtation ſome of the reformers inſpired their followers with againſt the ſign of the croſs? this was another extreme. Amongſt the proteſtants, either in *Switzerland*, or the ſeven provinces, there is not a croſs, nor a crucifix to be found in any family; and wherever you ſee the picture of either, you will not err once in fifty times, if you pronounce the people to be papiſts. Is not this folly? but was it not much more madneſs

F

neſs in the firſt reformers to break and deſtroy every thing that had a croſs or crucifix upon it, or was made in reſemblance of it? would it not be an odd way of paying reſpect to the memory of a prince, if we ſhould demoliſh his ſtatues, or cut his pictures in pieces wherever we met with them?

I cannot leave off yet. Does their averſion proceed from the reflection on the uſe the papiſts put it to? why can't they as well conſider, that this was one of the reaſons why they parted from their communion; and that now they have left them they have no more to do with them as to divine worſhip, than they have with the jews, or the pagans? What is this to the croſs? no body bids them make it an object of idolatry, neither do I bid them make any croſſes, or the reſemblance of it. People may hate onions and not be able to give a reaſon for it; but I ſhould think him a mad-man, who ſhould have a real averſion to them, upon the account of the *Ægyptians* of old, who paid idolatrous worſhip to them. A man of any family, that has a coat of arms to boaſt of, has it

painted

painted on his coach in many places, and can't have a ſilver ſpoon but what bears the creſt upon it; and ſhall a chriſtian hate the reſemblance of a Chriſt crucify'd, and either tremble at the ſight of, or elſe ſpurn from him what is the emblem of his redemption?

THE ſame reflection I would have men make on the greateſt part of the liturgy and the common-prayer. I would have them conſider, that in all great enmities, each party, for fear of bordering too near upon the other, precipitates it ſelf to the oppoſite extreme, and very often with little judgment. The papiſts had innumerable ceremonies, many of them really offenſive and ſinful; therefore the exceſſive zeal of moſt proteſtants made them imagine, that there could be no thorough reformation, if they retain'd any thing their adverſaries did or ſaid, how harmleſs or becoming ſoever. This may be obſerved in the very dawn of chriſtianity; tho' I think they carry it too far who are of opinion, that the altering of the chriſtian ſabbath, and ſhifting it from *Saturday* to *Sunday*, was more owing to an antipathy againſt the jews,

F 2 and

and a fondness of differing from them in as many things as it was possible, than the reasons that are commonly given for that change.

AFTER this, I would shew our dissenters, that they were more rigid anti-papists than any calvinists abroad; for that the protestants in *Holland, &c.* tho' they have thrown by the mass-book, and the prayers of the church of *Rome*, shew no aversion to set forms of prayers; that in the seven provinces they have forms of them adapted to the ceremonies both of baptism and marriage; and that the ministers of the national church, not only make use of a certain form of prayer, compos'd by order of the government, before their sermons, but are likewise obliged to conclude all their prayers, their own extemporary ones not excepted, with that of our Lord.

NEITHER would I forget to tell them, that all protestants beyond the seas, allow of godfathers and godmothers; witness king *William,* who had the states *ge-*

3   *neral*

neral and others † for his godfathers: nor, that they make uſe of inſtrumental muſick in divine worſhip; that throughout the provinces they have organs wherever they can afford them, and thoſe in the new church at *Amſterdam*, by good judges, are counted the beſt in the world.

WHAT I have ſaid, (which I am ſorry I could not do in fewer words) I would have the diſſenters ſeriouſly to conſider, and pick out of it an anſwer themſelves.

FURTHER I would beg leave to ask a rich presbyterian, why there is as much gaudineſs and ſuperfluity in dreſs to be ſeen at their meeting-houſes, as in any of our churches? if he pleads the modes in being, and the faſhion of the country for himſelf, why does he affect ſingularity in the habit of his teachers? if the laity of a nation differ from each other in opinion, and yet wear the ſame cloaths, and conſult nothing in their dreſs but the modes

† *The others were the ſtates of* Holland, *thoſe of* Zealand, *together with the magiſtrates of* Delft, Haerlem, *and* Amſterdam. Aytzema, *Herſtelde Leeuw.*

in

in being; why should the dissenting clergy stand out, and not all follow in their habits the fashion of the same country?

But should he refuse to admit of any difference in dress, between the clergy and the laity; then, why must their ministers wear black, and not as well sky colour or scarlet? to answer this, he'll fly to decency, and must at last be obliged to appeal to the custom of the country, which at the same time he refuses to comply with.

I would ask him moreover, why, if he affected the primitive simplicity of christians, he ridicul'd the quakers? for they in their worship, as to outward appearance, keep up a greater resemblance of the apostolick times, than any other sect of christians. Tho' many of these likewise, I am afraid, mistake affectation for a christian virtue; and being part of our dissenters, I have something to say to them in particular as to ceremonies.

I would first entreat them not to think better of themselves than they do of other people, before they had well examin'd whether they deserve it; and put them in mind that to be purer in outward wor-

ship

ſhip would avail but little, unleſs the heart was leſs corrupt. After that I would tell them, that the plainneſs and ſeeming humility, in which they differ'd from others, was the eaſieſt thing in the world, when acquired by education, and made habitual by cuſtom. That the houſe-keeping of a quaker was generally as expenſive as that of a churchman, of the ſame fortune; that many of them eat and drank, and wore the beſt of every thing, were curious in their furniture, magnificent in their buildings, and extravagant in their entertainments, and every thing about them.

I could go further, and affirm to them, that a quaker might have a greater guard upon his words and actions, and yet as to himſelf, not be a better man than a perſon of looſer morals; that, when a man ſtrenuouſly aſſerts a thing, his honour engages him to ſtick to it; and that the more pride he has, the leſs he'll recede from the principle he pretends to be of; for ſhould once a vain man, brag of being leſs chilly than others, he would keep from the fire as long as he could, whilſt he thought himſelf obſerv'd.

F 4   I would

I would likewife ask them, whether, while they are diftinguifhing themfelves from others, they are always confiftent with their principles? for a man, who refufes to pay refpect to the civil magiftrate, ought not to require, much lefs exact it, from his coachman, and every fervant he keeps. I would ask a man of fenfe and probity, as a great many of them are, how he could pretend to renounce the pomp and vanity of the world beyond others, and have nothing elfe to fhew for it, but keeping on his hat, and the fcantinefs of his coat? for, that thefe two, and ufing the fingular number inftead of the plural, in their addrefs to others, are all the characterifticks many of them are to be known by, is undeniable. I would conclude with this queftion, how he could imagine that the voluptuous enjoyment of eafe and luxury could be aton'd for by the pitiful facrifice of a yard of cloth, and perhaps half a fcore of buttons in every fuit he wears; whilft his wife and daughters put in above three times the quantity of filk, of what, twenty years ago, the fame garment would have been thought to require.

THIS

THIS is the uſe I would make of what I have ſaid on ceremonies, in relation to diſſenters, and I would ſpeak with the ſame plainneſs to thoſe of our national church.

I would urge to them, that all ceremonies in uſe amongſt chriſtians, even the moſt decent and the leaſt liable to cenſure, muſt be own'd to be of human invention, and that we had none we could with any certainty call apoſtolical; that as our church pretends to no infallibility, we ought not to be too dogmatical and poſitive, in defending every part of the rites and ceremonies of it: That in my remonſtrance to diſſenters, I had been favourable to our church; but elſe, that we had ſeveral ceremonies and uſages not to be inſiſted on: nay, that we had retain'd what the church of *Rome* it ſelf had borrowed from paganiſm; I would not adviſe any proteſtant to juſtify this, as cardinal *Baronius* does; who having confeſs'd the feaſt of *candlemaſs* to be entirely pagan in its original, adds; *the like has often happen'd, ſeveral other gentile ſuperſtitions being laudably introduced into the church, and expiated and ſanĉtified*
by

by the chriſtian uſage. Nor as ſome others have done, by ſaying, that adopting the uſages of paganiſm, is employing the ſpoils of *Egypt* to adorn the jewiſh tabernacle; that it is following the example of *Solomon*, who borrowed the materials and builders of the temple of the true GOD from an idolatrous king: that *David* ſcrupled not to ſet the crown of gold on his own head, which he tore from that of the idol *Milcom*.

Such juſtifications I would deſire them not to lay great ſtreſs upon, and tell them further, that ſtanding to the eaſt at the confeſſion of our faith, and bowing to the altar might be omitted without any great loſs: that bowing at the name of JESUS, and not at that of CHRIST, is a childiſh interpretation of the text it is deriv'd from; and that thoſe ſticklers for the letter, who inſiſt upon the performance of that rite, might without any great cunning perceive, if they would, that it is only comply'd with in ſtriſtneſs by the women. That the ſtated fees, which, beſides their tithes and ordinary income, our clergy can demand for marrying, baptizing, burying, *Eaſter*
offe-

offerings, &c. bore an air of popery to those, who are not accustomed to the usages of our church, and that, even by good men, they might easily be mistaken for relicts of priestcraft.

I would inform them, that many things might in themselves not be really superstitious, and yet men be guilty of superstition in the use of them, by laying too great a stress upon, and paying a more sacred veneration to them than they deserve. If he should own to me his weakness, that nothing could raise his devotion equally to good musick, I would commend him for preferring cathedral worship to any other; but I would not justify his anger against his neighbour, because he is disturb'd at the sight of a chorister, whom he knows to be a lewd companion, that lets out his voice for every purpose it can be hired for; sings anthems one hour, and obscenities the next, and in the same afternoon serves the church of GOD, and the playhouse.

I would allow, that the loose becoming garment of white linen the priest is clad with at divine service, may, as an emblem

of

of innocence and purity, be of use to put the wearer in mind of what he should be, and as such be edifying to the people; nay, I would grant, that the sight of the surplice ought to have no other effect on a candid beholder: but I would have no body judge uncharitably of a man who should deny, that the dresses of the dean and chapter, the diversity of hoods, caps and cawls, with all the variety of vestments at some solemnities to be seen at a cathedral, either all together, or part of them, had any thing in them more holy or more necessary than the gowns of the judges, the sword-bearers cap of maintenance, or the habits of the yeomen of the guards; and consequently would look upon them no otherwise than men used to do upon all odd fashions retain'd from old custom.

I would desire him to examine himself, and the force of education, and put him in mind of the proverb of the new vessel, which will long retain the smell it was once imbued with. That it was not of yesterday the people they quarrell'd with began to dissent from us; that as our animosities were the fruits of the disputes

and

and contentions of our forefathers, the diſſenters had from their infancy been inſpired
with horror againſt many things which in
reality are indifferent, and which we from
the ſame cauſe have been taught as early
to over-value; and that if we found it difficult to conquer the prejudices of education, we ought not to propoſe it as an eaſy
task to others.

THUS I would ſpeak to thoſe of our
own church, and conclude with this admonition: if the diſſenters are deluded, let
us ſhew that we are wiſer. Is the continuance of their ſeparation obſtinacy in
them, let us avoid the ſame imputation, by
not urging the diſpute any further. If
to err belongs to human frailty, let us
bear with their errors, and for the future
reſolve to treat them with humanity; and
begin with three things that ought to be
eaſy to a chriſtian: let us forbear calling
names, aſcribing ſentiments to them, which
they utterly diſown, and laying to the
charge of any of them, what they have
not been perſonally guilty of themſelves.

THE more one really conſiders the difference between a churchman and a preſbyterian,

byterian, the more eafy it feems to heal the fore, if thofe who are entrufted with the cure, would throw by their corrofives, and but ceafe to keep open the wounds with fo much induftry and application. Let me illuftrate this with an example.

A churchman receives the facrament kneeling, a presbyterian fitting. Let us fuppofe, that out of curiofity they would fee the manner, after which it is admini-ftred in each other's communion. There is no doubt, but fuch a fight would be very fhocking to both. Now, (fays the churchman) I fee that thefe wretches are not only flovenly and difrefpectful in their worfhip, but likewife place a religion in affronting GOD, and prophaning every thing that is holy, or elfe how could they chufe the moft irreverend and fcandaloufly familiar Pofture that can be invented, to take the Lord's fupper in. This is his conftruction.

THE presbyterian feeing every body up-on their knees, cries out, idolatry! thefe people, fays he, believe in tranfubftantia-tion, or elfe they would never worfhip the creature: this is popery all over; and I

am

am fure they adore the bread as much as the papifts do the wafer. At this rate they muft never be reconcil'd; but how ftrangely it would alter the cafe, if each of them would calmly hearken to what the other had to fay in his juftification!

THE presbyterian would fay, that the gofpel was the ftandard of his worfhip, and that he could not find that CHRIST or his difciples at the firft inftitution of the Lord's fupper, made ufe of any other pofture than that ufual at meals; that in imitation of this, as far as was confiftent with good fenfe, he took the facrament fitting, becaufe that is the pofture ufed at meals in the country, and the time he lives in; as much as among other nations, it was formerly the cuftom to eat and drink half lying down, and half leaning on couches. This is a very good plea for fitting down; but the reafon the churchman would give for kneeling, is as weighty to the full.

I do not believe (would he fay) the real prefence more than your felf; but look upon the partaking of the Lord's fupper, to be, of all the chriftian rites, the moft facred;

cred; it fills me at once with thoughts of my own unworthiness, and an awful reverence for the holiness of GOD, and therefore I receive it in the most humble posture I am able. What barbarous notions must a man have of the deity, who could imagine, that, if both spoke sincerely, and otherwise took the sacrament conscientiously, tho' in different postures, GOD would be offended at either!

To destroy all hatred and animosities, especially such as are chiefly built on prejudices, and are daily kept up by the ill Offices of others, the first step is with patience to consider what our adversaries may have to say for themselves: the next is to examine our own conduct, with the same severity as we do theirs.

THIS would enlarge the mind, make men give allowances to each other for education and custom, and help to cure them of their bigotry to their own opinion. It would teach dissenters to distinguish between things indifferent, and those that are clashing with the gospel, and make them know, that many things of human invention may have their use in sacred matters, and be

bene-

beneficial to ſociety, without interfering with religion.

A preſbyterian that can rejoice, and treat his friends on the anniverſaries of princes, whom he thinks to have been more eminently ſerviceable to his country, can keep queen *Elizabeth*'s and king *William*'s birth-days with pleaſure, would be no longer angry with his neighbour for not forgetting the nativity of his Saviour.

THE ſtrict quaker would no longer ſhock the ſight of ſilly people, by opening his ſhop in the moſt oſtentatious manner, when all his neighbours ſhut theirs the cloſeſt, but by examining the motives of his heart, learn to diſtinguiſh between the ſpirit of GOD, and that of contradiction.

THE rigid churchman, by comparing his own ſtock of inward virtue, with the vaſt concern he ſhews at the ſinfulneſs of ſchiſm in others, would learn to enter into the real cauſe of his uneaſineſs, ſhake hands with perſecution, and no longer miſtake ſelf-intereſt for charity, or party-zeal for religion.

I ſhall end this chapter with putting both churchmen and diſſenters in mind, that to

G

make

make religious ſcruples, and be anxiouſly ſollicitous concerning things indifferent, is ſuperſtition ; and to have another principle at heart than what men pretend to act from, is hypocriſy ; that ſo the crime of either may not be imagin'd to be the characteriſtick of one party more than another.

C H A P.

CHAP. IV.
Of MYSTERIES.

 Have said in the beginning of the first chapter, that, to be christians, it was necessary men should believe the mysterious as well as historical truths of the gospel. The straining of this, whilst we require others to explain every part of holy writ our own way, is very destructive to charity, and a handle for every communion to deny the name of christian to all those that refuse exactly to subscribe to their creeds; for should we reject those, who differ from us in the doctrine of one Mystery, the *Roman* catholicks may imagine, that they might with greater right exclude us from flatly denying another mystery, which they adore. For this reason I said lower, that whoever allow'd of the old and new testament, how differently soever from others, he might construe some

passa-

paſſages of either, ſo he but believ'd the whole to be the word of GOD, ought to be call'd a chriſtian.

BOTH proteſtants and *Roman* catholicks perfectly agree, that all Myſteries tranſcend reaſon, and there are ſome popiſh divines, who acknowledge * the myſteries denied by the *Socinians* to be againſt reaſon : but whether any thing contradictory can be the object of our faith, will beſt appear from a view of the difference there is between knowledge and belief.

WHAT has been convey'd by our own ſenſes to our underſtandings, we are ſaid to know : the ſame may be ſaid of every thing, which, after due examination, our reaſon plainly demonſtrates to our judgment to be true or falſe. So when I hear a man ſpeak, and ſee him ſtand before me, I know that he is there. And again, if I can reaſon at all, and exiſt my ſelf, I may be aſſur'd from within, that there is a firſt cauſe ; and conſequently I

* Nicolle perpetuitè de la foix, *pag.* 118, 119. *E-dit.* 1666.

can

can prove to my self, that there is a GOD.

THIS then is call'd knowledge, but, when we admit any thing to be true or false, and our judgment is persuaded that it is the one rather than the other, on an authority from without, the action is call'd believing : of this there are many degrees, and the confidence we believe with is either strong or slight, according to the good or indifferent opinion we entertain of the authority, which was the first motive of our belief. Experience teaches us, that this opinion is much influenced by the fears, wishes, inclinations, and varies according to the capacity of the believer. The ignorant may have a great opinion of an authority, which a wise man shall altogether despise : and on the other side the wise man may find out reasons to believe, which the other cannot penetrate into. It is to be observed, that when men believe, as often they do, on bare suspicion, guesses and slight surmises of their own, in these cases, the circumstances their conjectures are built upon, are all the authority from without, which they have for their belief.

WHAT

WHAT I have said may seem too phi-
losophical to those who are not used to abstract thinking ; but every body who is
but in the least capable of observing what
passes within his own mind, must know
the difference there is between knowing
and believing, and perceive that the first
implies a certainty, superiour to any af-
surance ever receiv'd from the latter, because, for the first we rely on our own
testimony, and for the latter we must trust
to the testimony of others.   It is very
true, that our senses sometimes deceive us,
that our reasons are false, and our judgment errs.   This I confess is a mortifying
reflection ; but still the greatest certainty
we can receive must come from them ;
for when once we begin to doubt of our
reason, and our senses, we are no longer sure
of any thing, an immediate revelation from
GOD not excepted ; for how shall we trust
to a revelation, when we cannot depend
either on the senses by which we receive
it, or our reason, the only touch-stone,
by which we can assure our selves of its
being divine ?

IN

IN the idea we can form of the fupreme being, the firft attributes, we are convinc'd of, are his power and wifdom, though in a degree of perfection vaftly beyond our capacity to conceive; and if we continue in that contemplation, we fhall find, that the unity of a GOD muft be equally necef-fary with his exiftence: but as foon as we admit of reveal'd religion, and the gofpel, we meet with fomething that furpaffes, if not fhocks our underftanding, which is the divinity of JESUS CHRIST, and that of the HOLY GHOST. Men may cavil and wreft words to their own purpofe as long as they lift; but whoever has read the New Teftament with attention, and denies that he has found any fuch meaning hinted at there, muft be either very blind or very obftinate.

WHAT then muft we do in this dilemma? fhall we reject part of the gofpel, or fay, that there are three Gods, and fo fpeak not only againft the cleareft ideas we have of the deity, but likewife the plaineft doctrine of the fame gofpel, as well as of the old teftament? not to be guilty of either, we ought to treat this point with

the

the utmost diffidence of our own capacity, and fix our eyes on the eternal veracity, as well as the unfearchable wisdom of G o d; and when once we have affured our felves that he neither can have the will to deceive us, nor can contradict himself, we shall look upon the whole as a mysterious truth, which G o d has not been pleafed to reveal to us in a more intelligible manner.

T h e more we endeavour to explain this myftery, the more intricate we shall find it ; and it will lefs startle and fright reafon, when propounded in a few words according to the fimplicity of the scripture, than it does by that great train of explications, that accompany it in *Thomas Aquina*'s commentators. People may wrangle and quarrel about this article to the world's end; but it is impoffible men should ever entertain the fame fentiments of a matter, which is unintelligible in its nature; and it is to be admired how fo many men of fenfe, and good logicians, as this point has been controverted by for fo many ages, could ever imagine that any thing could be a fit fubject for difputation,

tion, which no language can give them the least idea of. If GOD has so far enlighten'd any one's understanding, that he can comprehend more of this mystery than another, let him pay his acknowledgment with gratitude and humility, but not haughtily dictate to the conscience of his neighbour, who confesses that he has not receiv'd so great a measure of the divine grace.

OTHERS may interpret for us as they please, and impose upon us what forms they think fit: but whoever will attend to what passes in his own mind, may soon be convinced, that believing is not a thing of choice. Our church pretends not to infallibility, which implies, that all her members are at full liberty to re-examine whatever she has taught them. No private man therefore ought to be too dogmatical in matters of faith: what to my understanding is difficult, and obscure, cannot be made otherwise to me by another's saying, that it is clear and easy to him; and let us hear what we can, every one at last must judge for himself to the best of his ability. *There are innumerable places* (says the learn-

H   ned

ned and pious bishop *Taylor,* * *speaking of the holy scripture) that contain, no doubt, great mysteries, but so wrapt in clouds, and hid in umbrages, so heighten'd with expressions, or so cover'd with allegories and garments of rhetorick, so profound in the matter, or so alter'd and made intricate in the manner, that they may seem to have been left as trials of our industry, and as occasions and opportunities for the exercise of mutual charity and toleration, rather than as the repositories of faith, and furniture of creeds.*

THE doctrine of the Trinity was not establish'd before the famous council of *Nice,* which every body knows was occasion'd by the disputes of *Arius* and *Alexander,* the one a bishop, and the other a priest of *Alexandria.* The fathers of the three first centuries had very imperfect notions concerning this mystery, and they very much differ'd in their opinions, when they began to treat of it, as appears from their various terms, of which several were unintelligible, and the confused expressions

---

* *In his treatise on the liberty of prophesying, printed in his collection of political and moral discourses.*

they

they made use of. It is evident, that *Constantine the Great*, how well soever he had been instructed in his new religion, was very little acquainted with the point in question before the meeting of that assembly, as is so visible from the long letter he wrote to the contending parties above-mentioned, in which he chides them equally.

FOR though each side treated the other with the odious name of heretick, and endeavour'd to shew, that the sentiments of the opposite party overthrew the christian religion, yet the emperor had no such apprehensions. *He found* (he said) *that the controversy had begun in this manner,* * *that* Alexander *having demanded of each of his priests, what they thought of a passage, or rather on an idle sort of question,* Arius *inconsiderately answered what he should not have thought, or rather conceal'd, if he had thought it ; that from thence had come his excommunication, and the division of the people ; and therefore he exhorted them to a mutual pardoning of one another, and*

* Euseb. in vita Constant. *c.* 64. Socrat. *l.* 1. *c.* 7.

to receive his opinion, which was, that it had been better not to have troubled the ecclesiasticks with this question, and that those who were asked it, should have held their tongues, because the matter concerned what was equally incomprehensible to both parties, and which served only to raise disturbance among the people. He could not conceive, how far a question of very small importance, and in which, if they well understood one another, they would find they agreed in the main, they should make such a bustle, and divide themselves in so scandalous a manner.

I do not say this (added he) as if I would constrain you to think of the same thing on a most vain question, or however you please to call it: for one may, without dishonouring the assembly, and without breaking the communion, be in different sentiments in such inconsiderable things. We have not all the same wills in all things, neither are we all of us of the same temper of body and humours.

THE emperor, it is probable afterwards, inform'd himself, that this matter was of great moment, yet in his behaviour

touch-

touching this controverfy, he was not always very confiftent with himfelf. When *Arius* was condemn'd, he banifh'd him, and order'd all his [a] books to be burnt; but afterwards recall'd, and invited him to come to court, at his [b] (that is the emperor's) charge: he likewife fhew'd little regard to St. *Athanafius*, who had been a great ftickler againft *Arius*; for when that bifhop, having, in his turn, been condemn'd by his enemies on another account, was fent in exile, and thofe of his party [c] in *Alexandria* ceafed not to implore the emperor, that he might be recall'd; *Conftantine* [d], in a letter, upbraided the people of that town for their lightnefs and folly, and enjoin'd the ecclefiafticks to remain quiet, declaring, he would not recal *Athanafius*, whom he treats as a feditious perfon; and the fame emperor anfwer'd likewife to *Anthony* the hermit [e], *that he could not flight the judgment of the council*

[a] Eufeb. in vita Conftant.
[b] Socrat. *l.* 1. *c.* 25.
[c] Sozom. *l. c.* 31.
[d] Eufeb. in vita Conftant.
[e] Eufeb. in vita Conftant.

H 3

of

of Tyre, *because, that supposing some among the bishops were passionate, yet it was not probable that so great a number of wise and learned bishops should all of them act by passion ; and that* Athanasius *was an insolent, proud, troublesome fellow.*

THE *Arian* heresy did not die with its author : the emperors *Constantius* and *Valens* [a] protected it, and tho' some people out of zeal for orthodoxy have maintain'd, [b] that *Arianism* never made a great body in the world, nor was of any long [c] continuance, it is certain, that that heresy subsisted above three hundred years [d] in splendour ; that it was for almost two ages the predominant religion ; that it was on the throne in the east and west ; and that it reign'd in *Italy, France, Pannonia,* and *Africa.* Several have spoke very slightingly of the fathers, that compos'd the council of *Nice* ; especially *Sabinus,* [e] a *Macedonian*

[a] See Trebellius Pollio in the life of Galienus.

[b] Jurieu vray systeme de l'eglise, p. 149.

[c] Nicolle, contre jurieu de l'unité de l'eglise.

[d] Janua cœlorum reserata, *printed at* Amsterdam, 1692. pag. 57.

[e] Socrat. l. 7.

bi-

bishop of *Heraclea*, a town of *Thrace*, who treats them as ignoramus's in his collection of Councils ; but *Eusebius*, bishop of *Cesarea*, who assisted at it, has highly [a] extolled their wisdom and capacity, and some learned men of the last century have spoke in defence of them. Be their praise what it will, this is evident from many circumstances, that their debates were as much influenced by private grudges [b] and personal hatreds, as the love of truth, or any real piety. When several of these bishops, after the council of *Nice*, were met at *Jerusalem*, on another troublesom affair, *Constantine*, who was so bigotted to the clergy, wrote to them, complaining, [c] *that in a time, wherein the* barbarians *began to acknowledge the true* GOD, *the christians, who would be thought to have the mysteries of* GOD *in their keeping* (for he durst not say that they kept them) *labour'd only to entertain divisions and hatred among them, not to say for the destruction of mankind.*

[a] Eufeb. in vita Conftant.
[b] Sozom. *l.* 1. *c.* 17.
[c] Eufeb. in vita Conftant.

H 4 THE

THE contentions about this mystery of the Trinity, begun by two clergy-men, have already at one time or other been the ruin of millions of laymen, and are like to do more mischief in the world, if the civil magistrate interposes not and hinders the clergy from ever reviving this affair. Happy had it been for christianity, had all the clergy been of *Sozomen*'s opinion, who said, [a] *that he did not dare to relate the creed of* Nice, *because some, his pious and learned friends in this matter, advised him to suppress the things, which the initiates and priests alone should understand, and that, according to their council, he had conceal'd what was to be kept silent.*

THE great danger there is in the quarrels of the clergy is, that there can be no drawn battle among them; being in all their contests both judges and parties, one side must fall, and there can be no peace without a conquest. Could clergy-men have been satisfied without crushing their adversaries, the *Arian* heresy might have been prevented; for when the *Arians* shewed, that they were ready to submit to a

[a] Sozom. *l.* 1. *c.* 20.

con-

confeſſion expreſs'd in the terms propos'd to them, the orthodox biſhops fear'd, [a] leſt they ſhould expound theſe terms in an ill ſenſe, and therefore made an addition to it more binding ; which, when the *Arians* likewiſe would have ſubſcribed to, the orthodox ſtill found out more hampering terms, till at laſt from an incomprehenſible myſtery they made it in the opinion of the *Antitrinitarians*, a plain and intelligible contradiction. If this expreſſion be thought too harſh, I deſire the reader to conſider, that it is no more than what the greateſt champions of the *Trinitarians* are proud to own. Hear what Monſieur *Nicolle* ſays of the doctrine of the Trinity, *It* [b] *confounds reaſon,* ſays he, *and prompts it to revolt. If there be any viſible difficulties, they are thoſe which are contain'd in that myſtery, that three perſons really diſtinct have one and the ſame eſſence, and that this eſſence being the ſame thing in each perſon with the relations that diſtinguiſh them, may be communicated without the*

[a] *Monſ.* le Clerc, *in the life of* Euſebius.
[b] *Monſ.* Nicolle, perpetuité de la foi, *pag.* 118, *Edit.* 1666.

com-

communication of the relations which distin-
guish the persons. If human reason consults
her self, she will rise up against those incon-
ceivable truths: if she pretends to make use
of her own light to penetrate into them, it
will furnish her with arms to engage against
them. Wherefore, in order to believe them,
she ought to blind her self, to stifle all her
Ratiocinations, and depress and sink her self
under the weight of divine authority.

To give effectual directions for believing of mysteries is almost as difficult as it
is to explain them. As to our duty, concerning this of the Trinity, I think we
ought to examine the scriptures and believe of it what we can conceive the word
of GOD would have us, without depriving
others of the same liberty. I would say
very near the same of most mysteries, tho'
I incur the censures of our zealous clergy,
who will call this the advice of a latitudi-
narian, if not worse: those gentlemen are
not always very consistent with themselves.
The protestants could never have withdrawn
themselves from the church of *Rome*, with
any shew of reason, without denying her infallibility; yet the reform'd in general are

so very uneasy at the loss of it for themselves, that there is hardly a sect of them,
but the zealots of it are angry with every
body, that will not submit to their authority.

THE moderate men of our church are
not so positive as to their own interpreta-
tions of the scriptures, and think that [a]
it is unreasonable to require all men, under
the pain of an anathema, to see, that one
particular position is the certain sense of
a passage really ambiguous and difficult.
It were fit, says bishop *Taylor*, that [b] our
confidence should be according to our evidence, and our zeal according to our confidence. I desire the reader to take the
sentiments of this learned prelate concerning private judgment and opinions on these
and all matters of dispute in his own words,
Since (says he) *there are* [c] *so many copies
with infinite varieties of reading ; since a various interpunction, a parenthesis, a letter,
an accent may much alter the sense ; since*

---

[a] *Bishop* Taylor *on the liberty of prophesying.*
[b] Idem ibid.
[c] Idem *p.* 493, *Edit.* 1657.

some

some places have divers literal senses, may have spiritual, mystical, and allegorical meanings; since there are so many tropes, metonymies, ironies, hyperboles, proprieties, and improprieties of language, whose understanding depends upon such circumstances, that it is almost impossible to know the proper interpretation, now that the knowledge of such circumstances and particular stories is irrecoverably lost; since there are some mysteries, which at the best advantage of expression are not so easy to be apprehended, and whose application, by reason of our imperfections, must needs be dark, sometimes weak, sometimes unintelligible: and lastly, since these ordinary means of expounding scripture, as searching the originals, conference of places, parity of reason, and analogy of faith, are all dubious, uncertain, and very fallible; he that is the wisest, and by consequence the likeliest to expound truest, in all probability of reason, will be very far from confidence; because every one of these, and many more, are like so many degrees of improbability and uncertainty, all depressing our certainty of finding out truth in such mysteries, and amidst so many difficulties. And therefore a wise man that

con-

considers this, would not willingly be prescrib-ed to by others ; for it is best, every man should be left in that liberty from which no man can justly take him, unless he could se-cure him from error.

THE same bishop having told us in a-nother place, that all the disputes concerning tradition, councils, fathers, &c. were not arguments besides, or against reason, but contestations and pretences to the best arguments, and to the most certain satisfaction to our reason, goes on thus. *But* [a] *then all these coming into question submit themselves to reason, that is, to be judg'd by human understanding, upon the best grounds and information it can receive. So that scripture, tradition, councils and fathers, are the evidence in a question, but reason is the judge : that is, we being the persons that are to be persuaded, we must see, that we be persuaded reasonably ; and it is unreasonable to assent to a lesser evidence, when a greater and clearer is propounded : but of that, every man for himself is to take cognizance, if he be able to judge ; if he be not,*

[a] Idem 507.

he

he is not bound under the tye of necessity to know any thing of it.

IN such lessons and considerations as these, how ungrateful soever they may be to fiery zealots, are contain'd a true preservative from falling into schism, and the greatest antidote against persecution; for, as on the one hand, they will mitigate the troubles of scrupulous consciences, so on the other, they will cure uncharitableness in those, whose sufficiency makes them incapable of bearing with any opinion but their own.

THEY will likewise help to draw men off from vain speculations and empty cavils, and to promote concord and true religion; for it is union and the practice of virtue we want: these are the national blessings we stand most in need of. It is not faith we are defective in: [a] the multitude in all countries, as well as our own, are apt enough to believe what is taught them by their spiritual guides.

NOTHING can be more shocking to human reason, than the doctrine of the

[a] *See pag.* 7, 8, *and* 17.

real

real prefence in the eucharift; yet we find not, that among the *Roman* catholicks, who maintain tranfubftantiation, or the *Lutherans,* who hold a confubftantiation, the people boggle more at the articles of their faith, than they do among others, by whom the words that have occafion'd that pretended myftery are taken in a figurative fenfe.

THERE is hardly a truth more eafily apprehended, or which we are more fully convinc'd of, than that two and two make four: yet were men to be taught from their infancy that it was a myftery, that on a certain occafion two and two made feven, with an addition to be believ'd on pain of damnation, I am perfuaded, that at leaft feven in ten would fwallow the fhameful paradox; and that if they had always feen others ill treated for disbelieving of it, by that time they were come to years of maturity, they would not only affert it themfelves, but likewife diflike, if not hate thofe, who fhould call it in queftion. We muft fuppofe, that it had been inculcated to them with application and affiduity by parents, nurfes, mafters, and

and all that had the tuition of, or any direction over them. Few people are acquainted with the force of prejudice: we are little capable of examining any thing which is rooted in us by education and custom.

BUT, that my reader may see the opinion of one of our greatest divines, concerning the effects of dogmatising in divinity, and the proneness of the people to believe, I shall quote part of what archbishop *Tillotson* says [a] of mysteries on account of transubstantiation, *We will suppose then,* says his grace, *that about the time when universal ignorance, and the genuine daughter of it, (call her devotion or superstition) had overspread the world, and the generality of the people were strongly inclin'd to believe strange things; and even the greatest contradictions were recommended to them under the notion of mysteries; being told by their priests and guides, that the more contradictious any thing is to reason, the greater merit there is in believing it: I say, let us suppose, that in this state of things, one or*

[a] *Archbishop* Tillotson *in his rule of faith,* p. 716, &c.

more of the most eminent then in the church, either out of design, or out of superstitious ignorance, and mistake of the sense of our Saviour's words, used in the consecration of the sacrament, should advance this new doctrine, that the words of consecration, &c.
———————Such a doctrine as this was likely to be advanced by the ambitious clergy of that time, as a probable means to draw in the people to a greater veneration of them.
——————Nor was such a doctrine less likely to take and prevail among the people in an age prodigiously ignorant, and strongly inclin'd to superstition, and thereby well prepar'd to receive the grossest absurdities under the notion of mysteries——— ———Now supposing such a doctrine as this so fitted to the humour and temper of the age, to be once asserted either by chance or out of design, it would take like wild-fire; especially if by some one or more who bore sway in the church, it were but recommended with convenient gravity and solemnity——— ———And for the contradictions contain'd in this doctrine, it was but telling the people then (as they do in effect now) that contradictions ought to be no scruple in the way of faith;

I

that

that the more impoſſible any thing is, 'tis the fitter to be believ'd; that it is not praiſe-worthy to believe plain poſſibilities, but this is the galantry and heroical power of faith; this is the way to oblige God Almighty for e-ver to us, to believe flat and downright con-tradictions———— The more abſurd and un-reaſonable a thing is, the more proper matter for an article of faith. And if any of theſe innovations be objected againſt, as contrary to former belief and practice, it is but put-ting forth a luſty act of faith, and believing another contradiction, that though they be contrary, yet they are the ſame.

No candid reader can imagine, that I would endeavour to make ſlight of faith, or leſſen the reverence that is due to the real myſtery of our religion, any more than either of theſe prelates; and I can aſſure him, that the great end, of what I have ſaid and quoted of others in this chapter, is to promote the publick peace and tranquil-lity, by ſhewing, how conſiſtent it may be made with our piety to GOD, and charity to our neighbours. For which reaſon, in the firſt place, I recommend the ſerious con-ſideration of it to thoſe of the orthodox, who

can

can accommodate themselves to every word of our creeds, conjuring them not to exact rigorously the fame of every body, who owns himfelf to be of their communion. When men are peaceable and quiet, without ever defiring to mention the fcruples, which perhaps they may labour under in their private opinion, they ought not to be forc'd to fubfcribe to every model of faith that others fhall conceive for them. Thofe trials are ever attended with human paffion, and generally end in perfonal hatreds. A man may believe the fame in fubftance with us, but have a fcruple concerning perhaps one fingle word in a whole article of faith: when we confider, that this article was drawn up by uninfpired men, and perhaps thofe words put in on purpofe to puzzle an adverfary, who had fhew'd a diflike to them; is it not unchriftian like, to drag fuch a man out of his clofet to make him fign to it, and not fuffer him to reft, till by his refufal we fhall have an opportunity of calling him heretick, and expofing him as an enemy to God and religion? but how inhuman! how execrable would it it be, should this ever be done with a design to rob him of his livelyhood, and the good opinion of his fellow christians, that are unacquainted with the controversy?

BUT then again I would not more earnestly persuade the orthodox rigorists to avoid all narrow scrutinies of consciences but their own, than I would exhort the admirers of human understanding, not to rely too much upon their own sufficiency. How useful soever philosophy may be to society, and the affairs of human life; it is the worst guide to eternity, and ought never to be mixed with theology. He that will admit of no proof inferiour to a mathematical demonstration can never be a christian, and there is no system found out yet, by which the *Socinians* themselves could explain, and salve the difficulties to be met with in the gospel, even according to their own interpretation. Every man of thought must be convinced, that there are truths for which it were ridiculous to expect demonstration.

I shall end this chapter, by setting forth in two easy instances the difference there

is,

is, between things that are above reason, and surpass our capacity, and such as are against reason, and contradict demonstration.

WAS I to hear of a man, who could see through an oaken plank two inches thick, every where solid and entire, I would refuse to believe it, even on the testimony of ten thousand witnesses otherwise credible: but had GOD revealed to me, that he had made such an one, I would immediately submit, and as soon as I was satisfied, that the revelation was really divine, would believe it as surely, and, if it be possible with less scruple than now I believe that there is such a place as *Japan*, which has been confirmed to me several hundred ways. I would laugh at any body, that should talk of strait pores, and what only would make things diaphanous; I would not hearken to opticks or refractions, and despise all reasoners, who should pretend to demonstrate the impossibility of it. Here a man would have nothing to do, but to conquer the good opinion he has of human understanding, the shallowness

of

of which, the moſt knowing are ſo well convinc'd of on thouſand occaſions. In this caſe I would not only call it preſumption, but the higheſt inſolence, to oppoſe the penetration of all the philoſophers in the world to the leaſt idea, a reaſonable man can have of the omnipotence of GOD.

THE proud naturaliſts and mathematicians, who ſhould endeavour to diſſuade me from my belief, I would lead into a contemplation of the immenſity, and the order of the creation, the union between ſoul and body, and other wonders of the univerſe, that are moſt obvious; and having made them ſenſible of the pitiful ſtock of real knowledge they are poſſeſſed of, I would aſk them, what it was he could not make, that had made heaven and earth.

BUT on the other hand, when a man once knows that two and two makes four, and yet aſſerts, that he believes that two and two on a certain occaſion may make ſeven; if he be ſincere, it is evident, that he either knows not what he ſays, or at

leaſt

leaſt underſtands not what to believe ſig-
nifies. For after all, tho' a man may believe a thing to be true, which he appre-
hends not at all, it is impoſſible he ſhould
believe the contrary of what he plainly ap-
prehends to be true.

C H A P.

C H A P. V.

Of Free-Will and Predestination.

W H A T we call the will is pro-
perly the laſt reſult of deliberation, either long or ſhort,
which immediately precedes
the execution of, or at leaſt the endeavour
to execute the thing will'd : I ſay the reſult, which immediately precedes the execution ; for, when a will or volition is
made long before the execution of the thing
will'd, it is only call'd a reſolution, and always requires a latter will to ſet about it,
and ſometimes a great many, or elſe will
never be executed. So a man, whoſe head
achs after a debauch, ſays, and perhaps
with great ſincerity, that he will live ſo-
berly for the future. But theſe might better be call'd wiſhes, than wills or volitions ;
which latter always imply an execution,

or

or at leaft, an endeavour for it : and thefe can never be free ; for as foon as the will is made, the thing will'd is determin'd, and before it is made, it is no will yet ; but only a deliberation, what to will.

THE reafon, why every body imagines that he has a free-will, is, becaufe we are confcious, that in the choice of things we feel a power (which we perceive not to be controuled by any thing) to determine our judgment either way. But when once we reflect on what paffes within us, and confider that in making this choice, at leaft in things of moment, and that are worth obferving, we confult all our faculties, and are forc'd in fpight of our teeth to chufe that, which, to our then prefent inclination, often to our vifible detriment, feems to be moft eligible. If we reflect on this, I fay, our wills fhall not feem to be fo free, as is commonly imagin'd.

EVERY body can wifh what he pleafes, but it is not fo with his will ; and, was the one as arbitrary as the other, there would be more virtue, and not half the mifery, and what are call'd misfortunes in

K   the

the world, of what we now see men labour under. There is hardly a person so debauch'd, but what has often wish'd, tho' but for his health's or fortune's sake, that it was in his power to lead a more regular life: what is it hinders him, but his appetites and inclinations, that influence and seduce his will, and do him the same prejudice he could receive from a fatal and unavoidable necessity of sinning?

THAT the true motives of our will so often pass by undiscovered, is to be attributed to the swiftness of thought, and the sudden diversity of our volitions, which often succeed each other so instantaneously, that when men are in haste and irresolute, we may sometimes observe one part of the body yet employ'd in executing a former will, whilst another shall be already obeying the commands of a latter: but when we act slowly, and what is call'd deliberately, the motives of every volition must be obvious to all that have the courage, as well as capacity, to search into them.

GIVE two men each a glass in his hand of some value, which, if he breaks it, he is to pay for: let the one be of a covetous nature, but no wrangler, and very pliable as to opinion; the other very poſitive, but laviſh of his money. Diſpute with either of theſe pretty warmly againſt free-will, and the power he has of dropping the glaſs, or keeping it in his hand. The firſt, depend upon it, will not let it fall; and, dare him to it never ſo much, he'll content himſelf with ſaying, that he is ſure he can do it if he will, but that he has no mind to throw away ſo much money to be laugh'd at. The other, 'tis ten to one, will daſh it to pieces, and if he dares ſpeak his mind, tell you, that he had rather pay for the glaſs, than not have the pleaſure to convince you of your folly, obſtinacy, or what elſe his paſſion or manners ſhall give him leave to call it.

I doubt not but both perſons would be fully perſuaded, and therefore might ſwear with a good conſcience, that they had acted from a principle of free-will, though it ſeems plain to me, that each of them was prompted to what he did, and over-rul'd by a predominant paſſion.

I

I know very well, that it is poſſible that the covetous man might have broke the glaſs as well as the other, but then his love for money muſt have been leſs, or his deſire of triumph greater than would be ſuitable to the character I required him to be of.

THIS may ſerve to put us in mind, with what care and vigilance we ought to examine and guard our ſelves againſt thoſe paſſions, which ſo covertly govern and hurry us away, even unknown to our ſelves. The ſolidity of which moral, I hope, will make amends for the meanneſs of the example, which ſome may imagine to be below the dignity of the ſubject I treat of in this chapter.

THE word predeſtination is ſo well un-derſtood by all parties, that it would be ſuperfluous to explain it further. That this is a doctrine openly laid down in the goſpel, is evident to all that can read; that it is likewiſe attended with difficul-ties inexplicable to human reaſon, is as undeniable. I ſhall only take notice of the chief objection that is made againſt it, which is, that it makes GOD the author

of

of ſin. The plainneſs with which this doctrine has been taught by St. *Paul*, and the terrible conſequences to be drawn from it by as plain a manner of reaſoning, have occaſioned innumerable hereſies and ſchiſms, each of which has, at different times, been the cauſe of thouſands of miſchiefs and calamities among chriſtians.

IT is certain, that whilſt we only follow the light of nature, nothing can be more inconſiſtent with the ideas we have of the juſtice and goodneſs of GOD, than that a creature ſhould be puniſhed for ſins, which from eternity it was decreed he ſhould commit. It is this that has produced the various ſyſtems of the more and leſs daring advocates for free-will ; but I ſhall endeavour to demonſtrate on the one hand, that the boldeſt aſſertors of human liberty, the *Socinians* not excepted, have not remov'd the difficulty as to the origin of evil ; and on the other, that all the ſolution and arguments of the predeſtinarians, drawn from human reaſon, have hitherto been inſufficient to anſwer the objections that have been made to them. And when from hence it ſhall appear, that the debate is

K 3   about

about the greateſt myſtery of our religion, I doubt not but to convince every reaſonable man, that it is a fitter ſubjeċt for our reſignation to the reveal'd will of G o d, than it is for quarrels and contentions with one another.

I t would hardly be poſſible to think of any thing, that in ſo many thouſand controverſies, as are to be met with on this head, has not been ſaid by one or other ; for this reaſon, I have in my eye a celebrated author, who was endu'd with a vaſt ſtock of learning, and no leſs penetration, and has treated of this matter with greater moderation and impartiality than any other. From him I ſhall borrow ſeveral paſſages, and often manage what I have to ſay in his words, with little addition of my own.

I t muſt be allow'd, that the hypotheſis of human liberty ſeems at firſt view to clear the doubt: but it only puts the miſchief farther off, and can never take it away. It is needleſs to run thro' the ſeveral degrees, and the different ſyſtems that have been made of it by the *Pelagians, Semi-pelagians, Originiſts, Moliniſts, Synergiſts, gifts*, and *Arminians*, and many others; ſince thoſe who ſuppoſe the moſt abſolute free-will, if they are cloſely purſued, muſt at laſt be involv'd in, and leave the ſame difficulties unclear'd, which frighten men from predeſtination. From the ſimple queſtion, what is the cauſe of ſin? the reſult of a thouſand diſputes muſt at long run be this. GOD is eternal, and a being infinitely good, ſo there could be no evil before the world was made; GOD created the world, then whence comes evil?

THIS, allowing the ſyſtem of the creation, being unanſwerable to human capacities, produced in the ſecond century the *Marcionites*, and after them [a] the *Manicheans*. Theſe hereticks denied the old teſtament, and, among other impieties, ſuppoſed two coeternal principles, the one of all [b] good, and the other of all evil: the good principle, they ſaid, would have made every thing good, if he had not been oppos'd; but the bad principle being as powerful, and equally deſirous to introduce

[a] *In the third century.*
[b] Auguſtin de Hereſ. *c.* 46.

K 4

evil,

evil, as the other was to do good, the good principle was forc'd to yield to neceſſity; and thus the world, which is a compound of good and evil, was, after many conflicts, produced by the agreement of theſe two principles.

How oppoſite ſoever this opinion was to reveal'd religion, and the cleareſt ideas we have of the unity of GOD, when once this monſtrous hypotheſis was admitted, it explain'd the phænomena of human life better than any other, and ſolv'd innumerable difficulties that were inexplicable to the orthodox, whilſt both parties confin'd themſelves to the light of nature. Nothing was more eaſy to the fathers of the church, than to overthrow theſe hereſies, when they attack'd them upon the abſurdity of their ſyſtem, and the orthodox were the agreſſors; but when the *Manicheans* made the attack, it was a very hard task to anſwer their objections, and the fathers would not have triumphed over them at ſo cheap a rate as they did, had the others known better how to puſh them home. Had *Cerdon*, *Marcion*, *Apelles*, and *Manes* been as able diſputants, as many have

have been in the laſt century among the jeſuits and janſeniſts, they would not have
been ſilenc'd as they were.

WHEN the hereticks, by way of oppo-
ſition, enquir'd into the cauſe of evil, they
were commonly anſwer'd, that man was
created by GOD in a happy ſtate; but he,
not following the light of his conſcience,
which was intended by the author of his
being to conduct him in the way of virtue, became wicked, and ſo deſerv'd, that
GOD, who was ſovereignly juſt as well as
good, ſhould make him feel the effect of
his wrath; ſo that GOD is not the author
of moral evil, but of phyſical evil, which
is the puniſhment of moral evil. When
this was anſwer'd them, or any thing elſe,
by which the cauſe of ſin was thrown on
the free-will of the creature, they had nothing to reply; but if they had asked why
this free-will was given to man, or if it
was given, why ſo good a judge as he
was, it ſhould determine his choice to e-
vil, more work would have been cut out
for their antagoniſts: for every man's reaſon, they might have ſaid, muſt ſuggeſt to
him, that if man was the workmanſhip of
a prin-

a principle infinitely good and holy, he ſhould not only have been created without any actual evil, but alſo without any inclination, or the leaſt propenſity to evil, ſince that inclination is ſuch a defect, as could not have ſuch a principle for its cauſe.

WHAT *Origen* told the *Marcionites,* *That* [a] *an intelligent creature, who had not enjoy'd free-will, had been immutable and immortal like* GOD, is likewiſe eaſy to refute. They need only to have ask'd *Origen,* whether the bleſſed in paradiſe are equal to GOD in the attributes of immutability and immortality. He muſt have anſwer'd in the negative, and conſequently it is not true, that a creature becomes a GOD, becauſe it is determin'd to do good, and depriv'd of that which he calls free-will.

THE anſwer of St. *Baſil* has the ſame fault: GOD, (ſays he) *would* [b] *not have us to love him by conſtraint, and we ourſelves do not think our ſervants well diſpo-*

[a] *In a dialogue againſt the* Marcionites, *attributed to* Origen, Sect. 3.

[b] Baſilius magnus, *Tom.* 1. in homilia quod deus non ſit autor mali.

ſea

ſed to our ſervice whilſt we hold them in chains, but only when they obey us from their own free pleaſure. What would St. *Baſil* have replied, if they had remonſtrated to him, that in paradice God is lov'd and ſerv'd perfectly well, and yet the bleſſed do not enjoy free-will, and that they have not that fatal privilege of the power to commit ſin? Muſt we therefore compare them to ſlaves? And again, what would he ſay to the righteous upon earth, who by the aſſiſtance of the divine grace love their heavenly father, and perform good works? Does the grace of God reduce the faithful to the condition of ſlaves? It is evident then, that without infringing the liberty of the creature, God could infallibly determine it to what is good, and therefore ſin does not proceed from hence, that the Creator could not prevent it without deſtroying the free-will of the creature; but we muſt look out for ſome other cauſe of it.

Some have urg'd, that God permitted ſin to manifeſt his wiſdom, which ſhines more brightly by the diſorders, which the wickedneſs of men produces every day,

than

than it would have done in a state of innocence: but this is inconfiftent with the
ideas we have of the juftice and goodneſs
of GOD, and would be to compare the
deity to a father, who fhould fuffer his
children to break their legs, on purpoſe to
ſhew all the city his great skill in ſetting
their broken bones.

MANY more reaſons have been alledged for the permiſſion of ſin; but the
beſt that human wit has hitherto invented, may be oppos'd by others more ſpecious and more agreeable to the ideas we
have of order, and the difficulty concerning the origin of evil remains the ſame
in natural as well as reveal'd religion;
for which reaſon the fathers had the
heathen philoſophers to anſwer on this
head, as well as the hereticks that ſprung
from the church.

SOME of the pagans have made weighty objections againſt providence: that of
Epicurus, as to evil, is of great force. GOD,
ſays he, is either willing to take away
evil, and is not able; or he is able, and
not willing; or elſe he is neither willing
nor able, or he is both willing and able.

If

If he is willing and not able, he is weak, which can't be said of GOD; if he is able and not willing, he is envious, which is equally abfurd to fay; if he is neither willing nor able, he is both weak and envious: and if he is both willing and able, which is the only thing of the four that can be faid of GOD, then whence comes evil? this concerns not moral evil; but, if it did, the argument would be ftill more perplexing. *Laĉtantius* anfwers, [a] *that* GOD *is able, but not willing to take away evil, without being envious for all that: for the reafon, fays he, why* GOD *takes not away evil, is, becaufe it gives us wifdom, and at the fame time more good, and more pleafure in that wifdom, than there is trouble in evil. It is through wifdom we know* GOD, *and through that knowledge we gain immortality, which is the higheft good; fo that unlefs we firft know evil, we can never attain to the knowledge of good. But this* Epicurus *fees not, nor any other, that if evil be taken away, wifdom is taken away in like manner, and there remain in men no foot-*

[a] Laĉtant. de ira Dei, *cap.* 13.

fteps

ſteps of virtue, the eſſence of which conſiſts in bearing and overcoming the bitterneſs of evil. Thus for a ſmall ſpace if we ſhould be without evil, we ſhould be deſtitute of the greateſt and real good that belongs to us.

THIS anſwer of *Lactantius* is not only pitiful and weak, but full of errors, and perhaps hereſies. It ſuppoſes, that GOD muſt produce evil, becauſe otherwiſe he would not be able to communicate either wiſdom or virtue, or the knowledge of what is good. It overthrows all that divines tell us about the happineſs of paradice, and the ſtate of innocence. Are we not told, that *Adam* and *Eve* in this happy ſtate felt, without any mixture of uneaſineſs, all the pleaſures which that delicious and charming place the garden of *Eden*, where GOD placed them, could afford them? Beſides, do not all chriſtians take it for granted, that, if they had not ſinned, they and all their poſterity ſhould have enjoy'd this happineſs without being ſubject either to diſeaſes or troubles, and that neither the elements nor animals had ever done them any harm? It was their ſin that expos'd them to cold and heat,

to

to hunger and thirſt, to pain and ſorrow, and to the miſchiefs, which certain beaſts do to us.

IT is ſo far from being true, that virtue and wiſdom cannot belong to a man without phyſical evil, as *Lactantius* affirms, that on the contrary it muſt be maintained, that man has been ſubject to this evil only, becauſe he renounc'd virtue and wiſdom. The ſtoicks had committed the ſame fault, as *Lactantius*, and maintain'd the uſefulneſs of vice, without [a] which, they ſaid, there could have been no virtue. But ſee how ſolidly they were refuted by *Plutarch*. *Is there* [b] *then,* ſays he, *no good among the gods, becauſe there is no evil? And when* Jupiter *having reſolved all matter into himſelf, ſhall be alone, other differences being taken away, will there then be no good, becauſe there is no evil? But is it true, that there is a melody in a choir, though none in it ſing faultily, and health in the body, though no member is ſick; and cannot virtue have its exiſtence without vice?*

[a] Aul. Gellius, *lib. c.* 1.
[b] Plutarch. Iſis & Oſir.

I

I wonder they do not say, that the consumption was made for the sound constitution of mens bodies, and the gout for the swiftness of their feet, and that Achilles *would not have had a good head of hair, if* Thersites *had not been bald: for what difference is there between such triflers and ravers, and those, who say, that intemperance was brought forth not unprofitably for continence, nor injustice for justice, that so we may pray to the gods there may be always wickedness?*

THE argument of *Epicurus*, without the help of reveal'd religion, is not to be answer'd by any other system, but that of the two principles, which immediately clears that and all other difficulties concerning the origin of evil. How strange and deplorable is the fate of human reason, that the worst of hereticks, nay the heathens themselves, should with an hypothesis altogether absurd and contradictory, be able to explain, what we experience, a hundred times better than orthodox christians do with a supposition so just, so necessary, and so true, of one first principle,

ciple, which is infinitely good and almighty !

THIS doctrine of two principles, which
is now known by the name of **manicheiſm**,
has often violently diſturb'd the **peace** of
the church. It ſettled in ſeveral provinces
of the empire, and ſome of the *Marcionites* were ſo zealous for this impiety, as
to die for it, which made them boaſt of
having had many martyrs. [a] St. *Auguſtin*,
among others, before he was converted by
St. *Ambroſe*, had embrac'd this hereſy, and
maintain'd moſt of the doctrines of it with
great fervency. The *Paulicians*, the *Carpocratians*, the *Gnoſticks*, and ſeveral other
Sects of hereticks among the chriſtians,
were all of this opinion; but the doctrine
it ſelf had not its riſe from chriſtianity,
and was much older. *It is* [b] *impoſſible*,
ſays *Plutarch*, in his treatiſe of *Iſis* and *O-
ſiris*, *that one cauſe alone, whether good or
bad, ſhould be the principle of all things together*; and having given ſeveral reaſons
and inſtances to prove his aſſertion, he adds;
For nothing can be without a precedent cauſe,

[a] Aug iſt. Confeſſ. *lib.* 6. *c.* 15.
[b] Plutarch. Iſis & Oſir.

L   *and*

and what is good in it self, can never be the cause of evil; nature therefore muſt have a principle, from which evil proceeds as its cauſe and principle, as well as another from which good proceeds: 'tis the opinion of the greateſt part, and the wiſeſt among the ancients; for ſome think there are two gods of different profeſſions, the one the author of all good, the other of all evil.

PYTHAGORAS and *Plato* held the ſame falſe tenet; but the firſt, who is known to have broached this doctrine, was *Zoroaſter*, king of the *Bactrians*. The good principle he call'd [a] *Oromazes*, the other *Arimanius*. He paſſed likewiſe for the firſt [b] inventor of magick. This *Zoroaſter* lived above eight hundred years (ſome ſay much [c] more) before the *Trojan* war, and has made himſelf one of the moſt famous men in the world. There are learned men [d] who affirm, that there

[a] Diogenes Laert. in prooemio.
[b] Juſtin. *lib.* 1. *c.* 1.
[c] Hermippus & Hermodorus. *See* Diogen. in Laert. in prooem.
[d] *Dr.* Hyde, Hiſtor. Religion. veterum Perſar.

re-

remain ſome of this ſect in the *Indies*, and other parts of *Aſia*, to this day.

IN *Europe* and *Aſia* the doctrine of two coeternal principles has not been maintain'd for many ages, though a manichean now-a-days would be more formidable than ever; and there is hardly an argument, that in the controverſy about free-will and predeſtination has been made uſe of theſe two laſt centuries, but what would ſtrengthen his ſyſtem, was nothing but human reaſon admitted of to judge by.

REVEAL'D religion therefore, the Old and New Teſtament, are only capable of cutting this gordian knot: for it is as great an abſurdity to ſuppoſe the ſupreme being to be deſtitute of infinite power and knowledge, as it is to make him cruel and tyrannical to the laſt extremity. But it is yet more unaccountable than either, that men ſhould be willing to give up a conſiderable part of GOD's knowledge and power, when they muſt neceſſarily ſee, that even by their own ſcheme they cannot clear the attributes they contend for,

L 2 and

and which to preſerve they are ſo ready to
ſacrifice any other.

THE *Socinians,* to extricate themſelves
from this difficulty, deny the [a] creation
out of nothing. They look for the origin
of evil into matter it ſelf, which they ſay
is uncreated and eternal. But GOD has
modified matter, endued it with motion,
and made a world of it. If he could not
deſtroy or root out theſe evil particles, he
has at leaſt ſo well diſpoſed of them as not
to interfere with the deſign of his workmanſhip, or elſe, what faults are there in the
univerſe? have they met with any flaws in
it? let them behold the firmament and
celeſtial bodies, conſider well the vaſtneſs
of their magnitudes as well as numbers,
the rapidity of their motion, and the
ſtability of that order, by which they
perform their different and unequal cour-
ſes with ſo much ſteadineſs and harmony. The laws of motion are not more
changeable or irregular here below, nor

[a] See Monſ. Bayle's *Dictionary in the Article of*
Epicurus, Remark S.

are

are the various forms we see it shape matter into on earth, less stupendous than what we see above: so that let matter have been either created or not, and as independent as they please; it is certain, that to make it what it is, and bring it into this fabrick, must have required a power and a wisdom so infinite, and so vastly transcending all imagination, that nothing but ignorance and stupidity can save a man from falling into extasies of admiration, whenever he ventures to think of it.

ORDER then and [a] beauty are conspicuous in every thing without us; and the least part of the universe (our selves excepted) bespeaks a GOD for its author. The only slur on all the divine works is to be found in man. In that lump of earth, from which omnipotent wisdom chose to form the most perfect of his labours, the particles of evil, that had been pliable in all the rest, were so stubborn and refractory as to elude all the skill and power of the great architect. Here they

[a] Baronius ann. ecclef. ad annum. 120.

re-

remain'd in ſuch a force and condition that they were able to pervert and turn to evil a virtuous and innocent, a rational, a knowing and well inſtructed being. What miſerable ſhifts men will make to compliment their own underſtanding! GOD would have remedied this ; but was not able.

BUT if GOD had had a preſervative, that would effectually have prevented this miſchief, is it agreeable to the notions we have of infinite goodneſs, that he would not have given it to man? yet this is the caſe: they can't deny, but that GOD might have aſſiſted our firſt parents with his grace : yet it is plain that he did not. Could not the fatal preſent of free-will, which GOD had given him, been re-call'd on ſuch an emergency? would a good mother, who had given leave to her Daughters to go to a ball, not revoke that leave, if ſhe was ſure, that they would yield to enticement and loſe their honour? Or, if ſhe had an infallible preſerva-tive againſt all temptations, that was like-wiſe extremely delightful to all that made

uſe

uſe of it, would ſhe ever ſend her daughters to this ball without it?

THE only thing theſe gentlemen keeping to their ſyſtem have left to anſwer is, that GOD would have aſſiſted them with his grace, if he had known what would have happened; but that it is impoſſible to foreſee events that depend upon contingencies. But even this is a poor refuge. Let us carry on the ſame compariſon a little further : if that mother ſhould go to this ball, and through a window ſhould ſee and underſtand, that one of her daughters defends her ſelf but weakly in the corner of a chamber, againſt the ſollicitations of a crafty deceiver : if, even when ſhe ſees, that her daughter is but one ſtep from yielding *to the* deſires of the tempter, ſhe ſhould not go then to aſſiſt her and deliver her from the ſnare; would the world ſtill count her a good mother? this is a repreſentation of the conduct which the *Socinians* attribute to GOD.

THEY cannot ſay, that he knew the ſin of the firſt man, but as a poſſible event; he knew all the particulars of the temptation, and he muſt needs have known

a mo-a moment before *Eve* yielded, that she was going to destroy her self : for they don't deny, but that GOD knew all the thoughts of *Eve*. He did therefore suffer her to sin; and this he did at the same time, when he foresaw that she would certainly sin.

THE sin of *Adam* was yet more certainly foreseen; for the example of *Eve* gave some light, the better to foresee the fall of *Adam*. If GOD had purposed to preserve man and his innocency, and to prevent all the miseries which were to be the consequence of sin, would he not at least have fortify'd the husband after the wife had fall'n? would he not have given him another wife sound and perfect, instead of that which was seduced? It is evident therefore, that the *Socinian* system, by depriving GOD of prescience, reduces him to slavery and a pitiful form of government; and does not remove the grand difficulty, which it should remove, and which forces these hereticks to deny the foreknowledge of contingent events.

A

A predeſtinarian likewiſe labours to as little purpoſe, who, by philoſophical reaſons, endeavours to make good his doctrine, and by dint of argument pretends to clear it from the difficulties it is liable to. When it is objected to him, that his ſyſtem is neceſſarily attended with this conſequence; therefore GOD is the author of ſin; he ought to drop philoſophy, and run to his bible; for here the light of nature will not ſerve him, but to render the charge againſt him the more evident, the more he wrangles, if he has an able antagoniſt. The beſt anſwer he can make is this: I ſee as well as you the connexion of my principle with that conſequence, and my reaſon, that ſees it, does not afford me a ſufficient knowledge to make me underſtand how I am miſtaken in ſeeing it; neverthelefs I am fully perſuaded, that GOD finds in the infinite treaſures of his power and wiſdom, a certain and moſt infallible way of breaking that connexion, though it be unknown to me, and exceeds the extent of my knowledge.

THIS ought to be the anſwer of a predeſtinarian. But, as we can follow no bet-

ter

ter guides than the apostles themselves, let us examine how St. *Paul* has behaved himself in this important matter.

HE establishes absolute predestination in the plainest and concisest manner. *He hath mercy on whom he will have mercy, and whom he will he hardeneth.* Upon this the apostle, who knew very well what would naturally be objected against such a doctrine, starts the difficulty himself, *thou wilt say then unto me, Why does he yet find fault? for who has resisted his Will?* No *Molinist*, nor the most acute philosopher of the *Socinians* could have said any thing to push the objection further. And neither St. *Austin*, *Luther*, *Calvin*, or any of the *Thomists*, *Jansenists* have ever said any thing, that GOD will have men to commit sin. Which will still be more evident, if we observe, that just before the apostle had put us in mind of the transactions between *Moses* and *Pharaoh*, where we meet with the most remarkable instance of the divine sovereignty, that is any where extant; as if it had been to hinder us from making any feint and evasive construction of what he meant by *Hardening*.

GOD

GOD we know had first hardened the heart of *Pharaoh* against all the threatnings and miracles of *Moses*, and afterwards punished him for disobedience. A conduct seemingly opposite to all our human notions of justice and goodness. I take notice of this to demonstrate how remote the apostle's thoughts seem to have been from mollifying the expression, or denying the fact. All the solution he gives to the objection proposed, is the sovereign power of GOD, and the right the Creator has to dispose of his creatures as it seems good to him, *Nay, but oh man! who art thou that repliest against* GOD? *Shall the thing form'd say to him that form'd it, why hast thou made me thus?* This the apostle insists upon, and in the next verse repeats the substance of it over again in a comparison, the most adapted to inspire us with humility and resignation.

St. *Paul*, inspired as he was, does not pretend, that he is able to account for it any other way. He is at a loss himself, the great apostle of the *Gentiles*, in whom human learning was join'd with divine inspiration. Mind the philosophy he makes

M 2

use

ufe of, *O the depth and the riches both of the wifdom and knowledge of* GOD *! how unfearchable are his judgments, and his ways paft finding out !* This ought to put an end to all difputes, and impofe a profound filence on our reafon. The fubtleft logician, or moft learned theologift after this can have no more claim or colour to be dogmatical on this head, than the fimpleft fhepherd, or the moft illiterate plowman; for in point of penetration into the reveal'd will of GOD, I will not ask leave to affirm, that the fuperiority which the ableft divine has over the meaneft peafant, is much lefs than what St. *Paul* would have had over the ableft divine the world has had to boaft of fince the time of the apoftles. Muft not both parties blufh, when they pretend to teach with clearnefs what was a myftery to St. *Paul ?*

As it is fuperftition to forge and multiply myfteries without neceffity, and where, by a juft interpretation, matters may be made intelligible to us; fo not to allow things to be myfterious, when the word of GOD exprefly teaches us, that they are fuch, is no lefs than renouncing

2   chri-

chriſtianity. The *Carpocratians* [a] ſtand
accus'd of having plac'd the image of *A-
riſtotle* next to that of JEUS CHRIST,
and paid equal adoration to both. If the
impiety of theſe hereticks ſeem ſtrange,
what muſt we ſay to thoſe, who pretend
to a profound veneration for a religion altogether built upon myſteries, and at the
ſame time refuſe to admit of any thing
which they cannot plainly apprehend by
the light of nature?

LET me adviſe thoſe idolaters of human underſtanding, not to forget humanity in another ſenſe, and once begin to think
of charity and toleration. The impoſſibility
there is in our little knowledge of reconciling
either the ſyſtem of predeſtination, or that of
free-will, to all the neceſſary attributes of
GOD, ought, if not to unite men, at
leaſt make them deſiſt from quarrelling,
and taxing one another with teaching of
impious things and horrid blaſphemies.
Thoſe who are againſt toleration of either
ſide, might be bore with, if they could
clearly prove their opinion, and anſwer

[a] Baronius ann. ecclef. ad annum 120.

M 3   all.

all objections after a convincing manner; but that men fhould anathematife, banifh and hang thofe that diffent from them, tho' to defend their own fyftem each party is forc'd to fly to GOD's incomprehenfibility, is a thing altogether inexcufable.

I fhall leave this fubject with a bright example of moderation and humanity, not common among divines of different opinions, but which it is greatly the intereft of every country, that all clergy-men fhould follow. *Melanchton* was the head of the *Synergifts,* [a] a fect of *German* divines in the fixteenth century, who, thinking that *Luther*'s hypothefis about free-will was too harfh, taught, that men are not converted by GOD's Grace, without the concourfe of their own will. Every body knows how abfolute a predeftinarian *Calvin* was, and what clamours were rais'd againft him on this head, that he was reprefented as having broach'd the moft monftrous doctrine, and making G O D the author of fin in the moft execrable manner.

[a] Micrelius Syntagm. hift. ecclef.

YET

YET *Melanchton* had a fincere value and a friendfhip for *Calvin,* and wrote in defence of him on feveral occafions. He knew, that that great man abhorr'd the impieties that were laid to his charge, and that in none of his works he had ever afcrib'd any thing to GOD, but what was juft and holy; but, that he had taught, that the conduct of GOD furpaffing finite capacities, was not too narrowly to be pry'd into; that his judgments are a myfterious abyfs we ought not to meddle with, and that his ways are incomprehenfible. This *Melanchton* demonftrated to the other's enemies, always extolling the piety and good intention of *Calvin,* notwithftanding the difagreement of their opinions.

CALVIN believ'd, that the fupreme empire of GOD, and the rights of a providence worthy of the infinite being, required an abfolute predeftination. *Melanchton* believ'd that the goodnefs, holinefs and juftice of the fupreme being requir'd we fhould be free in our actions.

---

a Beza in vita Calvin. ad ann. 1552.

Thefe

Theſe were their principles. Both aim'd at the ſame thing, the greateſt glory of GOD. The candid *Melanchton* being con-vinc'd of this, as well as the difficulty and inexplicableneſs of the matter they differ'd about, was always ready to do *Calvin* ju-ſtice, admired his vaſt parts and erudi-tion, and own'd him for his fellow labourer in the miniſtry of the goſpel.

C H A P.

CHAP. VI.

Of the CHURCH.

AS no civiliz'd nation ever was without religion, so divine worship has always been accounted the business of all mankind, and a duty in which the meanest, as well as the highest, from the prince to the beggar, are equally concern'd. This, and the respect due to the Deity to be ador'd, have been the reason that the edifices set apart for a general worship, were always not only spacious, but as soon as man could raise them, likewise fine and stately structures. As this must make the building of them very expensive, they are generally rais'd at the publick cost, and therefore temples are national, and only made use of to celebrate that worship, that belongs to the national religion, which the government

ment

ment, and the generality of a country profess.

ALL the world takes delight more or less in excellency and beauty, every one judging according to his taste and capacity, and the greatest part of the multitude have nothing to boast of of their own, that exceeds mediocrity; for this reason, the common people are fond of every thing that belongs to the publick, which is praise-worthy. Here every body counts himself a sharer; when one nation beats another in battle, the whole country rejoice; those who staid at home are as proud of the victory as the conquerors themselves, and a man that is bed-rid imagines himself to have a part in the honour of the day. This consideration may furnish us with one reason, why the poorest people, who, generally speaking, have no extraordinary dwellings to brag of, should have such an excessive value for their temples abstract from religion.

MEN don't stand calculating what proportion their persons bear to the whole, it is sufficient that they are sharers, and what is publick, all members of the society have

the

the liberty of calling their own; and no
human creature can be fo abject in a country, but he may have the pleafure of faying, our army, our fleet, our government,
our funds. It is likewife obferv'd, that
the love and value, which from this nota-
ble propriety men conceive for things that
belong to the whole fociety, are greater
or leffer, according as thofe things are
either foon perifhable or more lafting. One
ftorm deftroys a whole fleet, an army is
often disbanded in a day, and the publick
treafure may foon be fquander'd away or
exhaufted by neceffity; but ftrong edifices, fuch as temples and halls remain
for many generations. As great lovers as
men are of novelty, they look upon it as
a weaknefs, and all have a great veneration for things not eafily alterable, and
fuch as are known to have been of great
duration.

IT has been fufficiently fhewn in the
foregoing chapters, that inward religion
and fpiritual devotion, are not what the
multitude was ever much affected with.
They muft have fomething more grofs that
employs their fenfes, and therefore whenever

ever we would fpeak to the vulgar pathe-
tically about religion, we make ufe of the
words, altar and temple, things that are
vifible; or elfe ftrictly fpeaking, religion
it felf, efpecially the chriftian, has nothing
to do with temples, or any building, and
therefore our Saviour and his apoftles
preach'd and taught in private houfes, or,
when their followers were more numerous,
in the open air: they would invade no
body's right, and to fhew, that neither
great numbers, nor ftately ftructures were
of any confideration as to godlinefs, CHRIST
told his difciples, that where two or three
were gathered together in his name, he
would be among them.

THE affemblies then of the faithful a-
mong chriftians, whether they met in a
room or a defart, were, in the time of
the apoftles, call'd churches, and all that
believ'd in CHRIST, wherefoever difpers'd,
were counted members of his univerfal
church. As afterwards they encreas'd in
numbers, and were favour'd or tolerated
by the governors they liv'd under, the
chriftians built many meeting-houfes,
which, from the affemblies that met there,
were

were in tract of time call'd churches. The
fame name was beftow'd on fome of the
heathen temples, as foon as the pagans
were turn'd out, and the chriftians were
poffefs'd of them ; and upon all changes in
government, or publick worfhip, the priefts
in favour, all the world over, as well as in
the *Roman* empire, always took care of the
temples and their appurtenances. The
firft church dedicated to St. *Paul* in *England*, was originally a pagan temple, built
to the honour of *Diana*, and the chief
mofque now in *Conftantinople* was a chriftian church confecrated to St. *Sophia*.

THOSE who are but in the leaft acquainted with the hiftory of the third,
fourth and fifth centuries, cannot be ignorant how often the chriftian and heathen priefts drove out one another by
turns, according as the religion of the one
or the other prevail'd, fometimes with cruel perfecution, and fometimes with tolerable moderation, according to the temper
of the emperor or his favourites, and muft
know that the chriftian clergy were as in-
triguing as other priefts, nor lefs induftrious to promote their temporal intereft, and
th e

that as foon as it was in their power, they encourag'd the building of churches, fome of them not inferiour to the moft magnificent pagan temples, of which at laft they kept for their own ufe, out of prudence, thofe that had not been demolifh'd out of zeal.

FROM what I have hinted already we may fee, that when the name of the church is given to a temple, to the edifice it felf erected for divine worfhip, it is done by a figurative way of fpeaking ; but otherwife, that the word (by which literally and originally nothing is meant but congregation or affembly) in the plaineft as well as moft charitable acceptation fignifies all that believe in CHRIST, of what fect or perfuafion foever, and includes the laity as well as the clergy. This is undeniable, yet there is hardly a clergyman that will fubfcribe to it without exception. The ambition, envy and revengeful fpirit of fome, together with the vain glory, folly and impiety of others, have made fuch feuds and diftractions, rais'd fuch diffentions and real animofities among the feveral flocks that have been entrufted to

3   them;

them; that the piety, wifdom, eloquence, and all the other great abilities of the reft have not been able to this hour to hinder chriftians from refufing to allow thofe, that differ from them in opinion, to belong to the church of CHRIST, and every fect pretends to be the true church, whilft all the reft are antichrift, fchifmaticks, or hereticks.

WHAT is generally underftood by the church in every country, is that religion the government pretends to maintain, and the clergy whereof are in poffeffion of the national churches, and their revenues; and here the word includes church government with all the rites and ceremonies, as well as privileges and immunities the clergy can claim by law.

IN this fenfe the church varies in every country, and there are not two alike in all chriftendom. So both in *France* and *Spain* the religion is *Roman* catholick; but in *France* they have no inquifition, they differ from the other in church government, and are not fo flavifhly fubject to the pope. At *Venice* again, they have an inquifition

quifition as well as in *Spain*, but a noble *Venetian* is always to be prefent at all their tranfactions, and when he leaves them they are no court, which alters the nature of the thing it felf. In *England* the religion is proteftant and epifcopal; the fame may be faid of fome *Lutherans*, yet the churches are vaftly different, as well in doctrine as ceremonies and government.

WHEN church is ufed with refpect to the religion profefs'd, as fuch a one is of the church of *England*, it includes both clergy and laity; but, with refpect to the government and authority of the church, nothing is underftood by it, but the clergy alone, for the laity has nothing to do there, but to obey. When indeed the intereft of the church is mention'd, the word is more comprehenfive, and takes in, befides the clergy, all thofe that are well-wifhers to their temporal welfare and authority, whether they belong to the fame communion or not. So *Lewis* the XIVth has been look'd upon as the greateft friend of the church of *England* by many of her clergy; feveral popes have been in the proteftant testant interest, and the grand *Turk* has more than once been defender of the faith of the injured churches in *Transilvania*.

FOR want of understanding these various acceptations of the word church, men have often been guilty of impiety, and laid that to the charge of a holy religion, which has been altogether owing to priest-craft. The church of Christ, as it signifies the professors of his religion, was propagated after a miraculous manner, by mean illiterate men, who, by preaching up meekness, patience, obedience to the civil magistrate, and an intire resignation to the will of GOD, gain'd multitudes of souls without the assistance of the secular power, or any other arms or compulsion whatever: men who recommended every where peace, union and charity, and despising all worldly interest, ventur'd and laid down their lives for the welfare of others.

BUT the church of Christ, as it comprehends the extent of jurisdiction, the temporal interest and authority of the clergy, that profess christianity, has been propated by quite contrary means. They dif-

N   fer'd

fer'd and quarrell'd in the firſt century, perſecuted one another in the ſecond; and as ſoon as it was in their power, and they had inſinuated themſelves into the favour of princes, they made uſe of worldly honour and riches, and other artifices to draw men to the church; whilſt thoſe, who refus'd to be of their opinion, were with the help of the government compell'd to it by main force without any miracle at all.

If the word church always imply'd religion, the moſt profligate wretches could never be the greateſt ſticklers for it; yet this we may obſerve in almoſt every nation. Some content themſelves with ſwearing, drinking, and telling lies for the church; but others more zealous perjure themſelves, raiſe rebellion, murder their princes, betray, burn, and deſtroy their country for the ſake of it.

To account for this odd turn of the mind in human creatures, I muſt deſire my reader to look back on what has been ſaid, *pag.* 19 and 20. As hardly any of the multitude are ſo ignorant, or ſo wicked as not to have a notion of virtue and vice,

vice, heaven and hell, at leaft a confus'd
one, fo at one time or other they are troubled with remorfes, they have dreads and
perplexities, which are the reafon that many of them when they find themfelves
wholly fwallow'd up in fenfuality, and utterly incapable of performing any kind of
religious duties, feeking relief like drown-
ing men, take hold of a ftraw, and are fo
ftupid, as to imagin that to have an affection for the church, the edifice it felf, or
the name of it, the habit of a clergyman,
or any thing ftill more remote from, and
yet in their opinion belonging to religion,
will make fome atonement for all their
tranfgreffions. It comforts them in their
anxiety, and makes them eafy; and it is
this that often makes the moft abandon'd
in a nation fo zealous for the church, without ever going to its fervice, or obferving
its rules. For, whoever rightly confiders
the force of this fuperftitious awe, and adds
to it the reafon I mention'd in the beginning of this chapter, will eafily perceive,
that both join'd together muft in all multitudes render the efteem, the veneration,
and the fondnefs for the word church as

N 2   ex-

exceffive, as without that confideration it
is unaccountable.

THOSE, who diffent from the national
church, or rather fcruple to comply with
the rites and ceremonies of it, are by
their teachers continually fet againft it;
they are told of all the abufes of it, which
none can be without; and from their infancy generally they are encouraged to defpife, and in time, according as their anti-
zeal is work'd to a pitch, perhaps brought
mortally to hate it. The confcioufnefs
of this averfion to the church has the
fame effect upon the minds of many, that
the affection for it has upon others; but
notwithftanding this hatred and contempt
fome may artfully be infpired with againft
the church, the vulgar are never better
pleafed than when they are poffeffed of the
national churches. In all countries, where
there are religious quarrels, thofe who
hated the very name, whilft they were
kept out of them, are foon reconcil'd to
them, if upon any turn in the publick worfhip they get the better of their adverfaries. There is a kind of magick in a fine
church, that bewitches the mob. They
look

look upon it as a rampart againſt hell and
the devil: they rely upon it at all events,
and ſeem to imagine, that their veneration
for it, and conſequently their hatred to
them that ſpeak againſt it, is an abſolution
from ſin, and a ſecurity to be wicked with
impunity.

THAT I have dwelt ſo long on this
head ought to ſeem excuſable to all, who
conſider, that it is my intention to point
out thoſe things to which the court of
Rome owes its greatneſs, and the firſt is
this frailty of the vulgar; on which have
been built all the ſplendor and temporal
authority, not on'y of the *Pagan* churches,
but likewiſe the *Mahometan* and that of
Rome. The next, and which is not ſufficiently to be admired, is the unconceiv-
able induſtry, to which may be join'd the
heroiſm of the clergy, who from the moſt
barren ſoil have made the fatteſt land in
the world. One cannot reflect without a-
mazement on the inexhauſtible treaſure
actually in poſſeſſion of, and the boundleſs
power in temporals, claim'd by the ſuc-
ceſſors of the apoſtles; and yet nothing in
nature can ſeem leſs capable of yielding
ſuch

such a product than the gospel. To illustrate what I mean by the heroism of the clergy, I shall give some few instances of it from the multitude which history abounds with.

'Tis a difficult task to controul great men and favourites of princes, and always hazardous to rebuke the mighty: yet the daring St. *Ambrose* [a] opposed the emperor himself. As *Theodosius* was coming to church at *Milan,* that gallant bishop stopped him, and made him do penance with all humility, before he would suffer him to enter into it. To conceive rightly the danger, and consequently the bravery of this action, we ought to know, that such another attempt had been made once before at *Antioch* by St. *Babylas* [b] with very ill success. St. *Chrysostom,* tho' he was mistaken in the name [c] of the emperor, and the crime laid to his charge, has more than once display'd his

[a] Erasm. Epist. 3. *lib.* 28. & Epist. 69. *lib.* 29.
[b] Euseb. hist. eccles. *l.* 6. *c.* 34.
[c] *St.* Chrysostom. *Homily on St.* Babylas, item contra gentiles, & aliis in locis.

usual

ufual eloquence in the praife of that martyr.

THE characterifticks of chriftianity have abundantly teftify'd the divinity of our religion; and obedience to fuperiors, and the civil magiftrate, with a peaceful dif-pofition and charity to all men, fo much recommended by the gofpel, have ever been the fureft means to propagate it; but the early zeal of churchmen has often look-ed upon them as flow ones, and their pow-er has been rais'd by more active virtues than patience under perfecution, and con-ftancy in death. Chriftians have often been the aggreffors, even when they were ftran-gers and lived upon fufferance. In the time of *Theodofius* junior, they enjoy'd a full liberty of confcience in *Perfia*, when [a] *Abdas*, a zealous bifhop, had the courage to pull down one of the temples where the *Perfians* worfhip'd the fire. The *Magi* made their complaints to the King, who fent for *Abdas*, and demanded no other fatisfaction than the rebuilding of the

[a] Theodor. Hift. ecclef. *lib.* 5. *c.* 39.

tem-

temple: [a] *Abdas* refus'd it with scorn, tho' that prince had declar'd to him, that in case of disobedience he would cause all the christian churches to be pull'd down; which he did, and began a terrible persecution, in which the valiant *Abdas* fell the first martyr.

THE brave remainder of the faithful, that could escape the fury of the *Persian* priests, were not so dejected at their loss, but that, animated with the hopes of a noble revenge, they implored the assistance of the emperor, which kindling a long war [b] between the *Romans* and *Persians*, occasion'd a second deluge of blood in vindication of the gospel.

FROM these and other examples it is evident, that the church has not been wanting to shew her fortitude in attacking her enemies, and redressing misfortunes; nor has she neglected to improve her successes. It is this restless application, by which she is arriv'd to that height of worldly glory and sovereignty. To put a

[a] Theodor. & Socrat. hist. Eccles.
[b] Socrat. hist. Eccles. *lib.* 7. *c.* 18.

crown

crown on the head of a kneeling prince, and immediately with a foot to kick it down again, may be cenfur'd in a bifhop as an action on fuch folemnities more familiar than polite ; but it is an expreffive emblem of fupremacy, which nothing but treading on the necks of princes could exceed: the lordly enfigns of fuperlative grandeur which every body knows the *Roman* pontiffs have difplay'd in thefe inftances and a hundred more ; yet, what is moft wonderful, all the temporals, the fucceffors of St. *Peter* are poffefs'd of, have been obftinately difputed, and fuch by inch got from the laity: not excepting what they lay claim to by virtue of the donation of *Conftantine*, which has been ridicul'd even by *Italian* poets.

NOTHING is more diverting than to read the various and noble ftruggles the popes have had with the princes of chriftendom, till *Gregory* the feventh, with the utmoft intrepidity, and equal hazard and difficulties, eftablifh'd his fuperiority over their temporalities: that able and ftately prelate, who, in the midft of winter,

O made

made an emperor [a] barefoot wait [b] unattended in a hall, fasting from morning till night, for three days together, before he would admit him to his presence; [c] and was the first, who undertook to deprive his lord and master of the imperial dignity. There is hardly an emperor to be named, who has opposed the pope, and has not been a sufferer at last; and it is incredible what indignities some princes have endured from them. The most valiant, the craftiest, and the most resolute, have been overmatched by them. *Henry* the fourth of *France*, as great as he was, was forc'd to submit to the chastisement, [d] which, whilst the fifth *psalm* was singing, *Clement* the eighth, from his throne, inflicted by the stroke of a switch at each verse, on the persons of his proxies, as they lay kneeling and bending down their heads before him. The same ceremony,

[a] Henry *the fourth.*
[b] Maimbourg decadence de l'empire. *l.* 3.
[c] *Some add, that he waited with scissars, and a broom in his hands, as submitting to be shorn and whipt*; du Plessis mystère de iniquité.
[d] Botero's Commentar.

[a] it

[a] it is said, was repeated more privately between the legate and his majesty's person.

WHEN the lustre of a church is once established, the homage, which is reckon'd her due, ceases not to be paid to her even in adversity. *Leo* the tenth, before his pontificate, when he was legate to *Julius* the second, was in the army that was beaten by the *French* at *Ravenna.* Whilst he was a prisoner, cardinal *Palavicini* tells us, [b] the conquering soldiers express'd so great a veneration for him, that they humbly begg'd pardon for their victory, beseech'd him to give them absolution, and promis'd never more to bear arms against the pope. This brings to mind another, but more noble example of the vast respect and submissive awe, which the very sight of a prelate and his pontifical ornaments have imprinted, not upon the children of the church, but *Barbarians,* cruel persecutors, and her greatest enemies.

[a] D' Aubigné.
[b] Palavic. istoria del concilio di Trente.

AT

ATTILA having ᵃ reduc'd *Aquileia* almoſt to aſhes, ravaged all upon his march from thence even to *Pavia* and *Milan*, and now he had made himſelf maſter of thoſe two great cities, and treated them as he had done the reſt, laying them both in rubbiſh. So many diſmal meſſages arriving upon the back of one another at *Rome* caus'd a great conſternation. The ſenate was aſſembled to deliberate, whether the emperor ſhould quit *Italy*; for to defend *Rome* againſt that innumerable multitude of *Barbarians* ſeem'd utterly impoſſible. Nothing at laſt was thought more adviſable, than to ſend an honourable embaſſy to *Attila*, with the pope at the head of it.

ACCORDINGLY *Leo* the firſt undauntedly went out in ſolemn pomp to meet him. The *Goth* was ſtruck with the appearance, obey'd the prieſt, and retir'd inſtantly with his whole army in a panick fear. *Attila* was afterwards aſhamed of his weakneſs, which to palliate he had invention enough, or others for him, to

---

ᵃ Maimbourg decadence de l'empire.

make

make a miraculous ſtory of it: alledging, that, during the time *Leo* ſpoke, he ſaw a venerable old man ſtand by his ſide, who, holding a naked ſword in his hand, threaten'd to kill him, unleſs he granted all the pope deſired. A pitiful excuſe for a conqueror at the head of his army! the dreadful *Attila*, the ſcourge of GOD, the enemy to mankind, whoſe ſight alone ſtruck terrour into the moſt undaunted, and whoſe very name made all the earth to tremble.

IN the next chapter I ſhall endeavour to prove, that the policies and worldly wiſdom of the clergy have been employ'd as ſucceſsfully for the temporal advancement of the church, as their heroiſm; and with all theſe helps the raiſing of the church to what it is from ſuch a beginning ought ſtill to be look'd upon as the greateſt atchievement that human ſtrength has to boaſt of.

THE *Pagans*, whoſe religion was built upon poetry and fiction, had a wretched theology, that might be turn'd to any purpoſe, and the prieſts in their contrivances had no morals to cope with. In mahome-

tiſm

tifm there is more morality, and the notions of the Deity are better ; both which
it is in all probability beholding for to the
gofpel: but then the whole religion feems
contriv'd to engage the fenfual and voluptuous: in the alcoran it felf many
things are ludicrous and filly, and not a
few that are foothing human paffion. But
in the chriftian religion all is grave and folid; every part of it is worthy of the moft
ferious contemplation of a man, that can
and dares think freely and thoroughly.
The idea it furnifhes us with of the
Godhead is fublime, and as incomprehenfible as it fhould be: in the doctrine of
Chrift there are no worldly allurements to
draw the vicious, and all his followers are
ty'd down to the ftricteft morality: the
whole aim of the gofpel is divine, nothing
in it can poffibly be conftrued fo as to
encourage priefturaft, or be ferviceable to
footh any human paffion, without doing
the utmoft violence to truth and good
fenfe; and yet behold, what has been made
of it !

WHEN we confider, that the holy
founder of our religion commanded frugality,

gality, embraced poverty, difclaim'd as well as contemn'd riches and earthly dominion, and told all mankind in exprefs words, that his kingdom was not of this world. When we confider this, I fay, is it eafily underftood, which way, and on what foot thofe, who dare call themfelves his vicars, fhould have made themfelves in the face of the fun temporal princes, who live magnificently and luxurioufly, and pretend by their function to be invefted not only with holinefs and abfolute knowledge, (which they may fay came by inheritance) but what the apoftles never thought of, an unlimited jurifdiction, and general mafterfhip over all things under heaven? they alfo fuppofe themfelves the fountain of worldly honour, and beftow titles on fovereigns, or take them away at pleafure. That of moft chriftian king, [a] *Julius* the fecond is faid to have once been deliberating to deprive *Lewis* the twelfth of, and transfer it on our king *Henry* the eighth.

[a] Guiccairdin, *lib.* 11.

O 4 THE

THE Roman [a] *Pontiff, says* Allatius one of the library-keepers of the vatican, *holds of no body, he judges every body, and is judged by none; obedience is to be paid to him, altho' he governs unjustly; he gives laws without receiving any, he alters them as he pleases, he creates magistrates, determines matters of faith; he orders the great affairs of the church as he pleases; he cannot err if he would, for no infidelity nor illusion can come near him; and if an angel should say otherwise, being stor'd as he is with the authority of* JESUS CHRIST, *he cannot change.*

WHAT an extravagant power is this in human creatures! yet it is demonstrable, that nothing is more adventitious, and altogether owing to fruitful invention, than the infallibility of the pope. By testament the clergy cannot have it from the apostles, who own'd, that they had doubts themselves; nor will any man imagine, that they have derived it from the scriptures; when a cardinal [b] writes in de-

[a] Allatius de perpetua consensione *lib.* I. *cap.* 2.
[b] *Cardinal* Hosius.

fence

fence [a] of a controvertist, who asserted, *that was it not for the authority of the church, he would pay no greater regard to the bible, than he had for Æsop's fables*; so that in the opinion of this clergy-man the scriptures receive all their sanction from the church, and therefore not the church from the scriptures. This I think is reasoning consequentially, though at first view there may seem to be less weight than subtilty in the thought.

BUT, be this as it will, there is no protestant that will not concur with me in what I have said, that may be displeasing to the church, if I only mean that of *Rome*; but he'll be very angry, and perhaps endeavour to have me punished by the law, should I apply any part of it to the church he belongs to, and which he believes to be that of CHRIST; it would be much the same, whether I did it in *England*, in *Holland*, or in *Sweden*; and it is not more surprising to see how vastly protestants differ from one another, than it is to observe, how unanimously they agree in one

[a] Hosius, *lib.* 3. in prolegom. Brentii.

thing.

thing with the church they sprung from, which is, that, to vindicate the religion they profess, besides their proofs from scripture, and the abilities of their divines, all desire to have the assistance of the secular power, and there is no sect of protestants, where their opinion is the uppermost, that is not as willing to make use of it on all occasions as the papists themselves.

In the religious disputes in *Holland*, it has been practised long ago: the *Gommarians* incited the princes of *Orange* against the *Arminians*, and made use of the civil power at the synod of *Dort*, with little appearance of moderation. Other synods afterwards have been very zealous in setting the states against the *Socinians*, several of their books have been burnt, and their authors banish'd.

In the time of *Edward* the sixth, *Lascus* and *Micronius* [a] were ministers of the *Dutch* church at *London*; being forc'd upon

a Samuel Andreas *Professor of divinity at* Marpurg, *relates this in his* Epistola Gratulatoria & Apologetica, *against the* Dania Orthodoxa fidelis & pacifica *of* Masius, *Divinity Professor at* Copenhagen.

that

that king's death to leave *England*, they endeavour'd to eftablifh themfelves and their flock in *Denmark*, but the *Lutherans* oppos'd it, and alledging, that their doctrine ftood condemn'd by the confeffion of *Augsburg*, forc'd them to retire out of the kingdom in the midft of winter. *Micronius* fome time after at *Hamburg* conferr'd with one *Weftphalus* a *Danifh* divine, who immediately urg'd the confent of the *Saxon* churches as an invincible argument againft the *Calvinifts*. *Micronius* anfwer'd, that if the truth of opinions was to be determin'd by the confent of churches, the papal caufe would be triumphant. *Weftphalus* reply'd, that the *Saxon* churches were the church of GOD; and when the other urg'd that the church was not confin'd to any place, and that there was no church but what might poffibly err, as was allow'd by *Luther :* he reply'd, that the import of *Luther*'s words was not that the church of JESUS CHRIST could be miftaken, but that the popifh church might. *Micronius* forgot not to tell him, that the holy fcripture is the fole rule of faith, and infifting upon this continually, he was plainly anfwer'd,

fwer'd, it follows from your arguments, that his *Danish* majesty and the senate of our city, who have decreed against you, should be guilty of a great fault; consider that you are condemn'd by A DYET of *Augsburg*.

IT is plain what *Westphalus* would infinuate, and this we shall find throughout the world, that the national clergy in all countries endeavour to render it a crime against the state, how remote soever it be from it, to seek or believe what clashes with their system, and they cannot answer themselves. The arguments by which all churches in power prove their divinity, when they appeal to the senses, have a near resemblance together.

THE defenders of the religion of old *Rome*, in the beginning of christianity, boasted of the antiquity of their religion, the vast extent of it, the victories that had been gain'd by the assistance of their gods, and the miracles that had been wrought for them: these they said were things visible, and from so many excellencies, in which none came near them, they maintain'd that theirs was the true religion.

gion. The church of new *Rome*, after fifteen hundred years ftanding, has often
made ufe of the fame proofs ever fince the
reformation, but not always with fo much
juftice in appearance as the *Pagans*. For
as to victories, it is but an hundred years
ago, that on a fair account the ballance
would have been on the fide of the *Mahometans :* and as to extent of dominion, the
chriftians are exceeded by the fame *Mahometans*, though both of them together,
in this article, cannot come up to the
Heathens, even at this day. For to divide the globe in thirty equal parts, by
the beft computation, fix are reckon'd to be
Chriftian, feven *Mahometan*, and all the reft
Pagan.

WHICH of the proteftant communions
ought to be call'd the true church of
Chrift, a man may be fooner convinc'd
of within, than he can demonftrate it to
an adverfary. But be the religion of a
country what it will, it is always certain,
that the greater the authority of the church
is, the better the clergy are pleafed; and
it fails as feldom, that, wherever it is exceffive, the laity are flaves, and the government

vernment precarious, unlefs it be in the hands of the clergy themfelves. Of this the ftate of the church in *Italy* is a flagrant inftance; for throughout the patrimony of St. *Peter*, the priefts are abfolute mafters, and have all the fat of the land. The churches are magnificent and crouded with treafure, but the laity are poor, and the common people, in houfes and furniture, diet and cloaths, and all the other valuable comforts of life, the moft miferable in chriftendom, in the moft happy foil and climate upon earth.

DURING the happinefs of the *Jews*, before they had kings, GOD rul'd over them more immediately himfelf; or elfe thefe are the fruits of a hierarchy, which all governments muft degenerate into, where the ftate, unmindful of its own fafety, takes not a fufficient care to guard it felf both againft the fly and bold encroachments of the church, and either wants ftrength, skill, or refolution, to keep the clergy of all forts in due bounds of obedience.

THOSE who confult hiftory, or will but read *Herodotus*, or *Diodorus Siculus*, will

will be convinc'd, that I do not deceive my reader: they will find that the *Ægyptian* priesthood being in ancient times the most numerous in the universe, had a third [a] part of the country in possession, and at last arrived to such a height, as in a manner to have swallow'd up the state. That the Magi in *Persia* actually chang'd the crown into a mitre [b] and had once a fair chance for the universal sway of the world. In the wide *Æthiopian* empire likewise they'll find, that the authority of the hierarchy has been so exorbitant, that the priest usurp'd an arbitrary power over the lives of all the laity, their [c] kings not excepted.

DOMINION ever follows property: thus it has been; thus it will be: manners and customs may change, but human nature is much the same in all ages. Perhaps it never was try'd, but else one might defy the most learned champion of the clergy, to produce from *Adam*, to this day, one single instance, of a nation of

[a] Diod. Sic. *li.* 1.
[b] Herod. *lib.* 3.
[c] Diod. sic. *lib.* 3.

note,

note, where the clergy had the deference paid to them, which the generality
of them defire, and were fuffer'd as much
to aggrandize themfelves as they pretended
their religion required, for fifty years together, which upon due examination would
not be found to have been enflaved by the
church before half that time was expired.
On this head there is no difference between proteftants and papifts: rigid *Gene-*
va it felf affords us a remarkable inftance,
[a] wherein a difpute between the church
and ftate, purfued with warmth and obftinacy on both fides, the clergy got the
better of the government in a point of authority, and the magiftrate was forc'd to yield,
at the very beginning of the reformation.

AMONGST thofe communions of proteftants, that never yet had any government
or national fociety of their fentiments, the
teachers in general, I know, loudly ex-
claim againft the pomp and temporal authority of the clergy: as many of them are
men of worth and probity, fo I doubt not,
but their intentions may be honeft: but I

[a] *See the tenth chapter toward the latter end.*

must

muſt deſire ſuch well deſigning leaders not to boaſt too much of their maiden humility, before they have been tried. A woman may be conſcious to her ſelf, that ſhe is chaſte, tho' ſhe never was ask'd to be otherwiſe; but ſhe can claim no merit in having kept her virginity, if it never was in her choice to part with it.

WHAT ſect or perſuaſion of chriſtians has a better goſpel to preach, or a more diſintereſted, and well meaning principle to walk by, than what the church of *Rome* had her origin from? Wealth and power are tempting, they are ſnares to all manner of virtues, and the ſincereſt man alive cannot warrant for himſelf, or promiſe before hand, what his behaviour will be, when his circumſtances ſhall ceaſe to be the ſame.

P   CHAP.

CHAP. VII.

Of the Politicks of the CHURCH.

HE immortality of the soul, tho' it had been solidly asserted by *Plato*, and treated of by divers philosophers before him; yet it remain'd a disputable point among men of the greatest penetration many years after: but whatever sentiments men entertain'd of the soul's continuance after death, the notions they had of another life were either very confus'd, or very mean and fabulous before the light of the gospel appear'd; and CHRIST was the first, who plainly taught, that men shall rise again, and in another world be punished or rewarded for ever, according as their behaviour has been in this life. If we consider on the one hand the vast disproportion between the momentary duration of this

life,

life, and eternity, and on the other, that
the joys of heaven prepar'd for the juſt,
and the torments of hell to be endured by
the wicked, ſhall both be ſo exquiſite, as
to exceed all imagination; in all which
our Saviour likewiſe has fully inſtructed us;
if we conſider, I ſay, theſe things, we ſhall
find, that no argument could be invented
more cogent, to make men of ſound reaſon
to bear for ſo ſhort a ſpace with any ſuffe-
rings, that might be ſerviceable to attain
ſuch a bliſs, and reject all pleaſures, that
might lead to ſuch miſeries.

THE natural conſequence that ought
to be expected from ſuch a doctrine is,
what the goſpel exacts from us, the ſtricteſt morality, with an abſolute reſignation
to the will of GOD; yet it has been made
ſubſervient to every bad purpoſe, and all
manner of wickedneſs: when once men
were thoroughly perſuaded of rewards and
puniſhments in the world to come, the
clergy left no ſtone unturn'd, to make them
believe likewiſe, that the prieſts, as being,
the favourites of GOD, were the ſole in-
terpreters, as well as keepers of the ſacred.
oracles, and every man's cauſe would be:

mana-

managed in heaven, according as they should accuse or intercede for them. If this they could compass, they knew very well, that the mastery over every man's liberty, as well as purse, could not be disputed by them. Would sensual men, who bestow so much on their pleasures, not pay for the enjoyment of them with impunity, or the rich leave any passion ungratify'd; if they firmly believed, that money, tho' not parted with till after death, would atone for their sins?

How shamefully the church of *Rome* has play'd upon the superstition of the laity, and how little care at last they took to cover their avarice, is amazing. In the pontificate of *Leo* the tenth, the ordinary revenues not being sufficient to feed the luxury of his court and enrich his sister likewise, great sums were raised by farming out indulgences, and other branches of the sacred funds, which made those, who had advanced the money, put them off in such vast quantities, that in many places in *Germany*, says [a] *Guicciardin*, the powers

[a] Guicciard. *lib.* 3.

to

to releafe fouls from purgatory were play'd for in taverns and eating-houfes. But as improvements are made in all crafts, the *Mahometans* have outdone the *Roman* priefts in the way of affurance, if it be true what I have read, that the prince of *Baffora* fells places in paradice, which in goodnefs fhall anfwer what price their faithful are pleafed to beftow; and at the payment of the money, figns policies for them, that give great content.

I fhall fay nothing of the fham miracles, and prodigies, voices pretended to come from heaven, faints and devils perfonated by friars, letters fent from the virgin *Mary* her felf; the counterfeiting of relicks, and the impudent multiplication of them; of all which fo many inftances now are known, that would have remained fecrets, if priefts had never fallen out. I fhall omit likewife the artifices ufed in exorcifms, murders committed, and other villainous pranks that have been play'd between monks of different orders, to fpoil one another's trade. The tricks and ftratagems of clerick invention have been as vile as they are innumerable, and I care

not

not to rake in that *Augean* ſtable: no *Herculean* labour will be ever able to clear it; becauſe the ſorgeries of prieſts, when once received for truths, are almoſt immortal. They are monſters of ſtink and darkneſs, that may grow ſick at the appearance of light, and faint away at the ſcent of knowledge, but ſeldom die, whilſt they have a relation left to take care of them.

ST. *AMABLE*, who lived in the fifth century, is the patron of *Riom*, a city in *Auvergne*: it is reported of him, that going to *Rome* on foot, the ſun waited on him as a ſervant, and carried his cloak and his gloves in the air like an umbrella, during the great heat, and kept off the rain from him in bad weather. The wiſer ſort of *Roman* catholicks have long ago rejected this as a fable: yet the tradition is accounted ſo certain in that country, that they ſeldom draw St. *Amable*'s picture, without his gloves and his cloak, being ſupported in the air by a ſun-beam. How great an affront ſoever this ſtory may ſeem to put on human underſtanding, yet it was once ſwallow'd as a fact; and

who

who ever would reflect on the wit of the age, it was believ'd in, I defire he would not forget the modefty of thofe, who impofed it upon the people.

IT is the common opinion, that the Wars and devaftations, occafion'd by the frequent irruptions of the *Goths* and *Vandals*, introduced barbarifm into *Italy*, and were the only caufe of that profound ignorance, that fo univerfally overfpread the empire for feveral ages : but this is wronging the clergy, who thoroughly underftanding their intereft affifted the growth of it with fo much application: nothing was more obnoxious to all their enterprizes, than the *Pagan* philofophers as well as hiftorians, and the good fenfe contain'd in their works. Knowledge is the bane of prieft-craft; which made fome prelates, as foon as it was in their power, behave themfelves againft all human literature, and every thing belonging to arts and fciences, with an uncommon rage. They burnt fome of the beft books, deftroy'd pictures of ineftimable value, broke, mutilated, and defaced the fineft pieces of fculpture, and made away with, or buried

under

under ground, the noblest remainders of antiquity; and once all the writings that were not the product of christian authors, are said to have been in danger of being committed to the flames by one [a] of the greatest saints of the church, I mean *Gregory* the first, sirnamed *the great*; whose inveteracy against paganism and learning, was so excessive, that he not only was angry with an archbishop [b] of *Vienna*, for suffering grammar to be taught in his diocess, but studied to write bad latin himself, and in one of his letters boasted, that he scorned to conform to the rule of grammar, not in any thing to resemble a heathen.

In pursuance of this refin'd policy, the clergy has refus'd to recede an inch from what had been gain'd on the credulity of the laymen; and whoever attempted to undeceive the people, was always looked upon as a false brother, and render'd odious to the world. Whoever imagines from

[a] Vita D. Georg. ex Joanne Laziardo Cœlestin.
[b] Maimbourg Histoire du Pontificat de Saint Gregoire.

what

what he has read laft, that I endeavour to make allufions to latter times, knows not my aim; for to point at particular perfons is what I would avoid the moft : I de_fpife the very thoughts of a party-man, and defire to touch no man's fore, but in order to heal it. What I now charge the clergy with in general, they have been guilty of before the middle of the fifth century, and above ten thoufand times fince.

BEFORE the age I fpeak of, the then orthodox church had begun to reap the fruits from the feed of ignorance fhe cul-tivated with fo much care, and now among other dealings made a vaft profit from her traffick in relicks and the charity of devo-tees, that came to vifit the fhrines of the dead. *Vigilantius*, a *Spanifh* prieft thought this an abufe, as well as the prayers for the dead, and taught the people, what any of the apoftles would have juftified, that no religious honour was due to the afhes of faints and martyrs.

HOW this was relifh'd by the church, we may guefs from the extravagant ex-preffions, in which St. *Jerom* vented his

Q anger

anger againſt him : in one place he calls him [a] *Samaritan,* jew, filthy wretch, whoſe tongue ought to be cut out, and a furious monſter, that ought to be bound.   I know, ſays he in another, [b] what makes you write as you do. *It is the unclean ſpirit, that dwells in you, who is tormented by, and therefore dreads to approach the duſt of thoſe holy ſepulchres.*

ANOTHER piece of cleric policy is their ſticking cloſe, and obſtinately ad-hering to their friends, whether good men or bad.   The church is a bountiful and indulgent mother, that rewards well thoſe, who really ſerve her, and connives at all faults in her children, but diſobedience and want of reſpect to her ſelf.   Who-ever takes her part need not fear her an-ger ; and the greateſt profligate, if he'll promote her temporal intereſt, ſhall al-ways command her good word.   What incenſe of praiſe has been formerly, and is yet beſtow'd on the firſt chriſtian emperor, as if he had been the beſt of men ?   and

[a] Hieronim. Epiſt. ad Riparium.
[b] Idem Epiſt. adverſ. vigilant.

yet

yet it is manifeſt he was a wicked prince. I would not rely on the heathen [a] authors, who ſaid, that *Conſtantine* finding no ways to expiate the execrable murders he had been guilty of, in the *Pagan* religion, but finding ſome in the chriſtian, he forſook that of his anceſtors, and made himſelf a chriſtian. This we'll ſay was a falſe accuſation, but I can't help obſerving from it, that, whilſt that emperor was alive, and all the world was acquainted with his actions, there could have been no room for this calumny had *Conſtantine* been a good man.

EUSEBIUS wrote his life, which is full of encomiums upon him, but leaves [b] out, that he had put to death his wife *Fauſta*, and his own ſon *Criſpus*, from no other motive but jealouſy and revenge. In his chronicles indeed he relates it; but other fathers again have ſtrove to ſtifle thoſe facts, which every body knew to be true. In refuting the heathen authors I

[a] Soſipater *and others, whom* Sozomen *and Evagrius have wrote againſt.*
[b] Baronius ad ann. 324.

ſpoke

spoke of before, *Evagrius* [a] had the courage plainly to deny them: *Sozomen* had more caution; but being likewise unwilling to acknowledge them, he talks of something else, and only [b] proves, that *Crispus* and *Fausta* could not have been put to death but many years after *Constantine* had abjur'd the *Pagan* religion.

CARDINAL *Baronius* justly blames the writers of ecclesiastical history, who have suppress'd, or endeavour'd to refute those matters of fact, and makes a heavy bustle about it; which that the reader may not wonder at in a cardinal, especially such a high-flying one, I must acquaint him, that he did it not for nothing, and only exposed the nakedness of the fathers, because it serv'd his turn to support some traditions which are favourable to the see of [c] *Rome*. As the fathers, who laid the foundation of the temporal blessings of

[a] Evagr. Hist. Ecclef. *lib.* 3. *c.* 41.

[b] Sozom. Hist. Ecclef. *lib.* 1. *c.* 5.

[c] *He makes use of it to confirm the Acts of Pope* Silvester, *and to prove, that* Constantine *was baptized at* Rome *by this Pope a little before the Celebration of the Council of* Nice. *See the Remark B. of the Article* Fausta *in* Baile's *Dict.*

3   the

the church, prais'd their benefactors, so the fons have paid their acknowledgments to the fathers, and moſt of their lives, that have been written by modern divines, are rather panegyricks than hiſtories. *Hannibal* had but one eye, yet a flattering limner painted him with both: this *Hannibal* diſlik'd, but was very well pleaſed with another, who drew him in *profile,* an ingenious way of hiding a man's blind-fide without offending truth. The generality of the clergy ſtand not upon ſuch niceties, and ſcorn to be ſtinted in their commendations: when they have a favourite of the church to paint, they'll draw him with two eyes, though all the world knows he has none.

GREGORY the great, as cruel a perſecutor as he was of human wit, uſed more moderation in forcing men to the goſpel, than was generally practis'd in thoſe days: he likewiſe made ᵃ a great reform in the lives of the clergy, whoſe lewdneſs was exceſſive, puniſhed their incontinence with

---

ᵃ Maimbourg hiſtoire du Pontific. de S. Gregoire.

ri-

rigour, and was very fevere [a] againſt calumny. He undertook the converſion of
this kingdom, and happily effected it by
the monks he ſent us under the conduct
of *Auguſtin* their abbot. In the whole he
is reckon'd to have been a man of ſtrict
morals, and one of the beſt of popes. But
how little virtue or piety are regarded,
even by clergymen of good repute, when
the intereſt of the church is concern'd, we
ſhall learn from a ſhocking inſtance in the
life of this great pontiff.

THE emperor *Maurice*'s army being
revolted againſt him at the inſtigation of
Phocas, march'd towards *Conſtantinople*,
and took it without any difficulty. The
emperor [b] was deliver'd to *Phocas*, who,
by an unheard of cruelty, caus'd five little princes, *Maurice*'s children, to be murder'd in his preſence, before their father's
eyes. The nurſe of the youngeſt had
cunningly retrieved him from the maſſacre,
and ſubſtituted her own in his place ; but
Maurice, who perceiv'd it, caus'd his own

[a] Idem ubi ſupra.
[b] Idem.

child

child to be return'd to the executioners. *Phocas* no ways moved with so brave and generous an action, which melted all the assistants into tears, commanded this little innocent to be kill'd, and *Maurice* himself butcher'd upon the bodies of his five children.

THE eldest son of the emperor had a little before been sent into *Persia*, but being taken at *Nicæa*, was put to death, as were almost all the friends and relations of *Maurice*, and even the empress *Constantina*, and her three daughters, contrary to the promise *Phocas* had made to the patriarch *Cyriacus*. There never was more innocent blood shed in any reign than in his, nor a more infamous [a] tyrant than *Phocas*; a deform'd wretch, of a frightful aspect, without virtue, birth, honour, or merit: he was a drunkard, lascivious, void of humanity, and had all the ill qualities that may be set in opposition to those, which the historians have extremely [b] praised in *Maurice*.

[a] Idem.
[b] Ibidem.

A 3

As soon as it was known at *Rome* what had happen'd at *Constantinople*, and this monster was crown'd there, our holy pope sent congratulatory letters [a] to *Phocas* and *Leontia* his wife, wherein he rejoic'd for his accession to the throne, as the greatest advantage that could have happen'd to the empire; speaking of the usurper in the most advantageous terms, as of an admirable prince, who would make it flourish again, and thank'd GOD, that the world being deliver'd from so hard and uneasy a yoke, began to enjoy the sweets of liberty under his reign; without adding one syllable to express the least sorrow, that *Maurice* and his children had suffer'd death. The end of this base flattery was, what excuses all faults, the interest of the church. *Maurice* had declar'd for the patriarch of *Constantinople*, in a dispute concerning superiority; the pope overjoy'd to be deliver'd from an emperor, who had favour'd the patriarch of *Constantinople*, load-

[a] *Dr.* Cave, Hist. liter. Scriptor, Ecclef. ad ann. 603.

ed

ed this new prince with praises, to draw him over to his side.

THE excessive complaisance of this same saint to queen *Brunehauld* of *France*, may serve as another evidence of the church's small regard for truth, and her adherence to her friends with an affection so unmoveable, that no crimes or impiety can shake it. This queen, as most historians say, was the most [a] wicked woman in the world, yet St. *Gregory* bestow'd upon her all the praises that can be given to the most perfect princess, and scrupled not *to say in a* very positive [b] manner, that *France* was, of all nations, the most happy, since they deserv'd such a queen endu'd with all sorts of virtues and good qualities. What occasioned his esteem for the worst of women was, that *Brunehauld*, in the midst of her heinous crimes, shew'd an extraordinary [c] magnificence, towards churchmen, and in her foundations of churches and convents, not forgetting to make a devout request for relicks to the holy father.

[a] Maimbourg ubi supra.
[b] George. *lib.* 11. *epist.* 8.
[c] Maimbourg hist. du Pontif. de. S. Greg.

WHAT

WHAT *Philip de Comines* fays [a], was anfwer'd to him in *Italy*, will not feem foreign to our purpofe. In the *Carthufian* monaftery at *Pavia*, lies the body of *John Galeazzo*, a great and wicked tyrant: *Comines*, who went to fee it, hearing one of the *Carthufians* that fhew'd it him, call him faint, whifper'd him in the ear, and ask'd why he call'd him faint, when he might fee painted about him the arms of many towns he had ufurp'd, and to which he had no right? the other anfwer'd him foftly, In this country, we call faints all who are our benefactors.

As the worft of men, who would but promote or fide with the temporal intereft of the church, have never fail'd of her higheft commendations; fo the beft have never efcap'd her indignation and refentment, when they either oppos'd that intereft, or found the leaft fault with the clergy, how juftly or difcreetly foever it was done. Of this there are as many proofs as there have been wife princes, that were no bigots to the clergy, or elfe

[a] Phil. de Comin. Memoir. *lib.* 7.

the

the reformation alone would convince us of it, when we reflect on the furious calumnies the church of *Rome*, promifcuoufly attacking all fects, has belch'd out againft the proteftants in general.

THIS policy the church made ufe of early: when emperors were once become chriftians, the clergy receiv'd fuch power and other worldly comfort from their authority, that they could not think of living without, and therefore loft all patience when *Julian* was advanc'd to the empire. They did and faid againft him every thing that rage and hatred could infpire, and fix'd upon him the firname of apoftate, to render him odious, which has ftuck by him to this day. *Julian* had been differently educated, as well at *Pagan* as at chriftian univerfities, and at one time he had heathens, and at another chriftians for his tutors: but I never faw it prov'd, that he adher'd to chriftianity at a time he might with fafety have refus'd it. It muft be confefs'd, that as foon as he was mafter of his choice, he made the worft, and unfortunately embrac'd paganifm, becaufe it was the religion of his anceftors.

BUT

BUT let him be call'd heathen or apo-state, or what the clergy pleases, to judge of him impartially from history, we must own, that he was a virtuous and gallant prince, endu'd with wit and humanity, and more steadiness and moderation than any of his christian predecessors. In his letters he appears to have been a father to his people, and one of them I will take leave to insert here, which will make us perfectly well acquainted with the tolerating temper of that prince, and at the same time point at the real cause of the clergy's animosities against him.

JULIAN to the *Bostrens*.

I Should have [a] thought, indeed, that the Galilean leaders would have esteem'd themselves more indebted to me than to him, who preceded me in the administration of the empire: for in his time many of them suffer'd exile, persecution, and imprisonment. Multitudes of those, whom in their religion

[a] Julian's *Epistles*, *Numb.* 52.

they

they term hereticks, *were put to the sword; insomuch, that in* Samosata, Cyzicum, Paphlagonia, Bythinia, Galatia, *and many other countries, whole towns were levell'd with the earth. The just reverse of this has been observ'd in my time. The exiles have been recall'd, and the proscrib'd restor'd to the lawful possessions of their estates: but to that height of fury and distraction are this people arrived, that being no longer allow'd the privilege to tyrannize over one another, or persecute either their own sectaries, or the religious of the lawful church, they swell with rage, and leave no stone unturn'd, no opportunity unimploy'd, of raising tumult and sedition. So little regard have they to true piety, so little obedience to our laws and constitutions, however human and tolerating. For still do we determine, and steadily resolve never to suffer one of them involuntarily to be drawn unto our altars.* ***. *As for the mere people indeed, they appear driven to these riots and seditions by those amongst them whom they call* Clericks; *who are now inrag'd to find themselves restrain'd in the use of their former power, and intemperate rule.* *** *They can no longer act the magistrate,*

strate, or civil judge, nor assume authority to make people's wills, supplant relations, possess themselves of other mens patrimonies, and, by specious pretences, transfer all into their own possession. For this reason, I have thought fit, by this publick edict, to forewarn the people of this sort, that they raise no more commotions, nor gather in a riotous manner about their seditious clericks, in defiance of the magistrate, who has been insulted, and in danger of being ston'd by these incited rabbles. In their congregations they may notwithstanding assemble as they please, and croud about their leaders, performing worship, receiving doctrine, and praying according as they are by them taught and conducted; but if with any tendency to sedition, let them beware, how they hearken or give assent; and remember 'tis at their peril, if by these means they are secretly wrought up to mutiny and insurrection. *** Live therefore in peace and quietness! neither spitefully opposing or injuriously treating one another. You misguided people of the new way, beware on your side! And you of the ancient and establish'd church, injure not your neighbours and fellow citizens, who

are

are enthusiastically led away in ignorance and mistake, rather than with design or malice! 'Tis by discourse *and* reason, *not by* blows, insults, *or* violence, *that men are to be inform'd of truth, and convinc'd of error. Again therefore, and again, I enjoin and charge the zealous followers of the true religion no way to injure, molest or affront the* Galilean *people.*

THESE were the sentiments of this emperor, whom the clergy make such a monster, and whose very clemency they made a handle of for slander; complaining, that by his mildness and unlimited toleration he had done more prejudice to the church than others with persecution. He was a politick prince, yet the clergy proved too hard for him, and never ceas'd plotting against him, till at last, to the great joy of the orthodox, he was assassinated by one of his christian soldiers.

BUT if to this treachery we should give the name of religious zeal against a *Pagan*, what excuse can the church have for her violent hatred against her very pontiffs, whenever they have been men of

pro-

probity, and endeavour'd to curb the licentioufnefs of the clergy? *Hadrian* the
fixth was a prelate of vaft learning and
parts, of unqueftionable morals, and ex-
emplary frugality, and in fhort, one of the
beft popes that have fill'd the chair in thefe
latter times. He was chofe for his virtue,
and the fame of his great abilities, [a] whilft
he was abfent, and wholly taken up with
the government affairs of *Spain*. As foon
as he began to act, he was lampoon'd and
defpis'd, and in a little time (it is thought)
made away with. Since that, they have
even reproach'd [b] him with ftupidity, and
want of tafte, for the plainnefs of his dyet, and his averfion to luxury. Would
you know the reafon of this anger and inveteracy? He took notice [c] of the wicked
lives of the clergy, and would reform them.
See here part of the inftructions this pope
gave his nuncio to the dyet of the empire,
which was held at the beginning of the reformation.

[a] Paul Jovius in vita Hadrian VI.
[b] Chriftoph. Battus.
[c] Moring. in vita Hadrian VI.

You shall tell them, (says he) *that we freely acknowledge, that* GOD *suffers this persecution by the* Lutherans, *brought upon his church for the sins of men, especially the priests and prelates of the church. The scriptures declare, that the sins of the people are derived from the sins of the priest: for which reason, as St.* Chrysostom *tells us, our saviour, willing to take care of the infirm city of* Jerusalem, *went into the temple to chastise the sins of the priests first, as a good physician, who cures the distemper from the root. We know that in this our holy see for some years many abominations have been committed: abuses in things spiritual, excesses in ordinances, and that every thing has been altered for the worse; and it is no wonder if the disease from the head fell upon the members, from the popes to other inferiour prelates. All we prelates,* viz. *ecclesiasticks, have declin'd every one to his own ways, and this great while there has not been any that has done well, not so much as one.*

A proteſtant writer imagines, that the cardinals ſo ſtrongly reſented this pope's reflecting upon the honour of the church, and his burning a man for the crime of

R   beaſtibeaftiality, that they [a] fhortened his life.

H o w little, goodnefs it felf, and the effentials of chriftianity are thought to be required in the head of the church, we may learn from thofe who pretend beft to underftand her intereft. *Innocent* XI. dreaded the exorbitant power and ambition of *Lewis* XIV. and oppofed the profperity of *France*, as much as any proteftant prince, which made that nation very angry with him. Hear the fally of one of them, who heard fome body praife the piety and moral feverity of that pope in the year 1689. *The greatnefs and majefty, faid he, of the catholick church, require a head not endowed with the virtues of a prieft, but with the talents of a cunning politician. They require a head, who has the courage to damn himfelf for the good and encreafe of his dominions ; that is the way to perform the office of a good fhepherd, who gives his life for his fheep. A fcrupulous and devout pope, like good* Adrian *the VIth, is only fit to let the temporals of the church perifh, which are fo advantageous for the maintenance of the fpirituals.*

[a] Nov. ex Epifc. Belg. divifio.

THIS

THIS *Frenchman* was partial, or elſe he would have found, *Innocent* had no piety that made him neglectful of his intereſt; he ſhould have conſider'd, that the court of *Rome* is no leſs concern'd than others in maintaining a ballance of power in chriſtendom. But had the pope aſſiſted the *Turk* againſt *Germany*, he would have commended him for acting againſt the *Roman* catholick religion to maintain the power of the *Roman* catholick church. *Sixtus* the Vth did the ſame againſt *Spain* in favour of *England* and *Holland*; and it is not improbable what *Leti* relates of him, [a] that he kept a ſecret correſpondence with queen *Elizabeth* to the prejudice of the king of *Spain*, notwithſtanding the bulls of excommunication he thunder'd out againſt her. His politicks were juſt; 'tis a leſs diſadvantage to the pope not to be acknowledg'd either in *Holland* or *England*, than if by ſuch an acknowledgment any catholick prince ſhould be enabled to obtain all his demands at *Rome*, either by fair or foul means.

[a] Leti Monarchie univerſelle, tom. 2.

R 2 THIS

THIS ought not to to be look'd upon as a digreffion in a man, who is endeavouring to demonftrate the difference between religion and the church. It fhews, that whoever will be but mindful of the latter, fhall have the clergy's leave to be as carelefs of the other as he pleafes. The *Athenians* having been intent on nothing but religion for fome time, were bid to take care not to mind heaven fo much as to lofe the earth. I have often thought that this would be a needlefs caution to the clergy, who all make fure of their power on earth firft, whatever becomes of their intereft in heaven. Every body does not know that good popes are fuppos'd to be wicked of courfe, and that the church it felf has but a flender opinion of their falvation. Yet it is true, if you'll believe *Bellarmin. The Popes,* fays he, *are fo far from deferving to be canonized, that they can hardly keep themfelves from hell.* If the authority of a cardinal be not fufficient, I can back it with infallibility from the words of *Marcellus* the **II.** who one day cry'd out at table, [a] *I do not fee, how thofe,*

[a] Onuphrius in Marcello II. apud Ancillon.

that

that are feated in St. Peter's *chair, can be faved.*

AMONG the politicks of the church, pious frauds ought not to be forgot. I fpeak not of the petty inventions of monks, and little priefts to raife devotion for their own ends; but fubftantial calumnies rais'd by the fathers with the greateft air of fincerity. The *Pagans,* I have faid before, had a wretched theology; and no man could have wifh'd for a more inconfiftent fyftem to oppofe, than their religion; yet the fathers were not contented without making it worfe, by falfe accufations, than it was.

THE floral games were celebrated after a fcandalous manner, with odious obfcenities: [a] this is undeniable; but it is not true what *Lactantius* fays, that they were inftituted by a curtezan, call'd *Flora,* who, grown rich by her trade, left the *Roman* people her heir, and order'd that the revenue of a certain fund, fhe fpecify'd, fhould be employ'd to celebrate her birthday; neither is it true, what he adds, that

[a] Lactant. Divin. Inftit. *lib. cap.* 20.

the

the senate endeavour'd to hide from the publick the rise of so infamous a custom; that accordingly, taking advantage of the name of this curtezan, they pretended that *Flora* was the goddess of flowers? and, that in order to have a good harvest, it was necessary to honour that goddess every year, and to make her propitious.

In the first place, the worship of *Flora* was instituted in *Rome*, [a] by *Tatius* and *Romulus* his collegue, and divine honours had been paid to this goddess by the *Sabins* before the building of *Rome*. In the second, those games were for a considerable time only celebrated as the intemperature of the seasons requir'd it, or the books of the *Sybils* enjoyn'd it, and not every year, [b] before the year of *Rome*, 580, and then, the irregularity of the spring having prov'd very detrimental, a decree was made to have them exhibited yearly. From all which it is evident, that the superstition of the *Pagans* to the goddess of flowers, was no pretence but a reality.

[a] Varro *lib.* 4. de Lingua Lat.
[b] Vossius de Orig. Idolol. *lib.* 1. *cap.* 12.

Lastly

Laftly the fund, [a] to defray the charges of the floral games, was the money accruing from the fines of thofe, who had appropriated to themfelves fuch lands as belong'd to the republick, and not any thing left by a common woman.

VOSSIUS and others have taken notice of this flander, and the firft cautions us not to adopt for truth whatever the fathers have writ againft the gentiles. A man may relate a falfhood by miftake without any intention to deceive. This is pardonable, and poffibly may be the cafe of *Lactantius*; but the fathers have done it often wilfully, and what is worfe, boafted of it, when they had done, as if either force or deceit, or any thing had been fair againft a heathen. St. *Jerom*, carried away by the violence of this prejudice, has not fcrupled to tell us, [b] that the fathers were obliged to fay not what they thought, but every thing requifite to refute what the heathens believ'd. He endeavours to vin-

[a] Voffius ubi fupra.
[b] *St.* Hieron. Apolog. ad Pammachium pro libris adv. Jovinian.

dicate

dicate them by St. *Paul's* example, but *Blondel* [a] has taken him up for it as he deserved. No such conduct can be prov'd upon any of the apostles, and truth needs not, nay scorns, the support of falshood.

IT is a vulgar notion, that after the coming of Christ, or at least upon the preaching of the gospel, all the *Pagan* oracles immediately ceas'd; what father or priest was the author of it I know not. But it is manifest, that in the reign of *Constantius*, the son of *Constantine the great*, the oracle of the god *Besa* subsisted still at *Abydus*, a city of *Ægypt*, famous upon many accounts. The evidence to prove this is remarkable. That emperor was [b] a suspicious, credulous prince, of a mean genius, and being inform'd that divers people went to consult this [c] oracle concerning his life, and the name of the person, who should succeed him, he was in a great rage, and dispatch'd away a commission presently to try the guilty, which caus'd great disorders, and greater noise.

[a] Blondel de Sibylles *lib.* 1. *cap.* 26.
[b] Ammian. Marcell. ad ann. 359.
[c] Idem ibid.

THAT

THAT there were other oracles befides, .remaining long after the firft plant-
ing of chriftianity, we may learn from
Paufanias, [a] who affirms, that in his time
there was no oracle fo true as that of
Amphilochus, which was at *Mallus* in *Cilicia* ;
from which it is to be fuppofed that there
were feveral others. *Plutarch* likewife
tells us, [b] that this oracle of *Amphilochus*
was famous and flourifhed in his days.

As I have reafon to fear more fevere
cenfures than others, fo I muft take pre-
cautions, which otherwife would be needlefs ; when I fpeak of oracles remaining
after the coming of Chrift, I have no defign to affert the reality of them, I mean
only, that they fubfifted, as they had done
before, by the juggle and artifice of the
priefts who had the profit of them: and it
is my real fentiment, that they would not
have ceas'd to this day, if people had not
ceas'd to believe in them. I know it is
the opinion of many, that the devil was
at the bottom of all thefe oracles, and that

[a] Paufan. *lib.* 1.
[b] Plutarch de fera numinis vindi&.

S   feveral

several imagine him to understand futurity, and often to foretel things truly, that are to come to pass. But I confess, I do not think he was concern'd in them any further, than as he is charged in our indictments of felons; or that he can foretel things to come any more, than he can work miracles. None can work miracles but GOD, and those to whom he immediately delegates his power; and I cannot believe that his power ever was employ'd in favour of idolatry, tho' a worthy divine of our church seems to insinuate it.

WHAT I mean is this, *Brennus* [a] with an army of *Gauls* was in full march to sack and pillage the rich temple of *Delphos*. But by the way such a violent tempest arose of thunder and lightning, as consum'd him and all his sacrilegious host. The heathens, as men of all other religions would have done, had the case been their own, cried out, a miracle! The christians, not being able to deny the fact, laid it upon the old pack-horse, the devil: but Dr. *Prideaux*, not willing to at-

[a] Justin. Hist. *lib.* 24.

tribute

tribute fo great a power to the infernal fiend, is of opinion, that it really was a miracle, *and that* GOD *wrought it ª for the fake of religion in general.*

HERE we differ: for tho' I am of the dean's opinion, that *Apollo, Jupiter,* or any other of the heathen gods, empty founds, things without exiſtence, could not raiſe this ſtorm ; yet the more I think on the great indignation, which the jealous GOD on all occaſions expreſſes againſt idolatry, the leſs I can think, that he would have wrought a miracle to fave this temple. I would rather ſay, that this tempeſt had been an accident, which all hot countries are ſubjeƈt to, than aſcribe a conduƈt to GOD, which on feveral accounts is fo unworthy the idea I have of him. Theſe words, in the ſenſe I underſtand them, ſuppoſe a reaſoning of this kind. If *Brennus* robs and deſtroys this temple of *Delphos* with impunity, it may encourage others one day or other to attempt the ſame upon mine ; and therefore I'll puniſh all facrilege, that my own may be the more ſafe.

ª *D.* Prideaux's *Conneƈtions of the Old and New Teſt.*

But

But if the words, *that* GOD *did it for the sake of religion in general,* do not include this thought, I own that I do not underftand their meaning; and heartily beg that learned man's pardon, if he takes offence at any thing I have faid; as to my felf I am fure I defign none, and am oblig'd to him for his elaborate works.

The *Mahometans* have not been ufed much better than the heathens. *Mahomet* was an impoftor; his followers have afferted many falfities concerning him: But neither is all true that chriftians have father'd upon them: nothing is more generally believed, than that to counterfeit a miracle, the body of *Mahomet* is fufpended in an iron coffin by virtue of loadftones, artfully plac'd at *Mecca*: yet his body was buried at *Medina,* [a] where it remains to this day, without an iron coffin, and without any loadftones; and the ableft naturalifts affirm [b], that fuch a fufpenfion in the air by loadftones furpaffes all human skill.

[a] *Dr.* Prideaux *in the life of* Mahomet.
[b] *See* Bernier's *Abridgment of the Philofophy of* Gaffendus.

The

The story likewise of the pigeon that used to come to this false prophet's ears has likewise been reported with great confidence, and some famous [a] writers assure us, that the *Musselmans* make mention of this dove; yet if we believe Dr. *Pocock* none [b] of the *Arabick* writers say any thing of it. Other things more ridiculous have been told us, concerning the credulity of the *Mahometans*, which they never heard of but from us.

That the spirit of insincerity, which has haunted the church so many ages ago, has not been expell'd, or altogether laid, by the reformation, will be shewn in several places of the ensuing chapter: but that those who have no mind to enter upon a fresh chapter, may not go away dissatisfied, I shall give them an instance before we part. The protestants have long diverted themselves with the story of pope *Joan*, and several *Roman* catholics

[a] Gabriel Sionita & Johan. Hesronita in tractatu de nonnullis Orientalium Urbibus.
[b] *Dr.* Pocock Specim. Histor. Arabum.

have

have, for want of better enquiry, been forc'd to yield them this point, till at laſt *Blondel*, a *French Hugonot*, made it evident [a] that it was a falſhood. *Spanheim* and *Mareſius* have in vain ſhew'd a great deal of erudition to re-eſtabliſh the credit of this fiction.

THIS I don't diſcommend them for, neither do I care whether there ever was a ſhe pope or not: but I think it inexcuſable, that thoſe who were themſelves convinc'd, that *Blondel* was in the right, ſhould be offended at the diſcovery. All the *Hugonots* [b] were very angry, that a miniſter of the reformed church ſhould prove the falſity of a thing which the proteſtant intereſt required to be true; they blamed him [c] for carrying away the filth of the papiſts, and ſaid, that thoſe who did not ceaſe to reproach the memory of the reformers deſerved not that any one ſhould do them that good of-

[a] In *Lib.* de Joanna Papiſta.
[b] In Præfat. Apologet. apud Mareſium.
[c] Curcellæus in refutat. Sam. Mareſ.

fice.

face. This was the language of the moſt moderate; others were hotter, and cried out, [a] that he had betray'd the proteſtant cauſe, and was brib'd by the enemies of it.

[a] Sarravius Epiſt. 178.

S 4 CHAP.

CHAP. VIII.

Of SCHISM.

HE church every where is look-ed upon as entire as a garment without feam; and whoever dif-fents from what is believed in it, perfuading others to be of his opinion, tears and makes a rent in it, which is call'd fchifm. When men of forefight and great abilities are by a deep laid policy raifing a noble machine of power, it muft be vexa-tious to fee bunglers, either out of envy or ignorance, interrupt and difturb them in their hearty endeavours: for this reafon, the grand architects of the authority, and all the fecular bleffings of the church, were always fo incens'd againft thofe who oppo-fed them, and treated all innovators with fo much feverity. It is undeniable, that great impieties and many monftrous opini-

ons

ons have sprung up among christians, since the time of the apostles, and I am willing to believe, that most of those who broached heresies have had their by-ends that had no relation to religion; but then no heresy began, but had a specious pretence of advancing piety, or avoiding something that gave offence in the system of the orthodox.

The charity of a christian in construing the actions of others, can hardly be too extensive; and I believe that the body (for I have nothing to do with the heads) of most hereticks were better people than they have been represented to us. The terror men are under at the thoughts of holding an opinion that makes God the author of evil, has produced the *Marcionites, Manicheans, Pelagians, Arminians,* and many other sects. The clear idea men have of the unity of God gave the first rise to *Arianism,* and has so often reviv'd it under different shapes. When men of narrow views lye poring upon particular scripture places, and let go the main scope and drift of the gospel, they must commit errors, or when men, having in vain raised

all

all their faculties to render the infinite
sublimity of GOD and his attributes intelligible, and endeavouring to make him less
incomprehensible, pull down, as it were, the
Deity to the level of their weak intellects,
they fall into miserable mistakes. This
latter was the fault of *Origen,* who could
not reconcile the eternity of damnation
with the infinite goodness of GOD; and
since him thousands have and daily do split
on the like rocks.

THE searchers after truth are often labouring between a *Scylla* and a *Charybdis*;
if they steer not steady, and are frighten'd
too much from either side, they are infallibly lost. For fear of being scorch'd by
the fire, men have leap'd into the sea,
where nothing could save them.

WHAT strange turns of thought are
human minds liable to! The *Abelians*
were a sect of hereticks, that [a] would not
suffer man to be alone, and ordered every
one to take a woman for a help-meet; but
strictly forbad all carnal commerce. They
regulated marriage at the rate of the ter-

---

[a] *St.* Augustin. de Hæres. *c.* 87.

restrial

reftrial paradice, where there was only the union of the heart between *Adam* and *Eve.* When a man and a woman were enter'd into that kind of fociety, they adopted two children, a boy and a girl, who fucceeded to their eftate, and who were married together, under the fame conditions of not getting children, but to adopt two of a different fex: if thefe people were fincere, they muft have been far from lafcivious, and practis'd a world of felf-denial. We read of *Anchorets*, fo affectedly modeft, [a] that they would not behold their own nudities, nor touch their own obfcene parts but with a glove, and an ancient philofopher [b] would never touch them either with or without gloves.

THE *Adamites* were a fect of hereticks that likewife profefs'd continency, but condemned marriage: when [c] they affembled for the exercife of their religion, they pull'd off their cloaths, and men and women fat together ftark naked, the minifters as well

[a] Hift. Ludicra *of Balthazar's Bonifacius.*
[b] Zenocrates.
[c] Danœus in Auguft. de Hæref. *cap.* 3.

as

as the laity. After they had perform'd their devotion, they put on their cloaths again and went home; if any committed a fault, he was no more receiv'd into that assembly: they said, that having, like *Adam*, eat of the forbidden fruit, they were to be driven, like him, out of paradice, which was the name they gave to their church: St. *Epiphanius* alledges nothing against their chastity, but *Clemens Alexandrinus* [a] relates horrible things of them, and what might be fear'd from such a custom; but in thirty or forty years, a sect may much deviate from the principles profess'd at their first institution; having deriv'd their name from the stem of all human kind, these miserable people imitated the nakedness which our first parents lived in, during the state of innocence, and declin'd marrying, because *Adam* did not know *Eve* till after his sin, and after his going out of paradice; so that they believ'd, that if man had persevered in his innocency, there would have been no marriage.

[a] Idem ibid.

MEN

MEN may have extravagant notions, yet no criminal defign, till human paffion intervenes, and laying hold of the opportunity, turns that to wickednefs and abomination, which was begun with the moft innocent intention; witnefs the devotional watchings which were practis'd in the primitive church: as they were perform'd at night, and by great numbers, lafcivious perfons made an ill ufe of them; when it was found, that all the remedies, applied to ftop this evil, prov'd ineffectual, thefe publick watchings were entirely left off.

THE *Turlupins* were ftill a more infamous fect, in all refpects as impudent [a] as the *Cynicks* among the heathens. Among the proteftants there has been one *Picard*, [b] who over-ftretch'd the errors of the *Adamites*, in refpect to nakednefs; in a little time he got a great many followers from *Flanders* into *Germany*, as far as *Bohemia*, tho' fome *Roman* catholicks have given the

[a] Gerfon apud Prateol.
[b] Varillas, *The Hiftory of Wicklefianifm*, Part 2.

name

name of *Picards* [a] to all the proteſtants of *Bohemia* who oppos'd popery.

SEVERAL doating men likewiſe among the anabaptiſts [b] have affected to go naked, moſt of them more deſerving pity than puniſhment.   In the year 1535, *Adamites* have been ſeen at *Amſterdam* run ſtark naked through the ſtreets, that were rich, and of good families; and it is reported, that ſome were fanatical enough to climb upon trees, where they waited in vain for bread to fall from heaven, until they fell half dead to the ground: many ſchiſms ought only to have been ridicul'd, and the enthuſiaſtical innovators treated, as moſt parts of *Europe* did the *French* prophets ſome few years ago; but the clergy-men have no patience, preſently they are ſerious and fall to perſecution; when men run into errors, becauſe they are fools, it is wrong for wiſe men to be angry with and puniſh them, as if they were knaves.

THE ſchiſms of note that have infeſted the church, from the time of the

[a] Rudigerus *in his Hiſtory of the Brethren of* Bohemia.

[b] Lambertus Hortenſius *in his Relation of the Tumults of the Anabaptiſts.*

apoftles to that of *Luther*, are faid to have been [a] a hundred and fourfcore, whether more or lefs is not material to my pur-pofe, the church of *Rome* has quell'd and triumph'd over them all, till that, which fhe calls the northern herefy, and we the refor-mation: by this fhe receiv'd a ruder fhock than ever fhe fuftain'd before, and would have been deftroy'd, had the reformers been unanimous; nay, if among the pro-teftants the clergy could have but kept *half* the temper the princes endeavour'd to do, long before this time we would have known nothing of the pope or of the church of *Rome*, but from hiftory.

As the reformation could not be brought about, without the help of the fecular power, the laity was refolv'd to be no lo-fers by it; in all countries where it took place, the publick immediately recover'd the greateft part of the lands, the trea-fure and other poffeffions of the church, that many different ways had been either coax'd or extorted from them by prieft-craft: the fupremacy in ecclefiaftical, as

[a] Moreri.

well

well as temporal matters, which the pope claim'd as his undoubted right was injur'd, and in most places vested in the civil magistrate, by which those princes and states became the real sovereigns of their own dominions, without asking leave of the court of *Rome*; no infallibility of councils or of any visible church was to be allow-ed of, and consequently mens consciences were deliver'd from the tyranny the priests had usurp'd over them. And lastly, matrimony was made as lawful to the clergy, as it was to the laity.

IT was on this foot only, that the clergy, as well as the sovereigns of the reformers, thought it possible this great work could be accomplish'd; and had churchmen no more deviated from these principles, than the princes have done, the temporal advantages that would have accrued from the reformation to every society, without interfering with religion, would have been inestimable: nothing is more manifest than that, without taking away from the church its exorbitant power and authority, the reformation could never have been effected; for whoever acknow-

ledges

ledge's the popes supremacy, can never by
force of arms dispute his jurisdiction, without owning himself to be in open rebellion; and it is impossible to act more incon-
sistently, than to say that popes are infallible, and at the same time contradict them,
and shew that they have been guilty of many damnable errors.

YET as soon as an absolute separation
from the church of *Rome* was made, the
protestants had established their communions, and the reformed religion was maintain'd by the sovereigns in every country
that had embrac'd it, the clergy presently
grew weary of being too apostolick; for
as the first reformers had upon very good
grounds found fault with, and given their
sentiments against the then established
church, so many of their successors claim'd
the same privilege, and openly told the
world, that by the same authority, which
was that of the scripture, it was as lawful
for them to dissent from the first reformers, if they could demonstrate that they
had been in an error, as it had been for
the first reformers to dissent from the
church of *Rome.*

T

THIS

THIS not being eafily anfwer'd by a proteftant, without engaging himfelf in tedious difputes, the national churches, in all reformed countries when fchifmaticks arofe, wanted that power and authority to crufh them, which in the church of *Rome* they had call'd an ufurpation; and no clergy-man, who has the temporal felicity of his order at heart, will fcruple to own, that to keep up orthodoxy power is requifite, as well as argument, and that no national church can flourifh without it.

THE words infallibility and independency are odious, but if we examine into the behaviour of the clergy, we fhall find but few proteftant church-men, who would not be glad of fome equivalents: moft of them agree, that in all countries, the church ought to have a jurifdiction without appeal, that in all ecclefiaftical matters, the clergy are the undoubted judges of the laity, as well as of their own order: but that church-men fhould ever be tried by the laity, is not fo well approved of, and many of them find fault with it, even for crimes againft the ftate; clergy-men, they fay, ought at leaft to be independent

on

on the government. In their prayers,
and by way of compliment, a proteſtant
clergy may ſtile their ſovereign to be under **Chriſt** the ſupreme head and governour of the church: but if this head com-
plies not with all their demands however
unreaſonable, if he refuſes to proſecute
thoſe who diſſent from the national church,
as violently as the clergy require he ſhould,
he ſhall immediately be hated by them,
ſlander'd, vilified, and, on all occaſions,
treated with all the diſreſpect and ill language imaginable; how incens'd they will
be, how furiouſly they'll fly in the face of
their ſupreme governour, if at any time
he pretends to direct or admoniſh them,
tho' in the mildeſt manner; what clamours they will raiſe againſt him ſhould
he but hinder them from coming together
at ſynods and other aſſemblies, even
when all the world knows that they deſire
to meet from no other motive than human paſſion, and to gratify a vindictive
ſpirit!

PROTESTANT church-men may
likewiſe acknowledge, that it is not impoſſible they ſhould err, tho' I already

T 2   have

have given an inſtance of one who denied it, (*p.* 156.) but at the ſame time they require of us an implicit faith and ready aſſent, to every thing they ſhall advance. The national clergy in all countries hate arguing, they are always angry with thoſe who oppoſe them, or but call the truth of their ſyſtem in queſtion; and no church ever had the power to puniſh men for disbelieving her doctrine, without making a ſevere uſe of it on the ſlighteſt occaſions: from all which it is manifeſt, that if proteſtant church-men are ſo civil, as not to pretend to be infallible, they expect we ſhould return the compliment, and treat them as if they were.

THE lawfulneſs of marriage in the clergy, which was agreed to at the reformation, they have not yet made any attempt againſt; they are eaſy on this head for their own ſakes, for where incontinency is ſcandalous, and fornication puniſh'd, no clergy will live without wives; *Luther* allow'd two [a] to the landgrave of *Heſſe*, and ſeveral paſſages in his works ſeem to favour poligamy; this I

[a] *Varillas Hiſtoir. de l'Hereſie.*

have

have nothing to do with : what I shall observe is, that the liberty of marrying in church-men, is an article of the highest importance to us; the rigorous precept of celibacy has all along been look'd upon by the vulgar of the *Romish* church as a piece of self-denial, a mighty hardship which the clergy imposed upon themselves and underwent for the good of religion, whereas among all the machinations of the church, this was the deepest plot that has been laid against the wealth and property of lay-men.

THE reason alledg'd for it, that to keep the holy and immaculate office of the priest-hood at a Distance remote enough from uncleanness, this exquisite purity was required, is a pretence as false as it is plausible : Had chastity been the church's aim, she would not have conniv'd at the lewd transgressions of the clergy as she has done : In *Italy*, *Spain*, and *Portugal*, the indulgences for the sin of the flesh and all impurities, are cheap and easy ; and at the same time that they look upon continence as a thing impracticable, marriage in a priest is shocking and abominable.

THIS

THIS may be folly in the multitude, but in the clergy it is craft; they know that if a fociety of a hundred men, who have all vow'd celibacy, will keep up their number, and as any die, chufe other fingle men, under the fame obligation in the room of the deceas'd, it muft be immortal, and that if they have a certain income exceeding their yearly expences, tho' never fo little, and there is the leaft prudence and oeconomy among them, this fociety, at long run, will get into their clutches the greateft if not all the wealth of the country they live in. As the church had many artifices to fcrape riches together, this was the moft fuitable contrivance to keep them.

BUT as this piece of policy was by all means to be conceal'd from the vulgar, it was thought neceffary, to make fome fhew of virtue, and to produce fome eminent examples of chaftity among the clergy: for tho' the lewdnefs of priefts and friars, at leaft of the greateft part of them, was notorious whilft they were alive, it was no difficult matter, when they had been dead fome time, and their memory was forgot by the publick, to fay of them what they pleas'd.

pleas'd. There is hardly an order of monks, that has not done themselves this kindness in the romantick praises they have bestow'd upon their founders. St. *Ignatius de Loyala* was a soldier by profession, and had given proofs [a] of his valour, when suddenly he became a zealous votary to the virgin *Mary*, hung up, and all night watch'd his arms in a chappel consecrated to her, where with all the ceremonies, used in ancient [b] chivalry, he declared himself her champion, and dedicated the remainder of his life to her service. The holy virgin in return, if we believe his historians, bestow'd on him the gift of continence in such a [c] degree, that, from the time he became her knight to his death, he felt not the least symptom of an immodest Temptation.

A critick will say, that his panegyrists have over-shot the mark, that by endea-

---

[a] Ribadeneiro in vita Ignatii *lib.* 1. *cap.* 4.

[b] *He was converted by reading the Legends of the Saints, as* Don Quixot *was to Knight-Errantry, by reading of old Romances.* Stillingfleet, *of the Fanaticism of the Church of* Rome.

[c] Ribadeneir.

vouring

vouring to render his virtue too sublime, they left him none, that where there is no desire there can be no self denial, and that a man, who is not sensible of any temptation, can claim no greater merit from continence, than he can from frigidity. This fault is not to be found with the commendations bestow'd on St. *Francis* of *Assisi*, the founder of one of the four mendicant orders, whose chastity has been highly extoll'd, tho' the conflicts he had with carnal temptations were very severe. *At the beginning of his Conversion* [a] *(says St. Bonaventure) he would often throw himself in a ditch full of ice, that he might get a compleat victory over his domestick enemy, and to preserve the robe of chastity from the conflagration of pleasure. Being one day strongly press'd by a temptation of the flesh, he pull'd off his cloaths* [b] *and scourg'd himself soundly! After that he open'd his cell and went into a garden, where he threw himself into a great heap of snow.* The

[a] See Ferrand's answer to the apology for the reformation.

[b] Ibidem.

fever

fever of luft muft be very high, where fuch violent coolers are requir'd.

WE have had a monk of our own long before St. *Francis,* who made ufe of the fame potent remedies, and often flung himfelf [a] into cold water or fnow, to extinguifh the flames of concupifcence ; but with greater fuccefs as to triumph. For St. *Francis,* in the heighth of his eager defires [b] durft not come near women; St. *Aldhelme,* an *Englifh* friar, who lived in the eighth century, and was for his learning and piety made a bifhop, got fo perfect a maftery over the flefh, that [c] the fineft woman made no impreffion upon him: and not to flinch from the moft dangerous temptations, he went to bed to a young girl, and lying by her fide repeated the whole pfalter, whilft the motions of his heart tended only to heaven.

THIS invincible fortitude of St. *Aldhelme,* has been look'd upon as an example [d] ra-

[a] Wilhelm. Malmesbury, in vita St. Aldhelmi.
[b] St. Bonaventura in vita St. Francifc.
[c] Malmesbury ubi fupra.
[d] *Hiftory of the works of the learned for the month of* April, 1689.

U ther

ther to be admired than imitated; and I believe not, that many, who have hazarded themselves to such trials of virtue, are come off conquerors, tho' several experiments have been made of it since the time of this saint. About the year 1437. the countess of *Guastala* by the advice of *Baptist de Crema*, a jacobin monk, founded a [a] a society call'd, *That of the victory over ones self against the flesh.* To gain this victory, a certain lady named *Julia*, put a young fellow into bed with a young girl, and laid a crucifix as a barrier betwixt them; which, if it kept them virtuous, ought not to be omitted in the catalogue of the miracles that have been wrought by crucifixes. This society of *Guastalians* multiply'd prodigiously for some time, till being look'd upon as libertines, they were every where expell'd.

WHAT fine stories or legends soever we are told of later saints, it is certain, that all the ancient fathers, and others who have wrote with any sincerity, found no-

[a] Hist. de la Mappe-Monde Papistique *Page* 18. *Edit.* 1567.

thing

thing more difficult to conquer than the fin of the flesh. St. *Jerom* tells [a] us, that the touch of a woman ought to be avoided like that of a mad dog, a caution as terrible as could be given by any man, how feverely foever he had been bit by them. Yet the experience of St. *Jerom* in that affair, was not comparable to that of St. *Auguftin*, who owns to us, that in his youth he was exceffively addicted to women, and made ufe of a prayer, in which he defired GOD [b] to make him chaft, but not too foon.

IT is true, that this father repented of all thefe things; but he forfook not his lewdnefs at once: the firft fymptoms of amendment that he fhew'd, was [c] to fix his incontinency, which had before been rambling on many objects; he took a concubine with whom he was contented feveral years, and having refolv'd on matrimony fent her back into *Africk*, whence he had her. But he had contracted fuch a

[a] Heronym. *lib.* 1. contra Jovinian.
[b] Auguftin. Confeff.
[c] Idem ibid.

U 2   habit

habit of incontinency, even when he had renounced Manicheism, and prepar'd for his baptism, that he was forc'd to take [a] a new concubine in the room of her he had dismiss'd, till the maiden design'd for his wife should come of age to be married, for which he was to tarry near two years. No man has spoke with greater freedom concerning the force of concupiscence, and the extasies of lustful pleasures than himself, converted as he was; and this father has more than once express'd himself so lively on this head, that he is better let alone than read in those places by most people.

I have said thus much of the injudicious encomiums of the legendaries in relation to the chastity of some saints, and hinted at the dangers, which virtue runs in a forc'd celibacy, to make it visible, by what means the craft of *Rome* has weather'd all the storms, that have attack'd her before the reformation ; and desire every one to consider, whether a protestant ought ever to wish for the return of the wealth, the

[a] Idem.

authority, and the power the church had before she was reform'd, if these were the noxious weeds she was to be clear'd from? But if they are thought necessary and men will look upon them as the strong banks, that have stem'd the most raging tides of heresy; those who have overthrown them, ought not to wonder at the inundation of schisms, which has follow'd upon the destruction of them?

LUTHER was the first reformer, and had made a considerable progress before *Calvin* appear'd in that work: the church of *England* was the last, and before our reformation was in any forwardness, several schisms were already sprung from Lutheranism; tho' in the first fifty years they had not above twelve, of which that of the anabaptists was one of the first. Afterwards they very much encreas'd in number: different schisms likewise arose from Calvinism, and the anabaptists have been divided in a vast many sects, [a] some of them extreamly different from the others. In the beginning also of the reformation

[a] John **Henry** Ottius *Annals of Anabapt'fm.*

U 3   Arianism

Arianism was reviv'd, and many of that sect, imbued with other pernicious errors, came from *Italy* to *France, Germany* and *Holland,* but finding no refuge any where else, settled in *Poland.*

If we consider the principal sects of the protestants, with all their divisions and subdivisions, we shall find their number to be frightful; and if we reflect on all the manifold mischiefs of civil wars, massacre and ruin, they have been the occasion of, we shall have reason to say, that nothing under the sun is more destructive to mankind than schism. Many wise princes, and able statesmen have endeavour'd to remedy this evil, by uniting protestants together, but have always been hinder'd by the clergy, either of one side or other: and, if any church-men (for it is not to be done without them) ever engaged in so good a design, they have been constantly reproach'd, and call'd traytors, and false brethren for it, by the rest of their order.

PER-

[a] *FERRI,* [b] *Dureus,* [c] *Hottinger,* and several other moderate divines of the last century, who lamenting the divisions of the protestants, labour'd for an union among them, have all met with this fate; and long before them the same treatment was given to *James Acontius,* who receiv'd so many favours of queen *Elizabeth,* and was the author of the famous book call'd *The stratagems of the devil.* Some said of him, that he had a mind to reduce all sects into one, and [d] inclose them in the same ark, as *Noah* did all sorts of animals in his, wherein they were preserv'd, tho' sustain'd by different food : others accused him, that by reducing the points necessary to salvation to a small number, and

[a] Paul Ferri *a learned Divine, and a famous Preacher at* Metz.

[b] John Dureus, *a* Scotch *Divine, who travell'd through* Germany, *to negotiate an Accommmodation between the* Lutherans *and* Calvinists. *See his* Prodromus tractat. irenicor.

[c] John Henry Hottinger, *a* Swiss *Divine, who was made President of the Commissioners, who were to revise the* German *Translation of the* Bible. Heidelb. in vita Hotting.

[d] Isaac Junius in examin. Apolog. Remonstrant.

U 4 re-

requiring a [a] toleration for the particular opinions, which were againſt the other articles, he open'd a wide door to all manner of hereſies.

THE differences between *Luther* and *Calvin*, have above all the reſt been very fatal to their followers, becauſe the numbers are ſo formidable of each ſide. The valiant king of *Sweden*, *Guſtavus Adolphus*, labour'd hard in his time, to reunite them, but in vain; *and it is certain, that a re-union between them had been made long ago, had it depended only upon the princes; but becauſe that affair depends on divines, it never yet could take effect, and probably never will.* It is not a layman, who judges thus of theſe gentlemen, generally ſpeaking, but it is one of their own order, and he amongſt others, that can ſpeak beſt of it by experience.

HE [a] ſays, *that the buſineſs of the re-union ought to be principally committed to ſecular perſons, and not to eccleſiaſticks. The divines,* adds he, *are too much addicted to*

[a] Peltius in dedicatione Harmoniæ.
[b] Petrus Jurius de pace ineunda.

their

their own sense, and have but little equity for those that differ from their opinion. They should not dispute concerning the truth of the doctrines; for disputes rather create new wars than appease the old ones; the disputants are not for concord, but for victory. They, who find themselves worsted, grow more haughty and enraged. In an assembly, where a re-union is treated of, the divines should be reduced to the plain function of advocates. They should be heard, but not be judges: That quality ought to be left to statesmen, and it is necessary, that the divines should even take an oath, that they will submit to the sentence that the political judges shall pronounce.

SINCE then without tyranny and granting a power to the church, which is destructive to the state, it is impossible to make men agree in sentiments of things, about which from their cradle they have been taught to differ, and notions once embraced cannot be dropt, whilst there are clergy-men to uphold them; the wisest measures a nation can take for its tranquillity are, chiefly to endeavour two things; one of them is, to prevent, as much as pos-

possible, all further schism, every one in his own sect. The other, to watch narrowly and disappoint those, who would make a handle of their differences to do mischief. To do the first, nothing is more effectual than to make all confessions, and articles of faith, as comprehensive, and conceive them in as general terms, as the word of GOD will allow of. For when the rigorists of any sect begin to be too particular in explaining some scripture places, and never rest till they have so narrowly contracted the sense of them, that it is impossible to construe them any other way, than what shall suit with their private fancy; tho' at the same time the words, in which the holy writers have deliver'd them, may admit of various expositions; it is then that schism and mischief are a hatching; for whoever cannot concur with every word, the majority have agreed to state their explication in, is excommunicated and declared a schismatick.

BUT as the following of the first maxim chiefly concerns the clergy, the laity, who besides their wishes for the observance of

it,

it, can contribute but little to it, ought
to lay the greatest stress upon the second,
which is to disappoint those who would
make a handle of their differences to do
mischief; and this is altogether in their
power in every protestant country, if the
better sort and sensible part of them will
but steadily resolve, in the first place, never to believe, what different sects say of
one another, if what is alledged be not
plainly prov'd on the party accus'd; secondly, to prefer the discourses of JESUS
CHRIST to any modern sermons, they
can hear, and the charms of the peaceful
gospel to the distorted countenance of an
angry priest; to spend time in exhorting
men to the latter is an affront to christians;
but to shew the reasonableness of the first,
and the solid grounds there are for such a
resolution, I must beg leave to draw a little
sketch of the clergy's behaviour to each
other, when they clash in opinion, and
neither conferences, nor the interposition
of the government, can accommodate the
matter.

THE first onset of the war is commonly made by cases rightly stated, and vindi-
cations

cations on both fides; letters to a friend, anſwers and replies, and, where the preſs is open, pamphlets fly about like hand grenadoes in an attack. The firſt generally contain proofs, arguments and appeals to common fenſe; in the next you'll have cavils, and logical diſtinctions; till at laſt they end in calumnies and invectives.

THE firſt weapon in their artillery of ſlander, is the accuſation of atheiſm, blaſphemy, or a tendency to one of them; which is made uſe of by all parties, and as occaſion ſerves flung on tenets diametrically oppoſite. The doctrine of predeſtination has been beſpatter'd with it a thouſand times. *Martin Becanus* is more extravagant, who ſays, that the fruits of *Calviniſm*, are more pernicious than thoſe of atheiſm. *Arminianiſm* aſſerts freewill, and is in that point the reverſe of *Calviniſm*; yet *Vedelius*, a famous reformed divine, ſays, that the ſcope of it is to introduce a ſubtle atheiſm into the church.

A s there is nothing more generally abominated, or more juſtly deteſted than

the

the name of atheist, so it is often abused, and serves evil men for an instrument of slander, to defeat an enemy without any further trouble: no other calumny is counted so effectual to blow up a man at once, whether he deserves it or not; and as in this it is like gun-powder, so it is the same in its origin, which both owe to the clergy. Accordingly they have always claim'd that word of reproach as their property, and the divines of different sects and religions have constantly made use of it, either against the laity, whom they disliked, and would render the object of the publick indignation and fury; or else among themselves in theological warfare, and the zealous exercise of their superlative and proverbial hatreds of one another.

The next stratagem of the clergy is to fasten, if possible, some crime against the state on the tenets of their adversaries, that by the one they may render them as odious to men, as by the other they have represented them to be to God. So one doctrine is said to favour tyranny and arbitrary power, another to be antimonarchical,

narchical, and leading to anarchy. Du
ring the greateſt part of the two laſt cen
turies, the national clergy of *France* ex
claim'd with great violence againſt th
Hugonots, and loudly aſſerted, that the
were all republicans, and the greateſt ene
mies to the crown, whilſt themſelves ap
pear'd in arms againſt their princes more
than once, and were not only the open a
betters in aſſaſſinating two of their king
ſucceſſively, but [a] many of them likewiſe
have pretended, by their own tenets, to
juſtify theſe execrable murders.

THE other arms, which they diſplay in
calumniating one another, conſiſt in per-
ſonal reflections, falſe quotations, and
downright lyes. It is impoſſible for men,
unacquainted with religious controverſies,
to imagine what improbable falſhoods the
ſons of *Rome* have dar'd to publiſh againſt
the firſt reformers : their rage againſt *Luther* has been altogether ſenſeleſs, and
come up to frenzy. I would not ſpeak thus
of common detraction, but ſome have been

[a] *See* Thuanus Hiſtor. & Maimbourg. Hiſtor. de
la Ligne, Liv. 3.

fooliſh

foolish enough, seriously to assert, that an *Incubus* [a] begot him upon his mother. The very astrologers have thrown in their mite, and falsify'd the hour of his [b] nativity, to have an opportunity of drawing his horoscope to their mind.

THE *Lutherans* have been almost as violent again *Calvin*, who undertook to reform them; and a minister of theirs, one *Hunnius* [c], who was otherwise a man of learning, had his understanding so blinded by his zeal, as to accuse him at once of *Nestorism, Judaism, Mahometism,* and, to shew himself compleatly mad, [d] atheism; for a man in his senses would have known that the imputation of the last could not be true, if but any one of the other was.

THE *Calvinists* again have father'd many things upon the *Anabaptists* and other sects which they never dream'd of; and

[a] *See* Maimbourg. Histor. du Lutheran. & Spondan. annal ad ann. 1517.

[b] Seckendorf Hist. Lutheran. *lib.* 1.

[c] Giles Hunnius *a famous* Lutheran *Divine, Professor of Divinity at* Marpurg.

[d] *In a Book call'd* Calvinus Judaizans.

all

all of them in their differences and paper wars, dealt very unfairly with one another. But that I may not be thought to aggravate these matters, I shall quote the testimony of *Jerom Zanchius,* a protestant divine, who once was like to have fill'd a professor's chair in *England,* where he complains of the manner of writing used among the protestants, even those who would be counted pastors, doctors, and pillars of the church. *We often,* (says he) *that the state of the question may not be understood, wrap it up in obscurity. Things that are manifest we impudently deny; such as are false we affirm without shame: things openly impious, we obtrude as the first principles of faith; what's orthodox we condemn for heresy. We wrest the scriptures, according to our own dreams, as we list. We brag of the fathers, when there is nothing which we have less a mind to, than to follow their doctrine. To sophisticate, to throw calumnies, and call names, is familiar to us. So we can but maintain our own cause,*

good

good or bad, justly or injuriously, we care not what becomes of the rest [a].

SHOULD any one object, that this *Zanchius*, though he was a protestant, had been much abused by his brethren, and when he wrote this, had been led away by human passion and resentment; I shall only answer, that then he may serve me in a double capacity, and so make use of him for an example and a witness both; and being one of the most celebrated divines of the sixteenth century, if he be thought not so well qualify'd for the one, he must be more eminently so for the other.

BY this time, I hope, I have convinc'd my reader, that we ought not to believe what different sects say against one another without proof. I confess I need not have gone so far beyond sea for one single testimony of an author, who has wrote near an hundred and fifty years ago, when, to corroborate my assertion, I might have so many thousand living witnesses at home.

---

[a] *A Translation from the Latin quoted by Father* l'Abbe, in differt. de Script. Ecclesiaft. *tom.* 2.

X But

But I did it in behalf of those peevish gentlemen, that are always finding fault with the times, to convince them, that the proteſtants of our age are not worſe than they were at the beginning of the re-formation, and that clergy-men are now as they have been all along.

The benefit a nation will receive from the maxim I recommend, is plainly viſi-ble; for when each party ceaſes to believe the evil, which is ſaid of the other, the anger of both muſt ſoon be diſarm'd, and conſequently the firebrands, who by their ſtories and ſuggeſtions deſign to do mif-chief to either, or both, diſappointed. It is for want of this reſolution only that ſchiſm can be pernicious to the ſtate: but if we believe, without examination, what we are told of our adverſaries, there can be no peace, and our animoſities muſt be eternal, tho' in the main we quarrell'd a-bout nothing.

Our church and the presbyterians dif-agree about ceremonies, and way of wor-ſhip, but the religion of both is the ſame; for allowing the doctrine of a church and the government of a church to be

two

two things, one may be for, and another againſt epiſcopacy, without differing in religion, more than one divine of the church of *England* may differ from another, of the ſame church, which happens daily without giving offence; and I don't believe there are two chriſtians in the world, that have exactly the ſame ſentiments about every thing contain'd in the bible. Yet what a heinous ſchiſm is their religion! And what a monſtrous ſuperſtition is ours!

WOULD you know what presbyterians are? go to ſome churches and you may hear, that they are a wilful, ſeditious and perverſe people, a generation of vipers, the worſt of ſubjects; that all their pretences to religion are only hypocriſy; that they are of antimonarchical and king-killing principles; that they have been the occaſion of all the calamities that have befallen the land for above theſe hundred years.

BUT if they are repreſented to us in this manner, their miniſters have not been behind hand with ours, and ſome of them have drawn us to their congregations in no better colours. They ſay of us, that we are always talking of the church, and

X 2

none louder than those who never go into it; that our worship is half popery; that we never think a king the head of the church but when he is a slave to the clergy; that our church never flourishes, but when the state is in danger, and we never complain but in just reigns; that we laugh at passive-obedience, when it is not our turn to govern, and never preach up that doctrine heartily, but to impose it upon others; that unless our party is pleas'd, we stick at no mischief, and then lay the fault on our adversaries.

WHILST by such stories the dissenters are frighten'd from our church and communion, and our selves continue in the sentiments we are taught to harbour of them, it is not likely our breaches should ever be lessen'd. Is not the nation in general very much obliged to the clergy of both sides? One thing indeed may be said in behalf of the dissenting clergy, that cannot be alledg'd as an excuse for the national. Their ministers speak ill of us for their daily bread, and many of them would have their livelihood to seek, were our differences made up: It is not their interest

we

we should meet each other half way, more than it would be the interest of a ferry-man to have the two shores unite. Whereas the national clergy can have no such fears; their income is settled, and they might live as comfortably without calumniating their neighbours, as now they do with it.

CHAP.

CHAP. IX.

Of TOLERATION and PERSECUTION.

SCHISM is an ailment in the body politick, not to be extirpated but by an utter amputation of the limbs infected, and a steady cruelty, zealously pursued without pity or remorse. All petty severities, however wholesome they may appear, are quack medicines, which only put the patients to pain, without removing the distemper. It is a case in which no remedies are effectual but killing ones; and to persecute by halfs, is sprinkling water upon a coal-fire; a small quantity of it will encrease the flame, which a pail full would have totally extinguish'd.

IN

IN the latter part of the 'foregoing chapter, I have named a method how fchifm may remain, and yet the evils generally apprehended from it, by the prudence of the laity be prevented. If we confider how eafily it may be bore with, without any detriment to the publick tranquillity, and we compare the peaceful maxim laid down there to the height of barbarity, by which only fchifm can be cured, perfecution muft appear to us as a remedy abundantly worfe than the difeafe; and the more a man knows of the world, either from reading or experience, the more he fhall be convinc'd, that not only reveal'd as well as natural religion, but likewife humanity, reafon, the intereft of mankind, their peace and felicity, and almoft every thing in nature pleads for toleration, except the national clergy in every country.

THOSE who are the moft follicitous about the temporal intereft of the church, are commonly the greateft perfecutors. It is the opinion of *Leo Allatius,* the greateft champion of the papal authority, whom [a] I

[a] Page 137.

have

have quoted once before, *That hereticks muſt be proſcrib'd, exterminated and puniſh'd, and if they are obſtinate, burnt and put to death* [a]. Neither is this only a leſſon of the inquiſition, no where taught but in *Italy, Spain,* and *Portugal* ; the *Gallican* church, who treats popes with greater freedom, has preach'd up the ſame doctrine with no leſs violence againſt the *Hugonots*. Let us ſee what *Quintin,* a famous profeſſor of the canon-law at *Paris*, ſaid in a ſpeech he made in the name of the clergy, during the aſſembly of the ſtates at *Or-leans,* in *December,* 1560, the king and queen being preſent.

HAVING demanded, [b] *That all the in-habitants of the kingdom ſhould be obliged to be catholicks ; that the non-chriſtians, that is, the hereticks, ſhould not be admitted into the converſation and company of the chriſtian ſubjects, and that for the time to come all hereticks ſhould be forbidden to deal in any commodity, (whether it were books or any other thing),* he added theſe dreadful words:

[a] Leo Allatius de perpetua confenſione, *lib.* 2. *c.* 13.

[b] Preſid. la place de l'eſtat de la religion & re-publique Liv. 4.

3   *And*

And therefore our request is just, reasonable, holy and catholick, and grounded upon the express command of GOD, *who enjoyns you, Sir, to grant it us, repeating the same command in several places, and at several times. He speaks of the idolators and* Gentiles *strangers to the law; hereticks among christians are accounted to be such: these are the words of the said law of* GOD; *be sure not to contract any friendship, confederacy or marriage with them; don't suffer them to inhabit the country; take no pity on them, beat them, strike them to death.* Here follows the reason of that command, *lest they should make thee sin against me; if thou believest their opinions, which will be an offence and a scandal that will raise my fury against thee, and soon after I shall destroy thee. Sir, and you Madam, avoid those horrible and dreadful threatnings, for the salvation of your souls, and the preservation of your scepter. This is, Sir, what your clergy of* France *propose and represent to your majesty in all simplicity, obedience, humility and submission concerning the honour and service of* GOD *in your kingdom, and for the ex-*
tirpation

Y

*tirpation and abolition of what is contrary
to it,* viz. *of sects and heretics.*

IT is plain, that the most humble and
devout of the clergy, by this memorial, to
which he said they expected an answer,
were for shedding blood as a thing necef-
sary, since they minded the king of *Moses*'s
order and threatnings : and before what I
have quoted, *Quintin* had already said, *That
his majesty being strong, and arm'd with iron,
ought to oppose the hereticks ; that in order
to it, and for no other end,* GOD *had put
the sword into his hands, to protect the good,
and punish the wicked ; and that none can
deny, that a heretick is capitally wicked, and
consequently ought to be punish'd capitally ;
being liable to the sword of the magistrate.*

THUS freely church-men express themselves, before the secular power is wrought
up to mischief ; but when princes become
tyrants, and set about persecution in earnest themselves, the clergy desire to be
seen in it no longer. It is not forty years
ago, that the *Gallican* church in a speech
to *Lewis* XIV. made some months before
the revocation of the edict of *Nantes,* declared, *That she did not desire his majesty
should*

*fhould make ufe of his power for the ex-
tirpation of hereticks.* The *Hugonots* complain'd of this diffimulation, as may be
feen in the words of Mr. *Claude.*

WHILST *the thing,* fays he, [a] *was only preparing, the authors of the perfecution
did not conceal themfelves, but ufed their endeavours to make the king appear in it. When
things came to the laft extremity, and to
open force, they conceal'd themfelves as much
as they could, and made the king appear in
his whole extent. There was nothing to be
heard then but this fort of difcourfes. The
king will have it fo. The king is refolv'd
upon it. The king goes farther than the
clergy defire. By thefe two means they
have been fo cunning as to afcribe to them_
felves the leaft violent part of that perfecution, and to charge the king with the moft o_
dious part.*

THESE things may pafs in a *Roman*
catholick clergy. A church that claims
infallibility and fuperiority over all titles
and governments, and is in actual poffeffion
of wealth and a property, fufficient to make

---

[a] Claude plaintes de proteftants.

the

the laity dread her, may have some plea
for perfecution: but a proteftant church,
that has not only own'd that fhe can
err, and that the magiftrate is above her,
but likewife fuffer'd her felf to be ftript
of her treafure, one would think could have
no pretenfions to juftify, nor means to go
through with it. Yet there is no national
church among the proteftants, that has not
try'd to perfecute as far as the fecular
power would let her ; and a fingle pres-
byter, who has once been fuffer'd to
make himfelf popular, and the idol of the
mob, may render himfelf as formidable
to the ftate as a pope.

AT *Geneva* by the fole authority of
Calvin many have been profcrib'd, and befides *Servetus*, who every body knows was
burnt for herefy, [a] *Alciatus*, [b] *Blandrata*
[c] *Gribaldus*, and fome others, would have
met with the fame fate, if they had not
faved themfelves by flight, and even after

[a] John Paul Alciatus, *a Gentleman of* Milan.
[b] George Blandrata, *an* Italian *Phyfician, born in*
Tiedmont.
[c] Mathew Gribaldus, *a learned civilian of* Padua.

the

the life of that great reformer, [a] *John Va-lentinus Gentilis*, who, like the reft, was fled, and got into *Moravia*, ventur'd, upon the death of his moft dreadful adverfary, to return into *Switzerland*, but was laid hold of, profecuted by the Calvinifts, and had his head [b] ftruck off for oppugning the myftery of the Trinity in the territo- ries of *Bern*; glorying that he fuffer'd for the honour of GOD the father.

[c] *CASTALIO*, who likewife had been forc'd to quit *Geneva* on the fcore of he- terodoxy, publifhed a book a little after the execution of *Servetus*, in which he blam'd that action, and fpoke up for to- leration, [d] difguifing himfelf under the name of *Martinus Bellius*. This *Beza* wrote againft, maintaining, that [e] hereticks were to be punifh'd by the magiftrate. So that whether we judge from the example

[a] *He was a native of* Cofenza *in the kingdom of* Naples.

[b] Aretius. Hift. Reform. Polon.

[c] *A learned Savoyard, who was many years profef- fr of the* Greek *tongue at* Bazil, *where he dy'd.*

[d] Ant. Fayus. in vita Bezæ.

[e] Beza de puniend. Hæret.

Y 3 of

of *Calvin*, or the precepts of *Beza* his collegue, and greateſt champion, perſecution ſeems to be a manifeſt tenet of Calviniſm. Whatever piety, eloquence and erudition theſe mighty pillars of the reformed church might be endued with, they were not always govern'd by the ſpirit of chriſtianity; their zeal was often ſuperior to their charity, they were implacable to all adverſaries, and in the moſt important of their actions, they were over-rul'd by human paſſion.

SHOULD it be objected, that ſuch tempers as theirs were more prone to anger and perſecution than others; that among the Calviniſts there were meak and compaſſionate chriſtians, and that therefore the charge ought not to be ſo general as I have laid it, I would anſwer; that power and authority were dangerous tools in the hands of churchmen: that whenever they were warmly oppoſed they could never forbear making uſe of them, and that how juſt, humane and compaſſionate ſoever their natural temper might be, all clergy-men in power turn'd perſecutors, as ſoon as they were thoroughly anger'd. St. *Auguſtin* had

an

an incomparable wit, and an imagination happy and abounding. [a] He had all along entertain'd fentiments of mildnefs and charity concerning the courfe to be taken with hereticks: but the contestations he had with the Donatifts, heated him fo much, that he ran into the quite contrary opinion, and maintain'd ftoutly, that hereticks ought to be perfecuted.

The grand reafon chiefly alledged for perfecuting hereticks is, that God is offended at them, and will punifh a whole nation for fuffering them to live among them. The proofs to juftify thefe apprehenfions are always fetch'd from the Old Teftament, for a very good reafon, becaufe there are none in the New: but how fantaftical and perverfe are mens judgments concerning an affair which feems to require the utmoft impartiality!

In fome proteftant countries men fhall be banifh'd, and have their goods confifcated, or elfe be imprifon'd and more feverely punifhed, becaufe they refufe to believe

---

[a] *Mr.* Claude, *in a Letter written at* Switzerland, *printed at* Dort *in* 1790.

every

every comment fome divines have made on the gofpel, and will not acquiefce in all the creeds drawn from it by human invention, though they believe in CHRIST and his apoftles, and are perfwaded, the New Teftament, and every thing contain'd in it, to be the word of GOD, whilft the fame nation fuffers others to build ftately fynagogues where they lift, who do not only reject, but likewife defpife and fcoff at the gofpel and chriftianity, as much as the heathens, and allows a worfhip as publick and as undifturb'd as the church injoys to men, whofe religion could have no being in our days, if they did not as heartily believe JESUS CHRIST to have been an impoftor, as we do *Mahomet*.

IF this plea of the apprehenfion, that GOD's judgment will follow on the toleration of herefy and infidelity, had any fincerity in it, would not chriftians, more efpecially proteftants, make a difference between thofe whom they difagree with in the very fundamentals of religion, and others, who profefs the fame faith in every article, and only differ from them in church

church government, and outward ceremonies? And could a national clergy behold chriftian princes confer honours, and confequently publick marks of efteem on jews without the leaft complaint, and at the fame time be' as loud as thunder in preffing them to degrade presbyterians? but jews cannot interfere with the temporal intereft of the national clergy; fchifmaticks may. Here is the danger; from this corner the evil is expected which they dread.

We often value our felves on our zeal againft popery, and that no proteftant church has produced more able divines to oppofe it, and refute the champions of it, than that of *England.* This is true, and no proteftants have ftood more in need of them; for the court of *Rome* has taken more pains to regain this kingdom than they have beftowed on any other proteftant country. But when that is over, and the danger of popery feems to be remov'd further off, our clergy exert themfelves with the fame warmth againft any other adverfary who dares to diffent from them, to difturb their tranquillity, and

roufe

rouse their anger, by denying their authority: many of them have not scrupled
publickly to profess a greater aversion to
presbytery, than they had for popery,
and construed the very proximity of their
opinions, to the disadvantage of their
antagonists; alledging, that the less the
difference was between them, the greater
must be the obstinacy of the dissenters in
refusing conformity.

NATIONAL churches only love and
hate occasionally, as it suits their interest,
and as every vice is made the worst, when
it is particularly preached against, so every adversary of a national church becomes
the blackest in his turn, when the clergy
have a mind more directly to vent their
anger against him. Murder and adultery
are heinous crimes; but what is so bad
as schism?—— But supposing it to be
such a damnable sin, as is told us with
so much heat and violence, it can only
be so to those who are the occasion
of it.

IF a man, led away by ambition, revenge, or any other passion to be grati-
fied, separates himself from the communion

nion he belong'd to for a trifle, infuses his notions into others, and endeavouring to gain proselytes to his opinion, by all imaginable cunning, draws great numbers from the national and established church, his crime is unpardonable, and himself a wicked seducer of the people. We will suppose likewise that his followers, who ran astray with him, are involved in part of his guilt; but it is not, like the sin of *Adam*, entail'd upon all their posterity to the world's end.

WHEN a schism has remain'd for several generations, has been examin'd, look'd into, and the sovereign power, having found it to bring neither dishonour to GOD, nor detriment to the society, thinks fit to tolerate it in an authentick manner, it then becomes a lawful worship, which it is criminal to disturb: nothing is more sacred to people than their religion; and a conscientious man, what sect soever he is of, will always take care to have his children, from their infancy, imbued with the doctrine which himself prefers to all others, and never suffer them to attend any other worship than what, in his opinion,

is

is the moſt acceptable to GOD.   Men
would not have children diſobey their
parents, or a pupil his governor, and before they are capable of judging for themſelves,   rather follow a ſtranger than
thoſe who are entruſted with their education.

WHEN people are arrived to years of
diſcretion, and begin to perceive they have
been brought up in an error, there is no
doubt but they ought to leave it;   and if,
being convinc'd of it, they perſiſt in it,
they commit a ſin;   but how ſhall we be
ſure that they are convinc'd of their error,
and how ſhall we know that their ſcruples are not really conſcientious ?   A national church ſeldom acknowledges the ſincerity of ſchiſmaticks ;   no proofs are convincing.   When they have made oath of
it,   the orthodox have told them they
were perjur'd ;   nay, ſhould they ſeal their
teſtimony with their blood, and dye for
their faith, they muſt expeĉt only to be
derided for their pains ;   for a ſchiſmatick
can be no [a] martyr.   Great numbers of

[a] Cyprian de unitate, Epiſt. 52. ad Antonian.

Mar-

Marcionites and [a] other hereticks, that were perfecuted by the orthodox of the primitive church, fuffer'd death for their opinions with great conftancy; but they never were ftiled martyrs but by their own fects.

THE crown of martyrdom can only be attain'd to by the orthodox: all the books of martyrs of the proteftants are defpis'd and fcoff'd at by the church of *Rome*, and the vaft multitudes fhe has maffacred for the reformed religion in *England, France,* and other parts of *Europe,* are in her language no more than obftinate hereticks, that have been punifh'd for their impieties. The proteftants had it not long in their power before they imitated the church of *Rome,* and the *Lutherans* in *Saxony,* and the *Calvinifts* in *Holland,* have treated the anabaptifts in the fame manner: thefe fchifmaticks, in the beginning of the fixteenth century, have publifhed two books of martyrs, one at *Harlem* and another at *Horn,* in which they complain as much of the tyranny of the *Lutherans*

[b] Eufeb. *and fee* Maimbourg's *Hiftory of* Calvinifm.

and

and *Calvinifts*, as thefe do of the papifts: but they have receiv'd the fame anfwer, that has been given to all hereticks a great many hundred years ago, which is the faying of St. *Cyprian*, *That* [a] *it is not the punifhment, but the caufe, that makes the martyr.* And what national church will allow the caufe of fchifmaticks to be a good one?

THE generality of men are fo wedded to, and fo obftinately fond of their own opinion, and a doctrine they have been imbued with from their cradle, that they cannot think any one fincere, who, being acquainted with it, refufes to embrace it. This holds in all religions, the *Mahometan*, and moft abfurd of the *Pagans* not excepted.

As there is nothing human minds may more widely differ in than in what concerns religious matters, fo there is no opinion fo monftroufly defpicable, but fome may adhere to it with zeal and fincerity; whilft others with the fame fincerity may have fentiments not perfectly agreeing with

[a] Cyprian ubi fupra.

any

any opinion, that is known. About the middle of the laft century, whilft the *Tri-nitarians* were accufing one another of believing *Tritheifm*, and the unity of GOD was ftrenuoufly afferted among the pro-teftants, the chevalier *Borri* [a] ftarted a no-tion among the *Roman* catholicks, that the Virgin *Mary* was a real goddefs, and a fourth perfon in the divinity. The empe-ror *Alexander* had in his palace an orato-ry, [b] where he went early in the morning to practife religious ceremonies in honour of the patrons he had made choice of. Here he had, with the effigies of his an-ceftors, thofe of very good princes, who had been deify'd, and other holy men, and among them *Apollonius Tyaneus*, JESUS CHRIST, *Abraham*, *Orpheus*, and fuch like gods, fays my author. Nothing can be more unaccountable than the mix'd worfhip of that emperor, or the notion he muft have had of the Deity; yet *Lam-pridius*, who wrote his life, and informs us

[a] *He was burnt in Effigy at* Rome, *with his Wri-tings, by the Hands of the Executioner,* January 3, 1661. Vita de Cavagliere Borri.
[b] Lamprid. in Alexand. Severo.

of

of this, speaks of him as of a virtuous, sincere and devout prince.

THE famous [a] *Hugo Grotius* had for many years before his death not been of any communion at all, [b] for which some have had a very ill opinion of him, and call him atheist ; but a learned apologist [c] of that great man has demonstrated how unjust as well as uncharitable, it is to fancy, that a man has no religion, when he joins with none of the factions that condemn mankind, and each of which pretends to be the only church of CHRIST. Fear and superstition may make men fly to devotions, that are inconsistent together, and a penetrating judgment may have scruples which others cannot see, yet both act with sincerity.

ONE of the greatest reasons why schismaticks and dissenters are call'd hypocrites by the orthodox, is, because, generally speaking, they lead better lives, or at least are more circumspect in their lan-

[a] *See a Book call'd*, Sentiments de quelques Theologiens d' Hollande.

[b] Idem.

[c] Idem.

guage

guage and behaviour. Those who would reform more strictly than others, must shew it in something: this nettles the orthodox, because they are obliged by it either to be more upon their guard themselves, or else run the risk of being thought worse of, than those they condemn. Wherefore to avoid the ill opinion of others, and likewise the trouble they find in amendment, they call their adversaries hypocrites, in hopes, that by undervaluing the strictness of their manners, they shall conceal the turpitude of their own.

How defignedly foever virtue and piety may be counterfeited by fome crafty deceivers, many of their followers, drawn in by outward appearances, may fet about reforming themfelves in good earneft, vaft multitudes may be new modell'd and reform'd after this manner by art and affiduity. The prince of *Conde's* army in *France* had more devout men, and was infinitely lefs corrupt in manners than the leaguers, and the round-heads of *Oliver Cromwel* were much lefs debauch'd than the cavaliers of the king. Such reformations

Z

mations may laſt for a while, but human nature of it ſelf will relapſe in time; and however, power, authority, victory, and ſucceſs, can never fail of relaxing mens morals.

B u t if hypocriſy be not laid to the charge of ſchiſmaticks, their actions at leaſt, even the beſt are diſcommended, if not miſconſtrued, and they can do nothing that is praiſe-worthy in the eyes of the orthodox. During the perſecution the anabaptiſts labour'd under beyond ſea, a-bove an hundred and fifty years ago, a moderate *Calviniſt* [a] enquiring into the reaſon how theſe deluded people could gain ſo many proſelytes, named three things, which he aſſigned as the chief cauſe of their perverting and ſeducing ſuch great numbers. The continual quotations of ſcripture texts their teachers made uſe of, the great ſhew they made of outward ho-lineſs, and their conſtancy in ſuffering and dying. By the firſt, he ſays, they make the poor ignorant people ſtand amaz'd,

[a] Guy de Bres, Racine Source & Fondement des Anabaptiſtes.

and

and imagine them to be great doctors, though what they quote is without fenfe, judgment or reafon: but he defires them to confider, that there never was any heretick in the world, but what made ufe of the fcripture, corrupting and wrefting it to maintain his blafphemies, though the fcripture gives no ground for errors and herefies; but that they proceed from a quite contrary caufe, as CHRIST fays, and here he quotes thefe words of our Saviour. *Do you not therefore err, becaufe you know not the fcriptures?*

As to the fecond thing by which they feduced filly people, their pretended holinefs, he proves by fome examples, that it is often the character of falfe doctors. To folve the third, he gives them the anfwer of St. *Cyprian,* which I have quoted above; and as for the reft, treats them with pity and contempt. The *Roman* catholicks have done the very fame to the Hugonots in *France:* the reformed, they faid, fpoke of nothing but of the bible, and quoted it continually. They were againft dancing, fine cloaths, going to the

Z 2

ta-

tavern, &c. and many of them suffer'd with conftancy for their religion. The difficulties were the fame, and fo were the anfwers to folve them. There are other countries, and of proteftants too, where the ufage of the orthodox to the fchifmaticks has not been very unlike to what I have mention'd. It is deplorable, that the proteftants are forc'd to make ufe of the fame arguments againft their fchifmaticks, which the papifts before have ufed againft the proteftants, and which fo many reform'd divines have fo fuccefsfully, and fo often refuted.

It is evident then, that there is no characteriftick to diftinguifh and know a true church from a falfe one. The arguments for toleration or perfecution, as they are occafionally wanted, are the fame in the one, as they are in the other; in the behaviour likewife between national churches, and thofe who diffent from them, countries differ but little. The language and actions are very near the fame throughout chriftendom. The fchifmaticks reject all human authority, quote fcripture, talk of reafon, and defire toleration:

3   leration:

leration : the orthodox ftand upon their
prerogative of elderfhip, punifhing of
hereticks, and defire the affiftance of the
fecular arm : whenever the fchifmaticks can make their opinion national,
they are orthodox, and ferve all other
innovators, juft as they were ferv'd before.

EVERY body knows how heartily the
French proteftants cry'd out for toleration
in their laft perfecution ; they would have
been fatisfy'd with a bare connivance, a
fufferance under penalties, or any thing
in the world to fave their lives and e-
ftates, without renouncing their religion.
Yet fome of them, who had narrowly e-
fcap'd the watchful dragoons, and thought
it a happinefs to become fugitives and re-
fugees in foreign countries, chang'd immediately with their circumftances their
tolerating tempers ; and one [a] of them,
who has made himfelf much talk'd of on
[b] another account, as foon as he was e-

---

[a] Peter Jurieu.
[b] *A Prophecy of the deftruction of the World, which
prov'd falfe during his Life-time.*

ftablifh'd

ftablifh'd in a great city of *Holland*, ª o-
penly preach'd and excited the civil power to perfecution with great violence, not
only againft the *Socinians*, but likewife the
Arminians, or as they call themfelves, *Re-
monftrants*, which latter are very numerous
in that place.

HE told the magiftrates, that it was
their duty to extirpate herefy and infidelity, that the true church could not flourifh
without the fupport of the fecular arm,
and that chriftianity it felf could not have
fpread, as it has done, if chriftian emperors and other princes had not affifted the
propagation of it by deftroying the heathen idols, diftreffing their priefts, and de-
molifhing their temples. What fervice
this language in the mouth of a refugee
muft have been of to the diftreffed brethren, he had left behind him, I leave the
reader to judge. What is true in *Holland*
muft be the fame in *France*.

IT is incredible, how all churches and
priefts have borrow'd of one another. The
fathers of the primitive church them-

ª Rotterdam.

felves

felves learn'd perfecution, and to juftify it, of the jews and heathens. I have faid more than once, what a wretched and despicable theology the *Pagans* had; and yet *Celfus,. Symmachus, Porphiry, Hierocles,* and other orators and philofophers who have wrote in defence of their national and eftablifhed church, and againft the innovations of the gofpel, have treated the chriftians with no more regard or ceremony, than a haughty rigorift of the orthodox would a fweet finger of *Ifrael,* a *French* prophet, or any the moft fenfe-lefs enthufiaft: one of thofe I have named, and who was a great courtier, had com-pos'd a book againft chriftianity, which *Lactantius* has anfwer'd, and Dr. *Cave* thinks, [a] but very indifferently. But the general account that father gives of it is worth reading.

H E *profess'd* (thefe [b] are the words of *Lactantius*) *that above all things it was the duty of a philofopher to affift men in drawing them from their errors, and call them back*

[a] *Dr.* Cave Hiftor. literat. Script. Eccl. in par-te 2.

[b] Lactantius Divin. inftitut. *lib.* 5. c. 2.

again

again into the right way which is the wor-
ſhip of the gods, by whoſe greatneſs and ma-
jeſty (he ſaid forſooth) the world was gover-
ned, and not ſuffer the ignorant to be drawn
away by the impoſtures of ſome men. That
therefore he had taken upon him that office
worthy of philoſophy, that he might carry
the light of wiſdom before thoſe, who were
in the dark; not only that by worſhipping the
gods they might be reſtor'd to their ſound
minds, but likewiſe that having laid down
their ſtubborn obſtinacy they might avoid the
torments of the body, and not chuſe to en-
dure the cruel manglings of their limbs for
nothing. But that it might appear what it
was, that had made him take the pains of
compoſing that work, he launch'd out in the
praiſes of the princes, whoſe piety and pro-
vidence (as he call'd it) had, as in all other
human affairs, been more eminently conſpi-
cuous in their defending the religion of the
gods. That at laſt, ſuch care was taken of
the intereſt of mankind, that, the ſuperſti-
tion, which was impious and only befitting
ᵃ old women, being ſuppreſs'd, the whole uni-

ᵃ Impia & anili Superſtitione.

verſe

verse should join in the true worship of the gods, and be made sensible of their mercies.

How many flatterers of persecuting tyrants have in later times copy'd after this *Pagan*, I shall not stay to examine; this I know, that what I have quoted would with little alteration have serv'd a member of the academy of sciences, in his addresses to the late grand monarch, after his extirpation of schism. But the chief use I would make of it is, to shew the possibility, that national churches may treat their betters with contempt; that it is no new thing for persecutors to pretend the good of mens souls, and their general happiness; and that no monstrousness or absurdity in publick worship, or established opinions, can ever hinder the champions of them from insulting, and assuming airs of superiority over schismaticks, tho' of the most rational and solid principles.

I am very much mistaken, if a serious reflection on what has been said hitherto, will not furnish a thinking man, with many arguments for toleration; what I be-

A a

gan

gan this chapter with is none of the leaft, I mean, that fchifin, where once it has been fuffer'd, can never be cur'd, but by an utter extirpation of the limbs infected, and a fteddy cruelty, zealoufly purfued without pity or remorfe. That this is not my own private opinion, one of the moft polite authors of the age fhall wit-nefs. [a] *Nothing (fays he) is more ridiculous in refpect of policy, or fo wrong and odious in refpect of common humanity, as a moderate and half way perfecution. It only frets the fore; it raifes the ill humour of mankind; excites the keener fpirits; moves indignation in beholders; and fows the very feeds of fchifm in mens bofoms. A refolute and bold fac'd perfecution leaves no time or fcope for thefe engendring diftempers, or gathering ill humours. It does the work at once; by extirpation, banifhment, or maffacre, and like a bold ftroke in furgery, difpatches by one fhort amputation, what a bungling hand would make worfe and worfe to the perpetual fufferance and mifery of the patient.*

[a] *Lord* Shaftsbury's Characterift. 3 *vol.*

In

IN *Italy*, *Spain*, and *Portugal*, where an heretick is knock'd down the moment he rifes, and the church has a proper power obey'd by the government, to enquire into a man's confcience before he opens his mouth, and punifh him for what the holy office fhall fancy him to think; a ftrict conformity in manner of worfhip, once eftablifh'd, may be maintain'd with little bloodfhed: otherwife it is never to be procur'd, but by the remedy prefcrib'd, *viz.* the utmoft violence and barbarity.

IT is evident then that the method now in ufe among the proteftant churches, to deftroy fchifm, is wrong; that their endeavours are fruitlefs, and as little likely to meet with fuccefs, as would be a man's labour, who, to make another his friend, fhould load him with calumnies, and flip no opportunity to vex him. The bold reformers, that could fway a ftate, are defunct. The ages grow wifer, and bigotry now is a rarity in princes. The reform'd clergy have given up their ftrength by their own act and deed. Men only expofe themfelves by threatning, what every body knows they can't execute.

A a 2 Rea-

Reasoning, good humour and persuasions are more likely to convince men, and draw them from their errors, than menaces without power. [a] *Mere threats,* says the learned nobleman I just now quoted, *without power of execution, are only exasperating and provocative. They who are masters of the carnal as well as the spiritual weapons, may apply each at their pleasure, and in what proportion they think necessary. But where the magistrate resolves steddily to reserve his fasces for his own proper province, and keep the edge tools and deadly instruments out of other hands, 'tis in vain for spiritual pretenders to take such magisterial airs. It can then only become them to brandish such arms, when they have strength enough to make the magistrate resign his office, and become provost, or executioner, in their service.*

BUT the greatest argument for toleration is, that differences in opinion can do no hurt, if all clergy-men are kept in awe, and no more independent on the state than the laity; whereas the calamities that may

[a] Idem.

attend

attend perfecution, are endlefs. I am not ignorant of the mifchiefs that are to be apprehended from an exceffive toleration, accompany'd with, or perhaps proceeding from, a remifnefs in the government; but this ought to be avoided as much as perfecution. Befides, when I fpeak up for a toleration of different fects, I mean only, fuch as fhall own the government to be the fupream authority upon earth, both in church and ftate, and have no other mafter abroad, that may make them plot againft our fafety. It is on this head only that papifts and *Non-Jurors* ought to be excluded; but this being the bufinefs of the ftate, the clergy has nothing to do with it.

I⊤ is the government and the miniftry of it, which ought to be watchful, and take care that the publick receives no detriment from fubtle ftratagems carried on under religious pretences. I can't help thinking in this place on the innumerable treacheries of chriftians, and the execrable manner, in which chriftianity has been propagated by the modern apoftles. That fcanty portion which *America* has

been

been blefs'd with, cofts them, befides all their immenfe treafure, vaft dominions, and their liberty, by the *Spaniard*'s own confeffion, the lives of twenty millions of *Indians.*

A *Spaniard* [a] being ask'd by the king of *Toffa*, how the king of *Spain* became mafter of fo great tracts of land in both hemifpheres, he too honeftly anfwered, *That he fent monks to preach the gofpel in foreign nations, and that after they had converted a good number of* Pagans, *he fent his troops, which, joining with the new chriftians, fubdued the Country.* This happen'd in *Japan,* and gave a plaufible pretence to the *Bonzes* to follicite the extirpation of the chriftians; which was executed, and has very much encreas'd the martyrology [b] of the Jefuits, by whofe induftry great numbers of the inhabitants had already embraced the gofpel. The *Japonefe,* it is certain, underftood not their fpiritual intereft: but confidering that thefe

[a] Hiftoir. des ouvrages des Savans. Sept. 1691.
[b] Ecclef. Hift. *of* Japan. *By* Francis Solier, *a Jefuit.*

ido-

idolaters knew not the true GOD, and the inftructive example they had of our converfions, and the fruits of them before their eyes, I don't fee, how we can blame their politicks, when they had nothing, but either an active or a paffive perfecution to chufe.

IF this be a digreffion, I hope it will not be thought an unprofitable one, as long as it reprefents to us the neceffity all governments lye under, of guarding themfelves againft the manifold machinations, which under the falfe appearances of piety and devotion, muft be deftructive to the ftate. I would have it likewife ferve to fatisfy the reader, that, when I advife the laity to keep the clergy in awe, I mean all clergy-men and religious teachers in general, and would by no means exclude the diffenters. No difcourfes nor even prayers, which have the leaft tendency to fedition, fhould be fuffer'd in any affembly: 'tis the bufinefs of a careful miniftry to look into thefe matters, and the leaft conventicle ought not to be neglected.

A a 4

WHEN

WHEN laymen, who cannot comply
with either the doctrine or rites of a
church by law establifhed, are not ftinted
in their birth-right, but enjoy all the temporal privileges and immunities in common with other fubjects, they ought to
ask for no more, as to fpiritual matters,
than that they may think what they pleafe,
ferve GOD, and educate their children,
their own way, without being difturb'd,
be inftructed by teachers of their own
choice, and have the liberty of building
houfes for divine worfhip, when and where
they think fit. If they make higher demands, which no layman would of himfelf, they ought to be deny'd and rebuk'd,
and their teachers, who put them upon
it, corrected.

A good government in all countries pays
a deference to the national church, and
no liberty of confcience ought to interfere with her juft rights. The publick temples and fchools ought to be facred to her,
and their revenues unqueftionably due to
thofe only who teach her doctrine. If it
be objected, that from what I have already proved from the temper of the

clergy

clergy in general, it muſt neceſſarily follow, that, where there is ſo great a toleration, the diſſenters will be encroaching, and never leave undermining the national church, and that what has been may be again, I readily anſwer, that this never was nor can be done, unleſs the laity join with their clergy in miſchief, which I would prevent.

IT is to deter men from this I take this pains. Had the laity refus'd to pull down the *Perſian* temple, when *Abdas* bid them, the chriſtians would have prevented a cruel perſecution. The buſineſs of clergy-men is to teach us our ſeveral duties toward GOD and man, to aſſiſt us in all the performances of religious worſhip, and ſhew us the way to ſalvation: whenever they talk to us of other matters by way of inſtruction, they exceed their commiſſion. But if at any time they would perſuade or exhort us to any thing, that may be deſtructive to the publick tranquillity, or leſſening the authority of the government, or mutual concord, we ought immediately to leave them, or elſe reſolve to be deaf to all the

flights

flights of either wit or eloquence, that might charm or feduce us.

ONCE for all, the gofpel teaches us o-bedience to fuperiors, and charity to all men ; and if the minifters of it will, to their own damnation, preach feditioufly, and be the trumpeters of rebellion, it is not our fault; but it is in our power to hearken to, or defpife them, as then they deferve we fhould. And what madnefs is it to liften to the *Syren's* fong, when fhe tunes her voice for our deftruction ? Civil wars may begin in the pulpit, but they are not decided there. All the loffes and calamities of them fall upon the people. The clergy may found to battle, but the laity muft fight it out. It is in vain like-wife to ask what principle the clergy are of, or whether they belong to a national or tolerated church, when once they are incens'd. In *France* the lawfulnefs of kil-ling of heretick princes, and paffive obe-dience, have been preach'd and maintain'd by the fame people in lefs than two years time. Whoever is openly infincere, can-not ask that we fhould believe him, and all who ftand up for the doctrine of paffive

obedi-

obedience to the civil powers in being from a principle of chriftianity, will never be active in offending it.

THE difference in the principles of the clergy, is not fo great as many imagine, and to underftand them is of no ufe to the laity in any country, when once they come to fight for them; for when half of a nation is maffacred by mutual fury, the defolate remainder will find but little comfort in knowing which party began the quarrel. There are eye-witnelfes yet alive of our paft misfortunes, and confufions from inteftine broils: may no futurity behold any other! but let us endeavour to forget them, and no pen be ever more employ'd to clear the doubtfulnefs of their caufes. We may, under a difcipline, lefs melancholly, learn wifdom from the folly of our neighbours.

IT will by many be thought injudicious, not to have ended this chapter before now; but a reader, as calm as my felf, will have patience, before we leave it, to read two or three fcraps of hiftory, which are not foreign to our purpofe.

THE

THE leapings [a] of *Macon* are very famous in *France*, and have been mention'd by more authors, than the cruelties of *Tiberius* in the isle of [b] *Caprea*. The place I speak of, is a city upon the *Soane* in the dutchy of *Burgundy*. The [c] *Hugonots* in the religious wars, in the year 1562, made themselves masters of it by force, broke down the images of the churches, and suppress'd the *Roman* religion. They took it in *May*, and it was retaken by the *Roman* catholicks in *August*, during which small time a vast treasure was heap'd up in it. It was sack'd and plundered; the exercise of the *Romish* religion was restor'd, and the priests and monks with their whores, of which they had abundance, return'd to their former state. To compleat the misfortunes of the reformed, the government was given to St. *Poinct*, a man of a sanguinary and cruel temper, who for his pastime, after he had feasted the ladies, was used to ask,

[a] *Call'd in French*, Sauteries de Macon.
[b] Suetonius in Tiberio.
[c] Beza Hist. Ecclef. *lib.* 15.

whe-

whether the farce, which was call'd the farce of St. *Poinct*, was ready to be acted. This was, as it were, the watch-word, by which his people were wont to bring out one or two prisoners, and sometimes more, whom they carry'd to the bridge of the *Soane*; and when they appear'd there with their wives, after he had ask'd them some pretty and pleasant questions, he caus'd them to be thrown down head-long, and drown'd in the river. It was also a usual thing, to give false alarms, and upon that pretence to shoot some prisoner, or any other of the reform'd religion whom he could catch, charging them with a design to betray the city.

T H E *Hugonots* perhaps might flatter themselves with a notion, that (as this was done by the papists) protestants could not be guilty of such enormities; if they had not upon record the barbarous treatment which the garrison of [a] *Monbrisson*, who, having compounded to surrender the town, was retir'd into the castle, received

[a] Varillas Hist. de Charles IX.

from

from a [a] proteſtant general; who would divert himſelf with ſeeing thoſe miſerable ſoldiers precipitated. They were brought to the top of the platform above the tower; thoſe, who had not the courage to precipitate themſelves, were caſt down headlong, and not ſo much as their chief, the brave *Moncelas*, was pardon'd. It is reported likewiſe, that the baron's ſoldiers, as barbarous as their general, receiv'd thoſe, who were thrown down from the tower, with horrid cries and ſhouts upon the points of their halberts and pikes.

THIS was done contrary to a ſolemn capitulation, and all the excuſe that was made for this breach of the publick faith, was, what, after the firſt unkindeſs ſhewn on either ſide, becomes immediately the common plea in all civil wars, repriſals. What he did, the baron ſaid, was to revenge in part the barbarities that had been committed after the ſacking of *Orange*: that city indeed had been the ſcene of

---

[a] Francis de Beaumont Baron des Adrets, *one of the Noblemen, whoſe Courage and Military Actions made the greateſt noiſe in the religious Wars under* Charles IX.

trium-

triumphant and elaborate cruelty, and all those, who had the misfortune to outlive the firſt fury, and fell not by merciful maſſacre, were reſerv'd for exquiſite torments, and the moſt ſhameful abuſes and mutilations. So ingenious was their barbarity, that to ſhew emblematically, that their quarrels were religious, ſeveral proteſtants of both ſexes were put to the fire, larded with ſlips of paper torn from *Geneva* bibles.

THESE are ſome of the fruits of the large crop, that may be gather'd from religious quarrels, the certain and undoubted offspring of the intemperate diſcourſes of ſeditious prieſts of either ſide, which if hearken'd to by the laity, can never fail of plunging them into civil wars. Oh! had I ſkill and eloquence to deſcribe them in their full and terrible extent, and inſpire my readers with a horror and deteſtation, ſufficient to guard them againſt the firſt approaches, and make them ſhrink from the remoteſt tendencies to thoſe unhappy wretched times, in which trade and all commerce are dead, and no merchandize valuable, that cannot be employ'd for the deſtruction

struction of ones country! When wealth
and property are precarious, and nothing
certain but ruin and devastation; when all
arts and sciences languish and are shov'd
aside by rudeness and brutality, and no wit
or ingenuity applauded, but what teaches
men how to be inhuman; till at last the
utmost barbarity and refined cruelties become the diversion of the most polite.

C H A P.

CHAP. X.

Of the Reciprocal Duties between the Clergy and the Laity.

AS in all univerſities, precedency, above other faculties, is given to that of theology, ſo the function of a divine, the miniſtry of the goſpel is an employment to which every member of the ſociety ought to pay deference and reſpect; and moreover, every clergy-man, who diſcharges his duty as he ſhould do, has a juſt title to the love and affection, as well as veneration and eſteem of the publick. In this place many perhaps will ſuſpect my ſincerity, and be ready to tell me, that had my deſign been to procure the clergy the favour or affection of the laity, I would have ſet them in another light than I have

B b   done

done. To remove this fulpicion, I muft put the reader in mind, that to judge impartially, we ought to view things on all fides, and that all men ought to be confider'd two different ways.

FIRST, as to their occupation, the ftation of life, which either choice or neceffity has put them in. And here we chiefly mind the ufefulnefs and dignity of their callings, their capacities, with all qualifications requir'd for the exercife or performance of their functions. In this view we have no regard for the perfons themfelves, but only the benefit they may be of to the publick, if they pleafe and their fervice be wanted; and they are only look'd upon as parts and members of the whole fociety.

SECONDLY, every perfon is to be confider'd as an entire individual, a wonderful machine, endued with thought and a will independent of any thing vifible from without. In this view we look upon him as a neceffitous being, fubject to hunger and thirft, and having many paffions to gratify, and at the fame time a vaft compound, a leffer world, with a fovereignty,

and

and court of judicature within, having a private welfare and prefervation of his own to mind, altogether abftract from the good of the publick.

MEN are naturally felfifh, unruly, and head-ftrong creatures, what makes them fociable is their neceffity and confcioufnefs of ftanding in need of each others help, to make life comfortable; and what makes this affiftance voluntarily given and lafting, are the gains or profit accruing to induftry for fervices it does to others, which in a well order'd fociety enables every body, who in fome thing or other will be ferviceable to the publick, to purchafe the affiftance of others in other inftances. And as all the conveniencies, and chief comforts of life depend, in a great meafure, on the labour and the fervices of others, fo he that is able to purchafe moft of them, is in the vogue of the world reckoned the moft happy.

THE ufefulnefs of fetting all mankind in thefe two different views, will foon appear, if we but confult our own experience, and take notice of what all mankind feems the moft inclin'd to. All the world agrees,

that

that the good of the whole fociety, or the majority of it, ought to be preferr'd to the advantages of private perfons, yet every body may find, that he loves himfelf better than he does all the reft of mankind. Nay, we are taught to do fo from our infancy; the firft thing our nurfes bid us is to take care of our felves. The fame charge we receive a thoufand times over from our parents, tutors, and all that are entrufted with our education. As foon as we truft children with money, we teach them to keep it. When young men talk of marrying, we bid them look out for a fortune, and blame them if they difregard it. A prudent father may caution his fon againft cowardice, fraud, or fordid avarice, becaufe thofe vices make men defpis'd in the world, but he won't bid him lavifh away his money, or be unmindful of his fafety.

ALL men are taught to difplay themfelves to the beft advantage, to defend themfelves againft injuftice and oppreffion, not to be neglectful of their eftate, their dignity, or their reputation in the world. This is call'd human prudence, and all the

he-

heroick flights of love and friendfhip, publick fpiritednefs to ones ruin, and the contempt of death to any extreme, are look'd upon as romantick notions only fit for knight-errantry, and are laugh'd out of countenance by thofe, who beft under-ftand the world. A good man it is likely will wifh that his children may be ufeful in their generation, and become remarka-bly beneficial to their country; and this he may do very heartily for his country's fake, for their fake, and his own: but whilft he is confulting what profeffion or employ-ment he is to bring them up to, what he looks for is to procure them a livelihood; his chief view is their maintenance and eftablifhment, with little regard to the publick.

HISTORY and experience teach us, that in purfuance of the maxims of this worldly wifdom, moft men have in all ages beheld themfelves in the fecond view, and every body looks upon his own dear per-fon, as an individual, if not independent being, which he is oblig'd every way to gra-tify and take care of, very often forgetting that they are members of the fociety. Men
can't

can't help thinking, that their employment, and the dignity of it, are as much
their own as their parts and features; for
which reafon the generality of them convert the whole produce, the fplendour,
the authority, and all profits and emoluments accruing from both to their own
private ufe and advantage, and moreover
count themfelves good honeft men if they
endeavour not to make more of either than
common cuftom, decency, and the laws of
the land allow of.

W E ought therefore to diftinguifh between the defign of an employment in its
original, and what it may be degenerated
into, between the real ufe and worth of a
calling, and what it may be perverted to;
and whenever it is objected, that the laity
can have no reafon, nor the leaft induce-
ment to love and efteem the clergy for
what I have reprefented them to be, for
fix chapters together, I fhall anfwer, that
if they had nothing but their faults, it is
true; but that the fame may be faid of all
profeffions, when we look upon the wrong
fide of them.

How

HOW can we like lawyers, who, if they dislike their fee, will neglect a cause, where your whole welfare, and perhaps the life of an innocent man is at stake; or physicians, who, for the same reason, will leave you to your self in a most dangerous illness, and let you dye rather than not gratify either their avarice or their pride? These things are often done, and chiefly by the most eminent in both professions.

NO joy is perfect, and nothing is compleat upon earth. The best of things are liable to flaws and inconveniencies. Men have been choak'd with bread. But what the necessity of human affairs requires, the society cannot be without, tho' it has its faults. An army of the best soldiers in the world is insignificant without a good general; yet, how many of these, when they they have been disgusted, have left their country exposed to the most imminent danger, and fought against it! But then on the other hand, how often has a general, in the most critical juncture, saved his country from perdition? Lawyers likewise and physicians are of great use to the publick; many cases made .... by il-

famous

lainous craft, are by able pleaders fet in their true light, in favour of juftice and honefty. The eftates of widows and orphans are often retriev'd by the vigilance and penetration of a learned council, and refcu'd from the ufurpation of the mighty, that without fuch an affiftance would have been loft for ever. Then what a faviour was the lawyer! So the moft dangerous diftempers are daily cur'd by the knowing, fagacious phyfician, that without his help would, in all human probability, have prov'd mortal. When this happens to a great and induftrious trader at a time his death would have been the ruin of feveral thriving families, or a man, whofe life afterwards proves advantageous to the publick in an extraordinary manner, then what a bleffing, and how God-like was the phyfician who faved him!

BUT if health and eftate are dear to us in this fhort ftage of life, we ought to have a much greater regard for a futurity, which fhall laft for ever. Few have leifure and ability both, to read and examine the fcriptures, as they ought, for the thorough underftanding of them; and all have

not

not knowledge fufficient to work out their own falvation. Vice fhould be continually expos'd, and finners reprov'd, and there is hardly a chriftian fo mindful of his duty, as never to ftand in need of admonition, or not to want fometimes to be exhorted to true piety and good actions. The rude multitude fhould be made acquainted with the heinoufnefs of fin, and thofe on whom the love of GOD has little influence, and the joys of heaven make no impreffion, ought to be fcar'd from evil-doing by the terrors of hell : for this reafon, no calling or profeffion is fo generally ufeful to a chriftian nation, as the miniftry of the gofpel, and no fet of men more abfolutely neceffary than fpiritual guides, to lead and encourage us in the difficult path of virtue, and fhew us the way to eternal happinefs.

MANY will wonder, why I fhould go fo far about to tell them what few people doubt of, that the function of divines deferves the higheft refpect, and is, in dignity, fuperiour to all other profeffions: but I defire thofe fuperficial judges to confider, that this was not the only thing I

C c
     had

had to mind. I very well knew what, in the foregoing chapters, I had said against the clergy; and how I have, in many places, endeavour'd to demonstrate, that soon after the time of the apostles, the holy order, set up by those true divines, degenerated from its glorious original; and that the christian clergy, when once the ministry of the gospel became a publick calling, an employ which men were brought up to for a livelihood, soon imitated the examples before them, behaved themselves like other priests, and studying more their own temporal advantage than the spiritual good of others, made their holy function, contrary to the intent of it, subservient to their own personal greatness, authority, and other worldly ends, and very often to the worst of purposes.

THIS, I say, I knew very well; and as I was likewise conscious to my self, that I had not done it with a design to render the clergy odious, I was resolv'd not to remain under the suspicion of it, and therefore was forc'd to avoid an imputation I did not deserve, to search further into human nature, and the origin of society it self,

felf, than otherwife there would have
been occafion for; that the knowledge
of what paffes in every one's own breaft,
might convince them, that I have faid
nothing of the clergy but what ought
to be expected from all mankind under the fame circumftances and temptations.

WE fee, that every body makes the
moft of his bufinefs for himfelf; that thofe
of the fame profeffion often combine together and form themfelves into compa-
nics and focieties, to confult and promote
the general intereft and welfare of their
profeffion, in order to render it as profi-
table and honourable to themfelves as it
is poffible: that, though the publick good
is the fpecious pretence for erecting of thofe
companies, what the governors and directors of them chiefly aim and drive
at, is, next to their private intereft, the
profit and advantage of the particular company they belong to: that fovereigns are
not ignorant of this, is manifeft from the
reftriction made ufe of, when they grant
any corporation the privilege to make
laws and regulations of their own, which

C c 2   is

is always done with a proviſo, that they
ſhall enact none that are claſhing, or any
ways interfere with the laws of the country, of which, if there was no danger, it
would never be mentioned.

THOSE who underſtand the world,
know, that there is a myſterious part in
every trade and profeſſion, beneficial to
thoſe only that are of it, and which moreover is abſolutely uſeleſs, if not detrimental to all the reſt of the ſociety. Therefore every ſhop-keeper has his mark, which
is allowed to be a ſecret ; and to enquire
into it, or but ſeem deſirous of knowing
it, is unmannerly and impertinent. The
intrinſical value and prime coſt of things
is what all ſellers endeavour with the utmoſt care to conceal from the buyers.

IF the ſpiritual power of the clergy be,
in vulgar eſteem, ſomewhat greater than
they are in reality poſſeſs'd of, it is an
heroick piece of honeſty in a clergy-man
to diſclaim it for himſelf ; but if a biſhop
ſhould acquaint the laity with this, and
undeceive them, it is very natural to imagine, that, tho' it could do no hurt to
religion it ſelf, the reſt of the clergy
would

would refent it. If we judge of others by our felves, we cannot think it pleafant to any profeffion to have their myfteries reveal'd. The poor have as much *Venice* treacle for a penny, as will make two half crown boluffes, if a phyfician prefcribes them to an alderman: this is very true, and the divulging it cannot do the leaft prejudice to any body's health whatever; yet no body expects to hear of it from an apothecary, and I am miftaken if the whole company would not call any of their fraternity a falfe brother, who fhould advertife it to the publick, more efpecially if he did it after he was made a phyfician.

AND as to the credit and dignity of employments, though the followers of it have vaftly deviated from the firft inftitution, yet we fee they are ever fond of retaining, even when the thing it felf is gone, if not the reputation, at leaft the name of their honourable original; as men of birth, and no merit, are proud of the titles that were given as a reward to their deferving anceftors. The great men of ancient *Rome* took inferiour citizens into

C c 3 their

their favour and protection : they pleaded their cause before the senate, if they stood in need of it, and assisted them, on all occasions, with their advice and authority, their eloquence, and often their purse. Those who enjoy'd the benefit of so generous a friendship, were call'd clients, and the honourable name of patrons was given to those noble benefactors. This custom has been out of doors a great many ages, and pleading of causes has been a mercenary employment time out of mind, that men are brought up to for a livelihood ; yet the names of patron and client are still retain'd by our modern lawyers, and 'tis not only, that the learn'd council, who give advice, and plead, make use of them, but every little pettifogger and hanger-on of the law has the impudence to call the customers he gets his bread by, his clients.

WHY should not the clergy have the same liberty ? Why not the cardinals, in all the splendor of ostentatious luxury; the bishop of *Munster* at the head of his army, or any other ecclesiastical prince, celebrating the carnival in masquerade, be

al-

allow'd to ftile themfelves the fucceffors of the apoftles? And why not the pope, in all his pontifical ornaments, be call'd fucceffor of St. *Peter*, and fervant of fervants, when he gives audience to the ambaffadors, or receives in ftate the adoration of a kneeling prince; or vicar of C H R I S T, whilft he lays claim to the fovereignty over all the kingdoms of this world? There is no doubt but that all of them are the fucceffors of the apoftles, as far as they are concern'd in the miniftry and promulgation of the gofpel; and they will never leave boafting of it, even if in their perfons, (which is hardly poffible) they fhould come ftill to be worfe than fome of them are now, or any have been yet.

THE captains, who divided the fpoil of the *Macedonian* conqueft, were the fucceffors of *Alexander*, though they did not inherit either his valour or magnanimity. The moft defpicable crafts-men have their founders upon record, if it does honour to their occupation, and never forget what once could be faid in praife of their calling. The gardener boafts of the antiquity and innocence of his employment, and,

C c 4   when

when tir'd, finds relief by thinking how the father of all mankind earn'd his bread. The wool-comber is proud that he can name a bishop for the inventor of his art. And if you attack a poor stocking-weaver on the meanness of his trade, he'll interrupt his work, though half starv'd, and take the pains to tell you, that he can name you a nobleman who had serv'd his time to the knitting frame.

THE apostles were the messengers of GOD, the clergy are the successors, and therefore they ought to be call'd the messengers of GOD; but as the same word, which in *Greek* signifies messenger, may likewise be translated ambassador, considering the veneration due to that character, and the dignity of their own order, most clergy-men are of opinion, that instead of messengers, they should be stil'd ambassadors of GOD, and on all occasions they esteem every body to be their friend, who entertains the most favourable sentiments of the honour, spiritual power and authority of their profession. What calling is there of the laity, that would not do the same? Ambassador is a modern word,

and

and not founding amifs, the ufe of it may
eafily be allowed them as a piece of civility, without looking too narrowly into the
real fign fication of it, or teafing them with
the confequences that might be drawn from
their pretenfions to the title.

FOR though every one loves to hear
the profeffion he belongs to well fpoken of
for his own fake, few defire it fhould be
to their coft. If a man would urge the
original relation between patron and client
to one of our moft eminent barrifters, it
would avail but little; and fhould he make
fuch a remonftrance to fave a fee, he would
only be laught at for his pains. In like
manner, to alledge the fpiritual wifdom of
the apoftles, the powerful influence of their
preaching, and the many miracles they
wrought as fo many teftimonies, that
confirmed the divinity of their miffion,
and require the fame credentials of the
clergy, would be thought unreafonable.

YET that the church of *Rome* has not
wholly quitted this point, is evident from
their frequent canonizations, to infinuate,
that the fame virtue and power of the apoftles ftill continue among her clergy. She
ad-

admits of no faints, unlefs it be known firft, that they have wrought miracles, either before or after death. But as the proofs of them are always made among friends, and deferr'd fo late, the worft of it is, that they are not convincing to their adverfaries, and all the proteftants openly proclaim them to be forgeries.

HAVING once renounc'd an expedient fo long made ufe of by the church, the reform'd clergy has been forc'd to make fhift without; and to folve all objections of that nature, they content themfelves with anfwering, that, though GOD had affifted the firft promulgation of the gofpel with miracles, and the apoftles had, for that purpofe, in all their tranfactions been influenc'd by his immediate power, yet after them it had not pleas'd the divine wifdom to infpire any of their fuceffors in fo vifible a manner. It would likewife be thought too rigorous to expect in them the fame holinefs that adorn'd the lives of the apoftles, the examplary patience with which they underwent all labour and difficulties to propagate the faith, the contempt of honour and riches, their firm-

3   nefs

nefs in perfecution, and conftancy in death.

THE clergy are not afhamed before the world to indulge every appetite they are able to gratify, refufe no conveniencies of eafe and luxury, and fhew the fame fondnefs of worldly pleafures as the laity; and no lefs uneafinefs when they are forc'd to go without. Should they be asked, if they would practife no felf denial, nor fhew any forbearance beyond the laity, why fo many of them fhould be haughty, covetous, prone to anger, and violent in their refentments, and not a few more notorioufly vicious; they would readily tell us, that the good things of this world were made for the ufe of man, and that the moderate enjoyment of them was by no human or divine precept denied more to the clergy than the laity; and for the reft, that we ought to confider, that clergy-men are made of the fame mould, and have the fame corrupt nature with other men; that they were born with the fame infirmities, fubject to the fame paffions, and that confequently they were liable to the fame temptations.

AND

AND if any should be guilty of crying sins, and be profligately wicked, they would assure us, that it was the highest injustice to charge this on the whole order. As to the scandal such examples might occasion, that it was only the ignorant and unthinking this could be prejudicial to, and that therefore all wise and considerate men ought for the sake of religion it self, and the good of society in general, rather stifle and help to conceal from vulgar eyes, the frailties of the clergy, than to proclaim and expose them to the world; and after all, that it was the general opinion of protestants, as well as papists, that the wickedness of a clergy-man render'd not his ministry ineffectual to those of the laity, who would vouchsafe to be good themselves.

FROM all which it is manifest, that the clergy would insinuate, that they may be beneficial to the society, notwithstanding they are bad men; that, whilst they trespass not against the laws or common decency, we ought not to find fault with their lives; and if they do, we

ought

ought to connive at them the beft we can: we are in the wrong therefore to look for more intrinfick worth, virtue, or felf-denial in the clergy, than we expect to find in the laity. It is an error likewife to imagine, that the impofition of hands, or any other ceremony, adds holinefs to a clergy-man, or renders the invocation of the Holy Ghoft effectual on a wicked prieft. This is afcribing greater virtue and efficacy to rites and ceremonies, than we really find in the very facraments of CHRIST, which are often adminiftred to fuch as prove the greateft profligates; or elfe how could men be perjur'd, or commit adultery, who have been partakers of the Lord's-fupper, and turn houfe-breakers and murderers after they had been baptized?

ST. *Cyprian,* it is true, in his letter to *Pupianus,* affirms with warmth, that [a] to fufpect a prieft to be polluted, is to judge GOD, and to call in queftion the teftimony of CHRIST who ordain'd him: but I muft beg this father's leave to diffent

[a] Cyprian Epift. 66.

from

from him in this opinion; for whatever excellency the clergy receive from ordination, experience teaches men, that it does not preserve them always from committing the worst of crimes; they are not less covetous, neither do they envy or back-bite less, and they hate worse than the laity. The monks and friars are remarkable for their lewdness, and the bishops of *Rome* have been noted for their luxury [a] so long ago, that *Ammianus Marcellinus* has upbraided them with it in his [b] time. Many clergy-men have been drunkards, and for their cruelty, where it has been in their power to exercise it, theirs has been more remarkable than any other profession.

In the days of St. *Lewis*, when the clergy had the power of life and death over their vassals, the chapter of *Paris* put all the inhabitants of *Chatenay* in prison, where, wanting the necessaries of life, they were [c] in danger to be starv'd to

[a] Ammian. Marcell. Histor. Rom. *lib.* 27.
[b] *The Fourth Century.*
[c] Jonville Hist, de St. Louis. *liv.* 10.

death;

death; and feveral actually dy'd either with famine or by the inconveniencies they fuffer'd by heat in a place hardly able to contain them. It is incredible what the Moors, Jews, and Pagans, have fuffer'd from the *Roman* clergy in *Spain*, *Portugal*, and *America*; to fay nothing of the affaffinations, private murders, and more private maffacres they have been guilty of, under pretence of promoting orthodoxy, againft the humble and credulous chriftian laity.

IN ripping up all thefe faults, I have no other defign than to convince the reader, that the clergy are men, as others are, neither better nor worfe than the laity; and that it is only fear and fuperftition, which for reafons above [a] mentioned, make the vulgar have a greater opinion of their fanctity, and rely on their influence in heaven, and fpiritual power with more confidence than they deferve. This over-rating of the perfonal worth of the clergy, is the occafion of a double evil: on the one hand it makes

[a] Pag. 21. 133. 143.

the

the laity have greater expectations of them, than they are either willing or able to anſwer, and on the other it prompts the clergy, at the expence of the publick tranquillity, to ſeek their own private ends with greater licentiouſneſs, than is allow'd of to any other calling.

THERE is no ſubjeƈt among the laity ſo great, that ſubmiſſion and obedience is not required of him to the laws and the ſupreme power ; becauſe we don't think any ſo virtuous or honeſt, but that ambition, avarice, or ſome other paſſion may induce him to prefer his own private advantage to that of the publick without juſtice or moderation. Both reaſon and experience teach us that we ought not to judge more favourably of the clergy. And yet their fair out-ſide and plauſible pretences impoſe upon, and hinder us from rightly diſtinguiſhing between that part of their funƈtion, which conſiſts in being ſerviceable to us in attaining eternal happineſs, and that part of it, which they employ for their temporal intereſt, which diſtinƈtion is yet very neceſſary ; for if

myſti-

mystically they are the succeffors of the apoftles as to the firft; they are more vifibly the succeffors of the jewifh and heathen priefts, in regard of the latter. There is no fhape or colour of drefs, no mien, nor outward modefty that is indued with any holinefs. A grave look often hides a voluptuous heart, and a man may be as wicked with a ftarch behaviour, and an auftere crabbed countenance, as he can with the moft rakifh air.

VIRTUE is fcarce every where, and a well-bred man may as much want real probity, as the greateft clown. Porters and carmen are reckon'd the rudeft and moft uncivilis'd part of the nation; the reverfe of them, and moft polite part are the courtiers; yet I don't think, that there is more religion in a hundred of the one, than there is in the fame number of the other. I am far from thinking, that the laity are better than the clergy, yet the one ought to be as dependent on the government as the other, and neither of them have any privilege or immunity to be mifchievous to the whole. All lawful employments are alike as to juftice and honefty,

D d

nefty,

nefty, and if in any calling, men are worfe, for the generality, than they are in others, it is only, becaufe they have a greater opportunity of being fo with impunity. Pride and ambition are fo riveted in our nature, that there is no profeffion, nor no fet of men, but what would lord it, and tyrannize over all the reft, if they could.

THE reafon why we ought to apprehend the encroachments of the clergy more than of any other profeffion, is, becaufe they have greater opportunities, and are lefs miftrufted. When a man has the power to harangue the multitude at his pleafure, where it is criminal to interrupt him, it is dangerous that he fhould have likewife the liberty of faying to them what he pleafes, without being liable to be call'd to an account for what he fays. Lawyers and phyficians often prove great burdens to a family; but then phyficians are never fent for, but when we are ill; and whilft GOD gives us health, we have nothing to do with them. Lawyers likewife are only made ufe of on occafion, and many live happily to a great age without ever employing any. But whether we

are

are fick or well, live in peace or difcord, the intercourfe between the clergy and the laity is continual. For, befides their officiating every day at divine fervice, we can do nothing of moment without them, and they affift us through every ftage of life. As foon as we are born they come to chriften us, and when the nurfe has had the greateft trouble with us, and we can help our felves, the clergy defire to have the tuition of us, till we are men. The next thing then to be thought on is matrimony, which we can't enter upon without them. In ficknefs they come to comfort us, and claim a right to examine our confciences when we are in health. They ftill vifit us on our death-beds, even when the phyfician has left us; and, after we have taken our leaves of them and the whole world, they won't yet part with us before they have feen us in the grave.

WHEN all thefe things are taken into due confideration, the clergy carefully reftrain'd from doing mifchief to the fociety, and the publick every way guarded againft them, as if they were the worft of

D d 2   men,

men, I would not have them debarr'd from the comforts of life, and they should enjoy the world equally with the laity. But that no impartial man may have the least reason, any longer to suspect my sincerity, and to shew my sentiments in relation of the reciprocal duties I treat of, without being dogmatical, I shall explain my meaning in the following example.

I don't think it easy to name a great city better govern'd than that of *Amsterdam*. (I beg, no prejudice against the name.) The behaviour there, between the national clergy and the laity, towards each other is very commendable. In the salary of the ministers there is a perfect equality; they have about two hundred pounds sterling yearly each, which, without their asking for, is sent home to them by quarterly payments in a handsome manner: besides this the *East India* company make them a present every year of spices. There is hardly a minister, who has not some intimacy with two, three, or more families of the senators, where he is always welcome, and treated with the same deference, they pay to one another; on all

solemn

ſolemn entertainments, this clergy-man gra-
ces their table, and ſhares with them in
moſt of their diverſions, and what ele-
gant comforts of life a friend can enjoy that does not live always under the
ſame roof.

THE multitude pay them great reſpect,
and it is counted brutiſh among the common people, not to pull off their hat to
a miniſter, which is often done even by
thoſe, who are not of the publick church,
and is the more remarkable in a country,
where the vulgar are more fam'd for ſelf-
intereſt than civility. To be a miniſter of
the publick church at *Amſterdam* is the
higheſt poſt in presbytery, a *Dutch* divine
can arrive at, and reckon'd ſo conſiderable, that, tho' he has not a groat, if he
marries a fortune of eight or ten thouſand
pounds ſterling, it is counted an equal
match : their widows have handſom pen-
ſions paid them, whilſt they remain ſingle ; and their children have moſt of the
offices and places of profit beſtow'd upon
them, that are in the gift of the magiſtrate, at leaſt with equal merit they are
generally preferr'd to all others.

WHAT.

WHAT is expected from the clergy
for this, is a grave deportment, and the
folemn exercife of their function; by no
means to meddle with ftate affairs, and
with all their faculties endeavour to appear hearty for the government, and the
publick welfare.   They are, whilft in
health, obliged to preach twice a week,
tho' their fermons commonly laft an hour
and an half in the delivery, and often
longer.   Confidering how large the churches, and numerous the audiences are, preaching is a painful office, and would be almoft
infupportable, if the pleafure of being fol-
lowed by fuch vaft multitudes did not
help, by gratifying human frailty, to al-
leviate the burden.   They are allowed to
inveigh againft fin and the vices of great
men, as much as they pleafe, without
pointing at particular perfons.   Tavern,
or coffee-houfe, they never enter into;
which, how much it contributes to the
veneration the vulgar has for them, no
clergy can know but what has try'd it.

NOT to be tedious, I have omitted
feveral tokens of efteem and friendfhip,
which at the birth of children, and other
times

times they receive; but one of them is too remarkable not to be mention'd. At publick rejoicings, when bonfires are made for peace or victory, the magistrate sends in to every minister a handsome quantity of wine, and in the evening a certain number of pitch-barrels, fill'd with other combustibles, is at the publick charge rais'd before their doors on a scaffold, and burnt, in the same manner as is done before the houses of officers of note, and the magistrates themselves. From this the people have the pleasure to think, that the government has as great a reliance on the prayers and piety of their clergy, as they have on the conduct and bravery of their commanders, and that the clergy participate in the publick joy, and have no wishes that are different from the common good.

THEY are *Calvinists,* and consequently presbyterians, that are all equal without pre-eminence or subordination. I have already declar'd for episcopacy in the third chapter, and shall say no more on that head. What I would observe relates to the harmony between the clergy and the

laity,

laity, and their reciprocal behaviour to each other, and I would recommend it no farther, than as it might concern our inferiour clergy, and interferes not with our constitution, or church government as established by law. As to the bishops, I would have all that respect and deference paid them, which is due to them as the first members of the honourable house they sit in : but their place there, and the share they have in the legislature, belong to them not as clergy-men, but as lords of parliament, by the law of the land, and not by provision of the gospel. The bishop-ricks themselves I look upon as places of honour and profit, to reward clergymen of merit and capacity. Their number is very moderate, and therefore the expence not half so burdensome to a nation as ours, as they are serviceable to the encourage-ment of learning.

PREACHING at *Amsterdam* must be a labour, which every body is not robust enough to undergo ; but if we abate some-what of the fatigue in that part of their function, for the rest I think ministers of the gospel ought to be satisfy'd with such

usage

ufage, as I have mention'd. If not, it is manifeft, that they are unreafonably follicitous, either to enjoy their eafe and pleafure in general, or elfe to gratify fome predominant paffion. And when we fee, that they have no regard for our eternal welfare, the main part of their function, all their arguments for power ought to be fufpected : for the more narrowly we examine into their fpecious pretences, the more we fhall find, that all tend to promote their own perfonal greatnefs, and temporal advantage, and that they only ftrive to have the whip-hand of the laity, to be their own judges, and wholly independent on all rule and government, but their own.

RELIGION requires no fuch thing. Ecclefiaftick cenfures are perpetual torments to the laity: the chief ufe they are of, befides puffing up the priefts with pride, is for envious and malicious people, when they want a handle to be vexatious to their neighbours, and it feldom happens, that courts of judicature, where clergy-men prefide, are not fad grievances to a nation, let their religion or church

E e

go-

government be what it will.   That presbytery is not eligible before episcopacy, we may learn from the use the clergy of *Geneva*, and the kirk of *Scotland*, have all along made of their jurisdiction.   Such a power must make all clergy-men tyrants, and would do the same to all professions, or any other set of men, invested with the like independent authority the clergy claim; and I would as soon trust the inquisition of *Spain* for lenity and discretion in punishing,   as I would the rulers of the independents in *America*, if not sooner;   for the more men are obliged to keep up a pretence to virtue and religion, true or false, the less fit they are to judge others. The reason is plain: hypocrites are under greater temptation to be cruel, than other sinners;   because they are always in hopes that we shall judge (as many are fools enough to do) of the holiness and purity of their hearts from the hatred and strong aversion they outwardly express against vice, which must make them unmercifully severe against the least frailties of others.

THE

THE civil magistrates ought never to part with their fasces to any function or profession whatever, but keep in their own hands the sole power of punishing offences, be the crime what it will. We don't live in such days of ignorance, that none but clergy-men can read: a government that is able to detect the intricate machinations of plotting statesmen, ought to be deem'd wise enough to know what is blasphemy or prophaneness, without asking a priest; and where immorality is discountenanced, and vice punish'd by wholesome laws, religion will never suffer for want of power, or any worldly greatness in the clergy. If they will think otherwise, let them; but if they complain of it by way of appeal to the multitude, they ought to be immediately stopt. When men offend by speaking, the first and mildest punishment they can expect, is to be silenc'd, which, if others will not take warning by, they ought to be more severely treated.

WHEN once it is manifest, that they only labour for their own worldly ends, we ought to be very cautious how and

where

where to believe them. They'll tell us, that without having the liberty to preach what they pleaſe, they cannot diſcharge their conſciences, nor perform their duty; they'll give us the examples of *Samuel*, of *Nathan*, and other prophets, and inſtance the noble freedom and becoming boldneſs with which they ſcrupled not to reprimand kings themſelves. They will add, that the clergy ſpeak on the part of GOD, as well as the prophets did, that they are the ambaſſadors of heaven, and that as ſuch they ought not to be limited or controul'd by any power upon earth.

THESE are ſpecious pleas; but before we are ſway'd by them, we ought to examine into the lives and actions of the clergy; and if we find that the greateſt part of them are very neglectful in every branch of their duty, that has any relation to the good of others; that there is not the leaſt reſemblance between the functions or perſons of the chriſtian clergy, and the prophets of the Old Teſtament, that there is no ſymptom about them to make us imagine, that they are inſpired by the

Holy

Holy Ghoſt, as they all were, whom they inſtance in, as having ſpoke to kings from GOD; and laſtly, that moſt of them are wholly taken up with worldly cares, and mind themſelves, their eaſe, their pleaſure, and earthly comforts more, ten to one, than the cauſe of GOD or religion. If we find, I ſay, theſe things, we ought to be deaf to the moſt plauſible of their pretenſions, and take care of our ſelves in defiance of all their deceitful eloquence.

As to their being the ambaſſadors of GOD, I have ſpoke of it already, and therefore, if they will compliment themſelves with the title, without laying any ſtreſs on the ſignification of the word, they may, but they muſt draw no conſequences from it: rhetoricians may have leave to uſe figurative ways of ſpeaking, that in the ſtrict ſenſe are not to be allow'd of. But how little the clergy reſemble either the apoſtles of Chriſt, or earthly ambaſſadors, may be eaſily ſhewn, without upbraiding them with their want of credentials. The apoſtles were viſibly choſen by our Saviour himſelf; the clergy are brought

up

up to their function for a livelihood : they disclaim'd all earthly power ; these are always grasping at it, and never more uneasy, than when they are restrain'd from the use of it : in short, the apostles voluntarily renounc'd the world ; and the greatest complaint of the clergy is, that they can't have enough of it.

As to earthly ambassadors, they are only sent to sovereigns that are altogether independent on him who sends them. What relation this has to the Creator of the universe and his creatures, whose very breathing depends on his preserving power, I can't well conceive. This is certain, princes send no ambassadors to their subjects, but when they want power ; and therefore, if the clergy will fancy themselves ambassadors to us from above, they must ascribe to the sole monarch of heaven and earth, who is jealous of his glory and sovereignty to the highest degree, what would be counted an unheard of and shameful condescension in a mortal and earthly king : a mean ill-advis'd conduct, that would infallibly tend to the dishonour of the most limited, and most precarious
world.

worldly prince. If every thing is blaf-
phemy, which detracts from the wifdom
and glory of GOD, what muft we fay of
their pretenfions?

BUT to return to the fubject of preaching, I conjure all civil magiftrates to believe, that nothing is more deftructive to
the peace of the fociety, or more dangerous to the publick welfare in general,
than to let the clamours and audaciouf-
nefs of malecontent clergy-men go unpu-
nifhed when they become criminal, and
tamely to fuffer that men, who, by their
function, ought to ftand by and ftrengthen
the authority of the government in every
thing that is not clafhing with the laws
of GOD, or their country, fhould openly
traduce, and endeavour to render it odious
to the people.

BUT as for want of fufficient proof it is
not always in the power of the magiftrate
to convince clergy-men of crimes, which
they have been actually guilty of, the laity ought ever to be upon their guard a-
gainft preachers when they know them to
be difpleas'd. When a government appears refolute in oppofing the leaft ten-

dencies

dencies to fedition and civil difcord, the difcontented clergy learn to be angry with difcretion, to make ufe of fly infinuations, and vent to their audiences in couch'd expreffions what in words at length for fear of condign punifhment they dare not utter.   In fuch conjectures every good fubject ought to beware himfelf, and ufe all his endeavours to caution others, his family, his friends, his neighbours, and every body he has any influence o-ver, how they give ear to fuch preach-ing.

To render fermons not unprofitable to us, it is a chriftian's duty in going to church to banifh, as much as he is able, from his heart all envy, jealoufy and re-venge, that he may at laft carry a difpo-fition capable of receiving the doctrine of peace. Would men comply with this, they might be furnifhed with a certain rule, by which the meaneft capacities would be able to judge of the integrity of their teachers, and have an infallible touchftone to know, whether they en-deavour'd to eftablifh fentiments of union and concord among their hearers, or by sowing the seeds of contention, spur them on to hatred and indignation against any of their neighbours. Where that care I recommend has been taken, let every person re-examine himself after sermon, and if he finds all calm within, and his mind not more disturb'd with anger, aversion or other symptoms of animosity, against those of different opinions, or against his superiours, in going out than it was at coming into the church, the minister has acted the good shepherd, and done honestly by his flock, and we may be satisfy'd that his discourse was not design'd to destroy or endanger the publick repose: but if after the same precaution, you feel in your bosom some rancour or ill-will, either against the government, or any of the ministry, or against others whom you disagree with. If you feel a desire of revenge, and your charity to any sort of men is sensibly decay'd, you may immediately, unless there is another visible cause of your change, lay the fault on your minister. 'Tis he who has seduc'd you from CHRIST, and you may assure your self, that, to gratify some passion,

or

or ferve fome other worldly end, he has endeavour'd to difturb the tranquillity of the people.

THERE are a thoufand artful ways, by which fubtle orators may prepoffefs men, raife their pity, anger, jealoufy, or any paffion they have a mind to, without fpeaking plain, more efpecially divines, who have fo large a field as the fcriptures to range in, from whence they may cull innumerable paffages, to be wrefted and turn'd to what purpofe they pleafe. With fuch a help, and a very little fkill, a preacher may infufe any ftrange notions into a vulgar audience, and either fet them on to, or deter them from things without naming them, or openly telling his hearers what he means, or what he would be at.

MANY things in the Old Teftament were only fpoke to the Jews, and could never relate to any other nation: many predictions, as thofe which foretold the deftruction of the city and temple of *Je-rufalem*, have been fulfill'd a great many ages ago. The fame muft be faid of every thing which has been prophefy'd con-

3   cerning

cerning the coming of the Meffiah, and whatever related to particular captivities and other calamities, which the Jews actually fuffer'd long before chriftianity; yet there's not a country in chriftendom where all things are not daily applied to the then prefent circumftances of the people, or made fubfervient (often very injudicioufly) to every end the minifter has in view, and what is a greater wonder, is, that by common confent this is call'd preaching of the gofpel.

I don't fay this to find fault with it, to deprive the minifters of the Old Teftament, or abridge their liberty of chufing their texts from any part of it as they pleafe, but to demonftrate the neceffity and reafonablenefs of a caution I am going to give, and which I would have all men make ufe of in hearing fermons. An allegorical expreffion often engages, and at once byaffes the hearers in favour of the preacher. How wonderfully is an audience often moved with the exclamation of a prophet, or a few words of a pfalm emphatically delivered, when at the fame time fhould the context be minded,

and

and all circumftances examin'd into, they would be found very impertinently apply'd. If men will fuffer themfelves to be drawn away by fuch random flights, their allegiance is always precarious, and they'll be perverted before they are aware, that the preacher has any defign againft the concord of the fociety.

In all profeffions men ought to do good, or at leaft to endeavour it ; and he is far from having difcharg'd his duty, who can but barely fay, that he has done no mifchief. A man who is entrufted with the cure of fouls, ought to examine into their frailties and fpiritual ailments, to adminifter proper remedies accordingly. When a minifter preaches to an incited rabble, it is not fufficient not to encreafe their fury; it is his duty to appeafe them, and turn their hearts from the mifchief, they are bent on, to the utmoft his abilities will let him. To act prudently with a mad-man, we ought not fo much as to mention the thing that diftracts him. It is very furprizing, that men of fenfe fhould fo often trefpafs againft fo plain a maxim, and (though as often admonifhed) ftill pretend

tend ignorance in the flagrancy of their guilt.

IN many cafes it is difficult openly to convince men of their crimes, as long as it is poffible for them to conceal, or but deny their evil intentions, and they often elude the force of a juft accufation by e-vafions, which their confciences muft up-braid them with. To exhort an audience to orthodoxy is laudable in a clergy-man; and to bid them beware of fchifm, and ftand up for the church, may likewife bear a very good conftruction; but if it makes the mob pull down a meeting-houfe in *England*, or abufe men for having com-mon-prayer books in *Scotland*, or commit fome other outrage, would not a minifter of the gofpel, if he was not pleas'd with it, on the firft opportunity undeceive his miftaken followers, reprove them, and in the moft ferious manner remonftrate to them, that they had mifconftrued his meaning? but if he takes notice of it, and goes on in the fame ftrain againft the fin of fchifm; if moreover his pleafant looks and a fignificant fmile now and then caft on the ring-leaders by ftealth, befpeak

his

his satisfaction, and far from reproving them, with unusual civilities he seems to reward their zeal; then what must we think of such a minister, or what can he say for himself? I should be glad to know what evasions he can have left, when thus far pursued.

I have hinted before at a conquest gain'd by the church over the state at *Geneva*. This victory was obtain'd by a sermon of [a] *Calvin*, which, to all outward appearance,

was

---

[a] *The Council of* Two Hundred *had made a Decree, that the final Judgment of the Causes of Excommunication should belong to the Senate, and that the Senate might absolve the Excommunicated, as they should think fit.* One Bertelier, *who had been excommunicated eighteen months before, sued to the Senate to be absolved.* This Calvin *strenuously opposed; but the Senate were for re-admitting him to the Communion, and by virtue of the Decree above-mention'd, the Senate granted Letters of Absolution to* Bertelier. *The Sacrament was to be administred to him within two Days.* When Calvin *came to hear what had pass'd, he soon resolv'd what he should do, and preach'd against the Contempt of the Sacrament; he rais'd his voice, lifted up his Hands, and said, That he would imitate St.* Chrysostome, *That he would not oppose Force to Force, but he would rather suffer himself to be massacred, than*

that

was full of zeal and piety, but in reality threatning the magiſtrate with an inſurrection, if they would not let *Calvin* have his will. The government took the hint, apprehended the danger, and the clergy gain'd their point.

To raiſe rebellion is a capital crime in any ſubjeƈt, but that a clergy-man ſhould prompt others to it, aggravates the offence: from the opportunities he has by his funƈtion, it is ſuppoſed to be always in his power, which, beſides the treaſon, makes him guilty of a breach of truſt, in perverting the deſign of his calling, to what is the leaſt ſuſpeƈted: It is the ſame as poyſoning in an apothecary, or cutting a man's throat in a barber. The laws therefore againſt ſeditious preaching ought to be more ſevere and extenſive than they are in moſt countries. For though many of the clergy are reſolute and audacious, yet great numbers contain themſelves within the limits of ſmall innuendos and remote ſug-

that his Hands ſhould preſent the Holy Myſteries to thoſe that had been judg'd unworthy of them. Beza in vita Calvin, ad ann. 1553.

geſtions,

geftions, who, were they not aw'd by the fear of punifhment, would openly vent their malice, ftick at no calumny, no bare-fac'd treafon, and make their pulpits, that fhould be the promptuaries of wholfome counfel, and fpiritual comfort, like the deceitful ᵃ veffels of *Hannibal*, yield nothing but poyfon and deftruction to fubvert a government they diflike.

I might urge this argument with ftill greater warmth, without contradicting what I have advanced concerning the fuperiority and pre-eminence of their profeffion; for nothing is more falfe, than that to bring a clergy-man to fhame is an affront to his cloth. As they won't allow, that the moft heinous crimes committed by a clergyman can caft the leaft fcandal on his calling, fo I can't fee why punifhing him as he deferves, fhould be counted an ignominy done to his whole or-

---

ᵃ *The* Romans *being Mafters at Sea, took all the* Carthaginian *Ships that came in their Way, which made* Hannibal *fend out fome fmall veffels on purpofe to be taken, as accordingly they were; but being carried home, they were found only freighted with Pots full of Serpents and Adders, and other poyfonous Vermin.* Plutarch.

der.

der. When a peer is put to death by the bafe hands of an executioner for a crime he was convicted of, no body looks upon it as an indignity offer'd to the honourable houfe of lords.

ONCE more I infift upon it, that to deftroy the power and authority ufurped by the clergy for their temporal intereft, and punifh them, when they deferve it, equal with other men, are not incompatible with the fincere refpect and higheft veneration that are owing to their holy function. There is no profeffion fo ufeful nor fo neceffary to the fociety as theirs; yet thofe who are of it owe as much obedience and fubmiffion to the laws and the civil magiftrates, as mountebanks or ftage-players. They are like fire and water, to be both valu'd and reftrain'd, the beft of fervants but worft of mafters; and I could heartily wifh, that all governments would treat the clergy, as, not to be wanting in either prudence or gratitude, I would a phyfician, who had faved my life. I would heap on him all the kindneffes in my power, and on all occafions he fhould command my friendfhip. I would not only believe, but obey

F f   every

every thing he fhould advife, relating to my health; but fhould he encroach on my goodnefs, I would fhew him his error in the mildeft manner, and fhould I do this in vain, I would have patience, and forbear falling out with him for a great while; but if after all I found he was incorrigible, and that nothing would ferve him but that he would have the government of my family, I would indulge him no longer, and at all events make him know I was refolv'd to be mafter at home.

C H A P.

CHAP. XI.

Of GOVERNMENT.

MANKIND agree in nothing more unanimoufly, than the neceffity there is of government in the civil fociety; but to this day it is undecided what fort of government is the beft. This is certain, that there is no form of government, but what has its peculiar grievances and corruptions, which others are not fo liable to, and confequently in every one of them fome inconveniencies are avoided, either wholly. or in part, that are more particularly or more eminently complained of in others. The fimple unmixed governments are monarchy, ariftocracy, and democracy. The fupreme and legiflative power of *Great Britain* is a compound of thefe three. I have often heard well-meaning people fay, that

E f 2   would

wonld every body be honeſt, ours is the
beſt conſtitution in the world. But this
is no encomium: where every body will
be honeſt, and do their duty, all governments are good alike. That is the beſt
conſtitution which provides againſt the
worſt contingencies, that is armed againſt
knavery, treachery, deceit, and all the
wicked wiles of human cunning, and pre-
ſerves ît ſelf firm, and remains unſhaken,
though moſt men ſhould prove knaves.
It is with a national conſtitution, as it is
with that of mens bodies; that which
can bear moſt fatigues without being diſ-
order'd, and laſt the longeſt in health, is
the beſt.

ALL ſubjects owe an unlimited obedience to the ſupreme power in all kingdoms,
ſtates and principalities whatever, and no
form of government can ſubſiſt without
an arbitrary ſovereignty. In any of the
three ſimple forms there is no queſtion
where this total ſubjection and unlimited
obedience is due; but in mix'd governments it often is the cauſe of fatal quarrels, as has manifeſtly appear'd in this
kingdom, where moſt calamities that have
be-

befallen either king or people, have been owing to this grand difpute. The flatterers of princes, among whom clergy-men never have been wanting, have ever afferted, that it was a fin to GOD not to pay it to the king. They maintain their argument with proofs from fcripture, the hiftory of all ages, and all the examples of abfolute monarchs, without taking the leaft notice of the conftitution, and the agreement between the king and the people.

As there was nothing fo fit to convey this doctrine among the people, and make it fpread, as the pulpit, princes, who had the misfortune of employing minifters that advis'd them to arbitrary fway, have made ufe of clergy-men to preach it. In the beginning of the laft century this doctrine had greater ftrefs laid upon it than ever had been before, and met with no great oppofition at firft; but a little after, as foon as fome untoward trials were made to put it into practice, half the nation rofe up againft it, and oppos'd this tenet with fo much violence, that it produc'd the moft fatal contentions. Both parties

were

were obftinate, and became daily more implacable to each other from the ill offices
of divines, the intemperate zeal of preachers on both fides, and the vindictive fpirit that reigned among them. As foon as
the affertors of the paffive doctrine loft
ground, ambitious men took advantage of
the opportunity, and carried their followers to another extreme, who joining force
to argument, maintained, that obedience
was only due to the people, and even
the king's perfon accountable for the
crimes of others, if committed by his
order.

THE affertors of liberty turn'd the op-
preffors of it, till monarchy was happily
re-eftablifh'd almoft by common confent,
and the doctrine of *Refiftance* became o-
dious in its turn, which it had not been
long, before the greateft part of the nation thought fit to make ufe of it again.
Notwithftanding the various turns of fate
thefe two doctrines have undergone, and
the many mifchiefs the difpute has occafion'd, the queftion remains ftill; and as
each party pretends to have the better of
the argument, the quarrel is undecided.

It

It would be endleſs to repeat a quarter part of what has been ſaid on this ſubject. I ſhall attempt no ſuch thing, but who-ever will examine all will find, that the great difficulty of determining this affair, proceeds from the difference between the parties in ſtating the caſe rightly; for when that is fairly propos'd, I can't help thinking, but that the diſpute muſt ſoon be at an end.

IT is agreed on all hands, that an un-limited obedience is due, the queſtion is, to whom? To the higheſt, the ſupreme power, that is inveſted with the abſolute ſovereignty of the nation. If we agree, likewiſe in this, as I think we do, the matter is decided, as ſoon as this power is found out. This abſolute ſovereignty of our nation is either lodg'd in one per-ſon, or in more than one; if in one we have nothing to mind but the arbitrary will and pleaſure of that one perſon, and the words parliament, fundamental laws and conſtitution, are empty ſounds with-out any ſignification; but if the ſovereignty be really divided into ſeveral branches, and the ultimate and legiſlative power is

poſ-

poſſeſs'd by the conſtitution, in which that power is founded, the king, lords and commons, then our unlimited obedience is only due to ſuch commands, as ſhall appear to have been given by their joint agreement, without being revok'd and made void by the ſame authority.

AND here it is to be obſerv'd, that as the power to make laws muſt include likewiſe a power to preſerve them from being violated with impunity, ſo every branch of the legiſlature muſt have as great a ſhare in the one, as it is inveſted with of the other. For when the commons in parliament are aſſembled to act their part in the legiſlature, and by their authority give ſanction to what they ſhall think neceſſary, or uſeful, the repreſentatives of the people are come on a very fooliſh errand, if there is another power upon earth, that without their conſent can make void, and with impunity annul, perhaps the next day, what they have been enacting with ſo much ſolemnity, and after ſo mature a deliberation.

To exert the power, which comes to their ſhare in making laws, the lords and

com-

commons muſt be lawfu'ly call'd and aſſembled in their reſpective houſes: but
whether they are ſitting or not, the power
of enforcing and preſerving the validity of
the laws is entruſted to the king; by this
confidence the nobles and people repoſe
in their monarch, he becomes the guar-
dian and ſuperintendant of the laws, whoſe
ſacred office it is not only to require o-
bedience to them of all his ſubjects, without partiality, but likewiſe to promote,
and every way encourage the execution of
them, and lend his authority to thoſe who
are employ'd in it. The king at his co-
ronation takes an oath to diſcharge this
truſt ; which, whilſt he does, he repreſents the whole ſovereignty of the nation, and the ſame obedience is to be
paid to him, which is due to all the three
eſtates.

FROM what has been ſaid it is evident, that the chief end, why the king
is inveſted with this power, is to enable
him to maintain the laws; and ſince the
king has no prerogative but what is given
by law, it is impoſſible, he ſhould have a
power, without his parliament, to make,

G g   re-

repeal, or alter any; and nothing is more abſurd than to advance, that a perſon has a juſt authority to deſtroy what he has ſworn to keep. But to render it ſtill more manifeſt, that the king has no power to claim obedience, and that it is not ſo much as ſurmis'd, he ſhould require it of his ſubjects to any command that is unlawful, we are but to obſerve what every body knows, that all perſons are accountable for their own actions, and that no order of the king, how plain or expreſs ſoever, tho' produced in writing, and corroborated with his ſign manual, can extenuate a man's guilt, much leſs exempt him from it, if in executing that order he has acted againſt the law. Nay the king has no power to claim obedience to any command, that is not founded in law, that is, where there is not ſome law that requires obedience to it. If the king commands me to give him my eſtate, if I think fit to comply and give it him, I break no law; the act I do is not unlawful; but I am not bound to do it, neither in law nor in conſcience; becauſe there is no law that gives him authority to require it.

IN

IN times of danger, if the safety of the nation requires, that the executive power should be encreased, the people may enlarge the trust they repose in the king, by laying aside for a while the great buckler of their liberty, the *Habeas Corpus* act. But this is never done, but when conspiracies and rebellion are actually on foot, and the parliament is perfectly well assured of the good intention of the king and ministry. Even in the heighth of this confidence it is very visible, that this trust is limited, the power of arbitrary confinements is never given to the king; all that is done by so laying aside the *Habeas Corpus* act, is only suspending for a few months some privileges given to the subjects by that act; and if there be any further occasion to continue such suspension, the people again must be consulted; the necessity there is for continuing this confidence in the king, is to be examin'd and discuss'd in parliament; or else at the stated period, as soon as the time is expir'd, the act reassumes its force, whether the parliament be prorogued, dissolv'd or actually sitting; which shews, that this is an

G g 2   affair

affair look'd upon to be of that high importance, that no person or power upon
earth shall judge of it but themselves:
and consequently that a very considerable
part of the sovereignty remains virtually in
the people, even when they have no re-
presentatives, and have actually entrusted
the executive power beyond the usual limits; and at the same time it demonstrates,
that the law is a rule that binds the king
equally with his subjects.

WHAT is most beautiful in our constitution is, that these three estates, singly
invested with so great a share of sovereignty, can never interfere with each others
power, whilst the laws are held sacred by
all the three equally. All the shares of
sovereignty possess'd by the lords and commons notwithstanding, the same honours
and respect are due to the king, that are
usually paid to absolute monarchs, as much
as if the legislature and supreme power
was not divided. He likewise makes bishops, is the fountain of honour, and has
the sole power to bestow titles and digni-
ties. He names all officers both civil and
military, and the coin bears his effigy.
He

He makes peace and war, leagues and alliances with foreign princes; and the political administration, and management of foreign affairs, and the interest of the nation, in respect to other states and potentates, are likewise his province. As to the government of his subjects he has, as I have hinted before, the superintendancy over all the laws to render them effectual, and justice is administred in his name.

These high prerogatives and undoubted marks of sovereignty, belong to the king, and many more, but he has not one that can make him a tyrant, or his subjects slaves. The rights and privileges of parliament, and the liberty and property of the people are as sacred branches of the constitution as any thing the king can claim. If a subject offends, it is the law, and not the arbitrary will of the prince, or any of his ministers, he is to be punished by. He that is refractory against the law, is in many cases as rigorously dealt with, as if he had disobey'd the most arbitrary tyrant; but where there is no law, there is no transgression. As the greatest respect is due to our monarchs,

they

they ought to be treated with the height of good manners, and the people may affert their liberty without making ufe of odious terms: and they can want no coercive power over their kings, becaufe their name or authority is no fhelter to a man who acts illegally.

IF a man comes without any force to demand money of me in the king's name contrary to the law, or without law, I laugh at him, and fend him about his bufinefs ; but if he came with a troop of horfe, or any other fuperiour force, I would comply, not, becaufe he came in the king's name, but becaufe he would be ftronger than I. But when he has done this, the law is on my fide, I can call him to an account for it, and the king's order fhreens him no more from the law, than an order of the great turk, or the mayor of the leaft corporation in *England*. But if, refufing to part with my money, I am imprifon'd, without admitting me to bail, if fufficient, and proffer'd, and am deny'd a lawful tryal, or that I am tried by an illegal court of judicature, erected at the king's pleafure, then the rights and liberty

ty of the subjects are invaded, and in the first case the act of *Habeas Corpus* is violated. All this may be done, and the king not in fault himself: he may be wholly ignorant of such facts, or be misinform'd, and some of his ministers abuse his authority, and they may be prosecuted and punished, and compell'd by law to make me satisfaction.

But if after many remonstrances made to the king, or his council, the injuries are not redress'd, I am refused justice, and brow-beaten and oppress'd; and such ministers remain unpunished, and in favour, and parliaments are either dissolv'd, or not call'd at the times, which the law has appointed for their meeting, and other illegal means are put in practice to skreen such evil ministers from justice: if this becomes a general complaint, and the king still continues to cut off all hopes of redress, he then breaks his contract with the people. It is impossible, that this should be done, but all the world must know it, yet the enemies of our constitution, by way of objection, ask us, Who is to be the judge of this breach,

G g 4   which

which is the fame, as if they asked, Who is to to be the judge that it is day at noon?

WHEN a monarch is the abfolute lord of every thing in his dominions, and he has not made yet any folemn irrevocable grants of privileges, or immunities to any of his vaffals, his arbitrary will is their law, and an unlimited obedience is due to his commands, not interfering with the laws of GOD, tho' otherwife the moft unreafonable. But fuch an extravagant power never lafted longer, than the force to execute and maintain it, and experience has taught princes long fince, that tho' the law of GOD enjoins fubjects to obey them, it is not fafe to truft to fuch a flavifh allegiance. If therefore a prince of wifdom and penetration, confidering, that he has almoft every fubject to fear, and none he can really truft, fhould for his own fake be willing to defift from this right of abfolute fway, and fhare the fupreme power with his people in a manner and proportion, as he thinks fit, and they fhall agree to: if a prince, I fay, condefcends to this, I can't fee why a contract,

tract, thus ratified between him and his people, is not as binding as any other contract whatfoever. What men, who are not tied to any laws, are abfolute mafters of, they may part with and divide among whom they pleafe. If the fupreme power was the prince's property, and he thinks fit to beftow part of it upon the people, the fhare of it which he makes over to them becomes their property, as much, as it was the prince's before. This would be juft by the law of nature, tho' the prince had no reafon, or the leaft motive, but his caprice, for fo doing; but if he did it to rid himfelf of many fears and jealou-fies, if he did it for the better fecurity of his perfon and government, his quiet, his pleafure, and the fucceffion to his po-fterity, then likewife it becomes equitable according to the laws of nations and fo-ciety; becaufe it is evident, that the prince receives a valuable confideration for what he gives away.

THOSE difputants then, who in de-fending the doctrine of paffive obedience compare our kings to abfolute monarchs, and in fpight of all remonftrances are ftill

ap-

applying the examples of arbitrary king-doms, to be met with in facred and pro-phane hiftory, to our conftitution, feem to me to argue befide the queftion, and are to be treated as men, who deny firft principles.

ANOTHER argument of contention is taken from the fucceffion of our kings, and the right of inheritance. Both par-ties agree, that our kingdom is heredita-ry, but one fide will have it, that nothing can incapacitate the next heir in blood but idiotifm or lunacy; but the other affert, that there may be feveral other reafons to fet afide this right, of which being a *Roman* catholick is made one by law. They prove likewife, that it often has been fet afide among the Jews and other na-tions as well as our own. The advocates for hereditary right reply, that whenever this right was fet afide, it was done un-juftly; that kings have this right from GOD, and, that no acts of parliament can make any alteration in it. They add, that kingly government is of divine in-ftitution, and that confequently the peo-ple cannot deprive them of it. This muft

car-

carry us back where we have been before in queſt of ſovereignty and the ſupreme power.

KINGLY government is of divine inſtitution by the doctrine of our church: I heartily believe it, and that kings are GOD's vicegerents; but I hope this is not meant only in behalf of abſolute monarchy with excluſion of all other forms of government. GOD commands us to be obedient to the higher powers: this duty, I conceive, we ought to pay not only to ſovereignty it ſelf, but likewiſe to all magiſtrates and ſuperiours, all rulers and officers, that either repreſent or act by the authority of the ſupreme government of a nation: but if the divines, in compliment to kings, would inſinuate, that no other form of government had any right of exacting obedience from their ſubjects, I ſhould believe that our church had loſt her infallibility, had a canon been made to eſtabliſh that doctrine; for from thence it muſt follow, the Great Mogul and the Grand Signior have a divine right to claim obedience of their ſubjects, which the republick of *Venice*, the ſtates general of the

United

United Provinces, and the cantons of *Switzerland,* are deſtitute of. Kings then, that is, the higher powers in every nation, whether the ſovereignty be lodg'd in one or more perſons, are of divine inſtitution, and there is no doubt but the ſovereignty of all countries derive their right from GOD. But as to the divinity of hereditary right, if it was p ov'd, which I yet never ſaw, it would be ſubject to the ſame alterations that government is, as to its form. The ſame authority that makes common-wealths and mix'd governments from abſolute monarchies, may alter the right of inheritance, prefer females to males, poſtpone or exclude them, and make what other regulations they think fit. In ſhort, the ſame authority, that eſtabliſhed the regal authority, and the ſucceſſion here in *England,* can alter it whenever the publick good requires it.

I ſhould not think my ſelf impartial, if I ſhould leave this ſubject without mentioning a ſcruple that has been perplexing even to men of candour. They have acknowledg'd the contract between the king and people, and the abſurdity of maintaining

taining

taining that paſſive obedience can be due to any thing but the ſupreme power, the whole ſovereignty, and likewiſe own'd, that the great ſhare of ſovereignty the people are poſſeſs'd of, has been very viſible in all the tranſactions of the nation for above theſe hundred years; but if they trace the power and authority of the commons a little higher, they find it very mean and precarious, and the further they go, the more arbitrary they find our kings, and the leſs deference was paid to the commons. They may urge, that laws are never better underſtood, than at the time they are made, and therefore to judge well of the true intent and deſign of the conſtitution, we ought to look into the partition of power, as near the time it was made in as is poſſible.

SUCH another ſcruple may be moved in the affair of the ſucceſſion; for when we have agreed, that there is no expreſs law of GOD concerning the right of inheritance, and that the examples where the rule, by which the neareſt of blood inherit, has been follow'd, are hardly more numerous than the exceptions, where men have

have fwerv'd from, and difregarded it, we cannot find in our hiftory any thing comparable to what was done at the revolution, and foon after. In all the ftruggles that have been made by the princes and barons for the crown, the right of inheritance was always infifted upon, and never fet afide but by fuperiour force. That thofe who remain'd in poffeffion, always courted the confent of parliaments, was to ftrengthen their title, and to be the furer of the peoples allegiance that they might not revolt; but this precaution was always of little ufe, when a more powerful antagonift arofe. This is certain, that both the king and the lords feem to be invefted with much lefs authority than they were in former ages: and many think it as fure, that parliaments have never calmly difpofed of the fucceffion to the prejudice of hereditary right before the revolution : but this is a miftake. In the 35th of *Henry* the eighth, the parliament did in full time of peace, after the princeffes *Mary* and *Elifabeth* had been both declar'd illegitimate, fettle the fucceffion of the crown in default of all other iffue of *Henry* the eighth, male

or

or female, upon thofe two princeffes fuc-
ceffively; and they both enjoy'd it accordingly: tho' they could not poffibly be
both legitimate, and tho' neither of them
were fo accordingly as the law ftood when
they took poffeffion of the crown. And
tho' upon Queen *Mary*'s acceffion to the
crown, the act was repeal'd, fo far as it
declared her illegitimate, yet it never was
repeal'd to this day, fo far as it declared
Queen *Elifabeth* illegitimate: but in the
13th of her reign an act was paffed, where-
by the declaring, that the queen and parliament had no right to alter and bind the
fucceffion of the crown, was made, during
her life, high treafon, and, after her death,
forfeiture of goods and chattels.

To folve the other difficulty, and penetrate into the reafon of the change that
is obfervable in the authority of the three
eftates, we muft take a view of the nation's condition in refpect to the fituation of
property, and mafterfhip, among the three
eftates. At the beginning of our conftitution the king had vaft poffeffions, and a
great part of the kingdom was his property. The lords were few, had exorbitant
eftate

estates among them, and some of them were so rich in land, and powerful in vassals, that one or two of those barons often were a match for the king. The humble commons all this while were hardly a free people, and had not one inch of ground. The scene has been much alter'd long since; the kings have parted with considerable branches of their prerogative, and that crown lands are nothing to what they were, is no secret. The lords are numerous, and many of them not rich; the church has but little land left to what she had, and the commons have for some time been possess'd of three fourths of the whole.

THE constitution therefore may be the same, that is, the sovereignty is, as much as ever, lodg'd in the three estates, king, lords and commons; but considering the vast change that has been made in their possessions, it would be absurd to think, that the three powers should be the same they were in relation to each other. Time was, when the king and lords were both formidable, and each was jealous of the others power; for which reason neither

I
　　　　　　　　　　　　　　　　of

of the two would fuffer the other to op-
prefs the poor and helplefs commons: but
the face of things is alter'd, neither of the
two firft eftates has reafon to dread the
other's power, and both of them together
would not be an over-match for the
third. So true it is, that dominion always follows property, and that, where
the one is wanting, it will ever be impra-
ticable for any long continuance to enforce
the other.

FROM the abfolute fway then exer-
cis'd by our kings, and the vaft authority
of the lords in former ages, it does not
appear that the commons were not a branch
of the fovereignty, or had a lefs fhare in
the legiflature than they have now; their
right was the fame, but they had not the
tools to maintain it. When kings and barons made war at their own charge, they
had no occafion to confult or trouble their
heads about the commons, who could not
affift them but with t eir perfonal fervice, which they had without calling of
parliaments: but when great fleets are
to be equipp'd, armies rais'd and maintain'd, general officers are to get eftates,

and miniſtries to be ich'd, when all this is to be done, an he purſe of the commons is to pay for it, when the very expences of the court, and all the various penſioners that belong to it are chiefly de. fray'd by them, it is no wonder, that they are often wanted, and have the deference ſhewn to them, which is due to the con- ſiderable ſhare they have in the ſove- reignty.

As to the ſucceſſion the kingdom is hereditary, as much as ever it was; the hereditary right has been ſet aſide often, and as well formerly as at the revolution. All the quarrels that have been made a- bout the ſucceſſion, have ever been decid- ed by the longeſt ſword; and ſo was the laſt, with this difference, that the diſpute before was between the rival princes, and this was between the prince and the peo- ple. I know very well, that the conven- tion was no parliament, but when king *James* had abdicated the kingdom, we muſt have been in the utmoſt confuſion, if the great men of the nation had not taken care of the government; and future ages, when they ſhall read this part of our hiſtory,

and

and be acquainted with all the circumstances of it, will be forc'd to admire the wisdom of thefe times, and confefs, to the praife of thofe patriots who manag'd that affair, that to preferve the religion, the liberty, and likewife the tranquillity of a nation, human prudence has never exerted it felf more confpicioufly on any other Emergency. We are told fometimes that the king's abdication was not voluntary; but it is evident, that he was defired to ftay, and nothing drove him away but his own fears. He had claimed and exercifed a defpotick power inconfiftent with the limited authority of the regal power which the laws vefted in him. He knew that he had broke through the laws, and that he had defy'd, and on many accounts moft heartily provok'd, his fubjects, and would not truft to what they might do in their anger.

THERE is no fact fo execrable, but the memory of it may be ufeful to pofterity, and the greateft misfortunes that can befal a father, may prove inftructive to his fon. A prince who would be arbitrary, ought not to be hamper'd with the virtues of a pri-

vate

vate man. When minifters have been flavifhly obfequious to their prince's command, and not fcrupled to betray both the
nation and their truft, to ferve the ambition of their mafters, good natur'd princes
are apt to love them in return, and think
themfelves oblig'd to protect them : But
this is wrong, a king, who is influenc'd by
friendfhip, gratitude or generofity, ought
to curb his ambition, and content himfelf
with governing according to law ; but he
who can part with a favourite for a trifle,
and is ever ready to facrifice the deareft
tools of his ambition to his own fecurity,
may now and then attempt to encroach on
his people, without great danger to his
perfon. But that king, who lays a ftrefs on
the delufive promifes of paffive obedience,
and has too much confidence in his own
divine right, will find at laft, that he has
trufted to a broken reed, and that the
prince who will exert the utmoft of his
power to fave the head of a minifter, who
has forfeited it, can never, whilft the fituation of property remains where it is, be
fafe upon the *Britifh* throne.

I re-

I return to our difputes, and fhall now obferve, that where any are on foot, the moft doubtful caufe gets champions and a-bettors among thofe who are not concern'd in nor well acquainted with the quarrel. Thofe who at the revolution were either children, or are born after it, if their fathers agreed to or acquiefc'd in the alterations that were made in the fucceffion, are hardly excufable for difowning the prefent eftablifhment ; their fcruples are far fetch'd. If every body muft be a judge of what was well or ill done in matters relating to the fucceffion of princes, or the conftitution, we fhall never want malecontents ; and if there is no validity in the confent of the people affembled, and acting in the moft folemn manner, fome will find as much reafon to difpute the divine right of *William* the firft, as others pretend to have in difowning that of *William* the third.

THOSE, who during the life of king *James*, after his abdication, would not fwear allegiance to king *William*, and have ever fince refus'd to take the oaths either to queen *Anne*, or his late majefty, may have fome plea for their fcruples at leaft

there

there is a poſſibility that they may be ſincere : but vaſt numbers are enemies to our tranquillity, that are neither candid in the remonſtrance of their grievances nor conſiſtent with themſelves. At one time they deny the validity of all acts of parliament made ſince the revolution: at another, they are in hopes of mending themſelves by a change of parties, and complain of the *Septennial-Act*, without conſidering that the law for *Triennial* parliaments had no being before the reign of king *William.* Sometimes they are religious, and an indefeaſible hereditary right is the only bar that hinders them from coming into the preſent eſtabliſhment ; this they inſiſt upon, and are deaf to all remonſtrances : they can't be convinc'd; and many profligates that ſtick at no crimes, are in this point, and no other, conſcientious.

IF this indefeaſible hereditary right is ſuperiour to all other claims and conſiderations, why did moſt of the malecontents ſwear allegiance to king *William* and queen *Anne*, and why have the greateſt part of them taken the oath to his late majeſty ? If they anſwer, becauſe they are impos'd

pos'd under penalties, it is a sign they are
not to be depended upon, who will for-
swear themselves for interest, and the sake
of worldly conveniencies. An oath made
to a king is an indissoluble as well as sacred tye, whilst the prince continues in the
legal discharge of his office, or others by
his consent, and in his name, discharge it
for him. Those who talk of swallowing
and washing down their oaths, and make
a sport with them, ought, in return, never
to be treated seriously, and their very scruples of conscience, if they pretend to any,
be made a jest of.

To swear with mental reservation has
been counted abominable, even by heathens. When *Euripides,* in one of his
Tragedies made *Hippolitus* say, that he had
swore with his tongue, and not with his
mind, it mov'd * the *Athenians* with indignation: the thought seem'd so loose to
them, that though *Hippolitus* chose rather
to dye than to violate that verbal oath,
they call'd the poet in question for it:
the expression it self was shocking, and

* Barnes in vita Euripid.

they

they could not endure, that any one should be reprefented, even upon the ftage, with fuch words in his mouth. If it be certain, that he who has fworn has fuppos'd a fact, that is not actually fo, and that unlefs he had believ'd that fact, he would not have fworn; in fuch a cafe, fays *Grotius,* an * oath obliges not. What pity 'tis our oath-fwallowers have not fuch an excufe to make!

HEREDITARY right is what the favourors of the pretender, of late years, have laid all their ftrefs upon, as if his birth had never been fufpected to have been fpurious. The law, I know, which bars all papifts from the crown, is a fufficient guard againft him; but it is ftrange that a thing fo uncertain, (if not unlikely) as his legitimacy, fhould by time, and nothing elfe, be put all together out of the queftion. Among the feveral reafons generally alledged for *Pyrrhonifm* in hiftory, the remotenefs of the time which things were wrote in, is always reckon'd one of the chief; but in the cafe of the pretender, there is fuppos'd

* Grotius de jure belli & pacis, *l.* 2. *c.* 13.

fome-

fomething which feems to derive its certainty from nothing elfe, but that people have forgot, or elfe never knew, the circumftances that made it doubtful.

THE queftion is, whether the queen was deliver'd of a fon or not? thofe who maintain the affirmative, produce many witneffes of reputation both to the pregnancy and the delivery: They will not allow, that the oaths of *Roman* catholicks fhould be lefs credited than thofe of proteftants, becaufe both are of equal validity in law; for which reafon they affert, that the queen was actually brought to bed of a fon, and ask what evidence can be brought to the contrary. To this may be anfwer'd, that it is often impoffible to prove a negative, efpecially in fuch a cafe, if people may be allow'd to fuffer no body about them but of their own chufing; and as to the oaths of *Roman* catholicks, that notwithftanding their validity in law, it is certain that the popes not only claim a power to abfolve men of them, but have actually, as far as their authority could do it, forgiven as heinous crimes as perjury; that every ftep towards the reduction of

I i   fuch

fuch a kingdom as this to the obedience
of the holy fee, muft be look'd upon at
Rome, as a matter of the higheft concern
to the church.   I muft own, that was this
mighty work to be accomplifhed at the
expence of five thoufand falfe oaths, and
nothing wanting but a formal abfolution
to indemnify the jurors, fign'd by the holy father, and the whole college of cardinals, I fhould think *Great Britain* in no
fmall danger of popery.

THE reafons, which thofe who hold the
negative, offer for believing that a child
was impos'd upon the nation, befides fome
fufpicions and furmifes of things, that
cannot eafily be proved, are thefe.   In
the firft place they fay, that as foon as
it was reported that the queen was with
child, it was every where buzz'd about,
that it would be a prince, and that during
her pregnancy, the *Roman* catholicks, and
all who favour'd arbitrary power, were as
infolent upon it, as the certainty of the
thing could have made them: that before
the queen was near her time, fhe feem'd
very irrefolute in fixing upon a place
where to lye in, and at laft, when preparations

rations had been made, and all had been ready for some time in one palace, things were in great haste removed to another; that all this while there had been at court several starts and sudden motions; sometimes every thing appear'd gay and prosperous, at others the courtiers look'd as if all was lost, and there were such continual whisperings among them, as are observ'd where some mysterious intrigue, or deep design of great importance is carrying on; and lastly, that those, who by the law and custom of *England* should be present at the queen's delivery, were not there.

T H I S last they lay the greater stress upon, because the court knew, that all the protestants of *Europe* expected a cheat. What the other side replies to this is weak, for to say, that the duke of *Monmouth* being beheaded, the king had no body to fear, and that the queen was a haughty, imperious woman, who would not shew so much complaisance to the nation, as to satisfy them in this particular; and that, though the king knew that the law required the presence of several persons,

the

the queen was obstinate and ungovernable. To alledge this, I say, is not sufficient in a case of so high a concern; all *Europe* had their eyes upon them, had every thing been fair, no court in the world would have made such a false step, when they could not be ignorant that they were suspected. A woman is not fit to be a king's wife, who, on such an occasion, should scruple to admit a hundred strangers if it was required. What would not a princess do on an emergency, where her glory, the welfare of her posterity, the peace of nations, her all is at stake! *Constantia,* ᵃ queen of *Sicily,* not to give the least suspicion, was brought to bed, and lay-in publickly in the plains and meadows of *Palermo.*

To this we must add the juncture of time it was done in. King *James* left no stone unturn'd to introduce popery, which would have signify'd little for his reign, if his successor had been a protestant: all the machinations of the priests would have been in vain, unless a male heir could be

---

ᵃ Brantome Dames illustr.

had;

had; it was the sheet-anchor of all their hopes. King *James* could not obtain his ends without arbitrary measures; he mistrusted his people, and would have nothing to do with parliaments, and there was nothing the cause stood in more absolute need of than the birth of a prince, that at once should blast all the hopes of the protestant heirs, and strengthen the king in the illegal courses he had resolv'd upon. It is easier for a nation to judge of a matter in dispute, when it happens, and all things relating to it are in every body's view, than when the thing is over, and the circumstances that accompanied it are lost out of sight; besides some have forgot, others never known any thing of them, but imperfectly from books or tradition, both of which are seldom otherwise than partial.

WHEN all these things are consider'd, the pretender's being born of the queen will not be so clear as many imagine. Eight in ten of the people then living did not believe that the queen had a child; how comes it that above three and thirty years after, it should be expected that the

same

fame nation fhould believe that fhe had, without receiving any further proof than what they had before? For what happen'd in *France* is as much an evidence againft, as it is for his legitimacy. When moft people fufpeſted him to be a fuppofititious child, and the fruitfulneſs of the queen was a thing much doubted of, nothing was more neceſſary than that fhe fhould have another, to remove the fufpicion from the firſt; and had the court art enough to procure fuch a male child in *England*, where they were watch'd, at a time it was fo much againſt the proteſtant intereſt they fhould have one, it was no difficulty to fuborn one of either fex in *France*, where no body over-look'd or obferv'd them.

I know very well, that all thefe things may be turn'd a quite contrary way, and be fet in another light; but I know likewiſe, that the probabilities are no more on that fide, than they are on this: the thing is doubtful, and fo it is like to remain. It was king *James's* fault, that the method the law prefcribes to clear the doubt was not put in practice, and we
                                        have

have no fuch obligation to his memory, as by an eafy credulity to fupply his want of precaution, which perhaps was part of the impofture.

No man is lefs bigotted to any party than my felf, but there are facts that are undeniable. About the time this pretended prince was born, the king of *France* was wholly bent on the execution of the fcheme he had fo long made for the univerfal monarchy of *Europe.* The court of *England* was one of his tools, the king then on the throne a weak, good-natur'd, eafy, fuperftitious prince, who was rul'd by his queen, a monftrous bigot to popery, a haughty, violent, crafty, *Italian* fpirit. All heads at *Rome* were at work, and all capable emiffaries employ'd, and they had all the affiftance the king and queen could give, to reduce *England* to the obedience of the holy fee. *France* had with her gold brib'd moft princes and miniftries in chriftendom into a lethargy. A ftrict friendfhip and alliance was made between that court and ours And now the flavery of *Europe* feem'd unavoidable. The knowing men of *England* faw this, were uneafy,

I i 4 but

but could not help themselves. King
James had erected an ecclesiastical court
to introduce his religion, and on several
other accounts violated the laws; but he
had a fine standing army, was rich himself, and receiv'd great supplies from *France.*
The only bulwark of the protestant interest were the states-general; but what
could they do against two powerful kingdoms?

IT was then the design of the revolution
was form'd, and happily brought about,
whilst the great genius of *William* the
third rous'd the courts of *Europe* from
their indolence, shew'd them the common
danger, and made several of them arm a-
gainst the delusions and exorbitant power
of *France.* Our posterity a thousand years
hence will find, that the wisdom and vast
abilities of this prince spoil'd and put a
stop to the grand design which *Lewis* the
fourteenth had form'd against *Europe*, and
sapp'd his deepest machinations. When
they shall see from the losses *France* has
been able to sustain, how vastly superiour
she was to all her enemies, how king *William* was perplex'd at home, how many
trea-

treacheries he had to cope with, they will be forc'd to conclude, that to have done what he did, he muft have been a prodigious man : no body then will doubt, that he was the preferver of the proteftant intereft, and the liberties of chriftendom. Thofe who are too fevere criticks on the actions of princes, and by bold conjectures fupply the gaps and hidden parts of hiftory, perhaps will fay of him, that he was of a reftlefs fpirit, more fit for war than peace, and that his perfonal enmity to *Lewis* the fourteenth turn'd his ambition the right way, which otherwife might have proved lefs advantageous to the liberties he afferted ; but they will be forc'd to confefs, that he was, as to perfonal expences, a frugal, a manly, laborious, heroick prince, and a confummate politician, lefs given to luxury and pleafure than any of his time.

To the forefight of this great king, the proteftant caufe is indebted for the exclufion of all papifts from the crown, and the eftablifhing the fucceffion in the illuftrious houfe of *Hanover,* who were the next proteftant heirs : and this fince, after
his

his death, has been confirm'd with all the folemnity and unanimous confent, that parliaments can proceed in.   During almoſt the whole reign of Q. *Anne*, the princeſs *Sophia*, of bleſſed memory, was the next and preſumptive heir to the crown; his late majeſty, by right of inheritance, as her eldeſt ſon, was poſſeſs'd of the throne, which the princeſs his mother muſt have fill'd by a parliamentary eſtabliſhment of almoſt thirty years ſtanding.   Theſe are truths that muſt be laſting, and which time or faction ſhall not erafe.

C H A P.

CHAP. XII.

Of National Happiness.

THAT *Great Britain* is a happy iſland, and well ſtor'd magazine of native bleſſings, whether we look on the ſituation, the ſoil, the climate, or the inhabitants of it, is undeniable. The firſt guards us from foreign inſults by the ſeas that ſurround us, and ſecures us from the rage of their incroaching waves, almoſt every where, by ſolid cliffs, and impenetrable rocks. The ſecond is fertile in moſt parts, and admits of many improvements. All the neceſſaries of life we have of our own growth, and many ſuperfluities. As we want olives, wine and ſpices, ſo we are free from the violent heats that are requir'd to produce them; but then of our own product we have generally ſuch a ſtore as is able to

pur-

purchase all the various implements of pride and luxury, from the richest nations and the remotest corners of the earth in a surprising plenty. Our climate is still more happy; it is the most moderate, at least the south part of it, in the universe, and no country has less cold in winter, that is not subject to greater heat in summer. What king *Charles* the second said on this head was very judicious: in his presence one day the weather happen'd to be the subject of the discourse; and as some foreign ministers complain'd of the uncertainty of our's, and were bragging of the serenity of the air in their own country; [a] *The best climate,* said the king, *in my opinion is that, in which a man may be abroad with comfort most hours in the day, and most days in the year.*

THE people of *Great Britain* are docile and industrious, warlike when occasion requires, and obstinate when provok'd: they are excellent artificers in most handicrafts, but more noted for improvements than invention. The most useful of them, that

[a] *Sir* William Temple's *Memoirs.*

is,

is, thofe inured to labour, are indefatiga-
ble, when employ'd to their mind. There
is no toil fo immenfe which they will not
undergo, nor hardfhip they will flinch
from, if they engage heartily in it, and the
wages or rewards are proportion'd to their
trouble. Their very diverfions are laborious, and few are flothful where profit or
a profpect of fome other advantage is
ftirring. The removing of merchandizes
of all forts, efpecially our fuel to and from
different places, require great flight, but
more robuftnefs, and on this account there
is more bodily ftrength exerted to the
beft advantage, and more work done in
London, than by the fame number of
hands you fhall find perform'd any where
elfe ; nor is there a place in the world,
where the flaving people of the loweft
rank, that will and can work, either get
and fpend more money chearfully than
they do in this city, where vaft multitudes are continually employ'd in mix-
ing hard labour with good fellow-
fhip.

In fhape and gracefulnefs of body, the
Britifh nation are fecond to none ; I

I   might

might ſay more of wit and beauty, but that I think them to be trifles, not always beneficial, and let who will count them among the national bleſſings, I ſhall always believe, that if we had leſs of both, we ſhould be more happy, and not half ſo fickle; but then to make amends for what we ſuffer by theſe, there is no nation, where good ſenſe is more generally eſteem'd at its true value, and very few, where ſo great a vein of it runs through the vulgar. But the moſt ſubſtantial bleſſing, and the peculiar happineſs we enjoy above all other countries, are the laws and liberties of *England.* Let ſlaves and flatterers of princes, with all the abettors of arbitrary power tell us, that what we call liberty is licentiouſneſs; an *Engliſhman* knows better, and can anſwer them, that whilſt we deſire no liberties, but what the laws allow, and every one obeys them in the ſtricteſt manner, the ſubject in our conſtitution receives a noble freedom from the ſame ſovereignty, to which he owes his allegiance. From page 337 to 344 I have hinted at what our great happineſs conſiſts in.

IN

IN *Switzerland* the bayliffs are petty tyrants in every diftrict, and in *Holland* the magiftrates of every city are arbitrary in many things, and men are capitally punifh'd without publick tryal : but what we, and only we may boaft of, is, that throughout the globe there is not a country, great or fmall, where the men of the higheft rank can do lefs injury to their inferiours, and even to the loweft with impunity than in *England.* This privilege, without which all the joys and comforts of life are precarious, is the grand characteriftick of *Englifh* liberty, and a felicity, which it is not in the power of wit or eloquence to over-rate.

SINCE fo many bleffings then confpire, what hinders us from being happy ; for it is certain we are not fo? A fincere man would no more flatter his country than he would the meaneft perfon in it. Our difcontent and grumblings are publickly known, and all *Europe* hear us murmur in the midft of fo much eafe, and greater plenty than any empire, ftate or kingdom now enjoys. Should any ftate phyfician behold our goodly countenance, and, having

ving

ving felt our low difpirited pulfe, examine
into the real caufe of all our grievances,
he muft infallibly pronounce the nation
hypp'd.   No woman in the height of va-
pours is more whimfical in her complaints
than fome of us,   and melancholy mad-
men have not more difmal apprehenfions
of things in the blackeft fits of the fpleen,
than our ftate hypochondriacks are daily
buzzing in our ears.   In diftempers, where
the imagination is chiefly affected,   men,
without any other remedies, may often reafon themfelves into health.

WHOEVER would be happy fhould endeavour to be wife;   and as this confifts in
having a diffufive knowledge of the real
worth of things,   and a capacity of chufing on all emergencies what to found and
unbyafs'd reafon would feem the moft eligible, fo it is by fhaking off all cloggs of
prejudice,   and fetters of human authority, by thinking freely, that men can only
mount to wifdom.   There is no better
way of curing groundlefs jealoufy and pan-
nick fears, than by daring to examine and
boldly look things in the face.   As with
this freedom, I have treated of the church,
diftin-

diftinguifh'd between that and religion, fpoke of government, and the obedience due to it, and briefly touch'd on our differences about the fucceffion of our kings, fo now I fhall with the fame liberty prefent my readers with an open view of courts and minifters.

KINGS that are abfolute, or would be fo, are dreadful creatures all the world over. Confidering their education as princes, and the flattery they are ever furrounded with, it is GOD's mercy that any of them are tolerable. In limited monarchies kings have greater opportunities of practifing felf-denial, and moderating their defires. As they are vaftly fuperiour to the higheft fubject, fo we ought not to judge of them as we do of other men, and the two greateft virtues our nation can pray for in a monarch, are, that he may ever delight in the true exercife of his great power, and always abftain from wifhing to encreafe it. Thefe, without any other addition, can never fail of making him a bleffing to his people, who, in return, owe him their homage and their hearts, which to exprefs, they ought cheerfully to be at

K k the

the charge of entertaining him and his family in diftinguifh'd magnificence, and take care that on all accounts he is ferv'd, approach'd, and addrefs'd to with the moft humble fubmiffion, and fuperlative refpeʧ, and nothing be wanting about his perfon of what fplendid affluence can procure towards the enjoyment of the moft delicious eafe and the height of earthly glory.   This we perform.

S o   many fervices require abundance of people of various employments, who are well vers'd in all manner of elegancy and politenefs ; the feveral branches of the publick adminiftration demand many officers of different ranks and capacities, all which make up a confiderable number of perfons, of whom feveral have large falaries and other emoluments,   and not a few great opportunities   of   enriching   themfelves. From what has been faid we may eafily imagine, that the courts of our king, how frugal and virtuous foever the monarch may be himfelf, muft be places of pomp and luxury, ftately academies of all manner of pleafure and diverfions,   where men learn to excite, as well as to indulge their

appe-

appetites, and all the paſſions and ſenſa-
tions are refin'd upon.

THOUGH every courtier in his turn has
a ſhare in theſe worldly enjoyments, yet
the whole machine ſeems only contriv'd
to do honour to the king, and every creature there appears in his ſtation, as if he
was only born to procure him either eaſe
or pleaſure. To make this not look as if
it was done in jeſt, the higheſt officers of
all are often oblig'd to a certain ſtrictneſs
of attendance and ſeveral ſervices, which
would be counted vile and abject if perform'd to any other. What makes the
men of the firſt quality amends for this
condeſcenſion, is, that the ſame complai-
ſance, and very near the ſame homage,
is paid to them by thoſe of the ſecond
rank, and ſo on ; which renders the whole
a gaudy ſociety of ſubordinate ſlavery,
where each member has an object to envy,
and none can ſubſiſt without the profoun-
deſt diſſimulation.

LET us now examine what ſort of people it is moſt probable would reſort to
ſuch places as I have deſcrib'd courts to
be, and we ſhall obſerve, that they either

are

are ambitious men, who are reſtleſs after greatneſs, and ſtrive in vain to find a comfort in being ever diſſatisfy'd with their preſent condition, or elſe thoſe of a more abject pride, who want to lord it over others, and from a baſeneſs in their nature, delight in being bow'd and cring'd to by all that ſtand in need of them : thoſe that are tainted with the vice of *Cataline*, and are greedy after the poſſeſſions of others, only to heighten the ſatisfaction they feel in throwing away their own : the covetous with mean ſouls and no conſcience, that will beg, if they cannot plunder, and do any thing to be rich.   Theſe, and the men of pleaſure and ſenſuality, are generally the perſons whom their inclinations drive to court; and, except ſome few, who ſue for places to be reveng'd on others, the reſt are commonly vain people, that love ſhew and gawdineſs, and from an idle and plentiful education, have learned to delight in nothing but the outſide of things.

I ſhall be ask'd, Are there then no ſtateſmen, no men of parts, of erudition, of capacity for buſineſs, that will be laborious ?

borious? Yes, feveral, that are guilty of the vices I named, are fuch at all courts, or elfe the affairs of ftate could not be ma-nag'd ; yet the greater the plenty is, gene-rally the lefs will be the application among them. But are there none then, who, be-fides thofe good qualifications, have noble fouls, and humanity, and are free from thofe vices ? Not many, and fuch of them as take it in their heads to be courtiers, are generally men eager after fenfual plea-fures, and perverting the accomplifhments of nature and learning to a wrong ftudy, fpend the beft part of their time in re-fining upon *Epicurifm* of all forts. Good men, that are lovers of their country, and fit to be minifters of ftate, are fcarce at all courts. A perfon who is contented with what he has, that hates noife and infincerity, and having no revenge to exe-cute, or other irregular paffion to gratify, is one who knows how to value his own liberty, and defires nothing flavifh of o-thers ; fuch a perfon, I fay, what fhould he do at court? For a man fo qualified, who has polite learning, and a good for-tune, if he underftands the worth of things,

and

and has a true taste of life, may better divert himself almost any where else.

THE men of the highest quality and ample fortunes by inheritance, may come to honour, and pay their respects to their prince, assist at councils and other solemnities where their presence is required by their birth, but they seldom offer themselves for the service of their country, when qualify'd as I describ'd. It is an ungrateful task, when well perform'd, and honest men generally fare the worst. As to religion and true piety, should any one who is but inclin'd to it, get into court, there's [a] half a distich ready, by its merit almost become a proverb, that will bid him go out of it the first thing he does.

IT is incredible what benefit may accrue to us from this thorough knowledge of courts: first it will take away at once all those heavy complaints we are always making against our kings about the choice of their ministers. There are good men at all courts, but not such a vast plenty of them as people imagine, and the best

[a] Exeat ex aula qui cupit esse pius.

judge

judge can chufe no better commodity than the markets afford. Secondly it will cure us of that mifchievous credulity, with which we are fo ready to believe, according as we are influenc'd either by love or hatred of a party, whatever is told us of the virtues or vices of minifters. He that knows how courtiers throw their own faults upon others; their artifices in fpreading reports; the faftening of flander; the mines they dig for one another's deftruction; the deep craft of their intrigues, and all other machinations in practice among them, will have but little faith in what is rumour'd about publick minifters.

THERE is nothing more difficult than to know a good man from a bad one, and the juggle of courts is to one who is not in the fecret, what a game of chefs is to a man wholly ignorant of it: as the one may fee the gamefters move every piece, and yet not underftand what is aim'd at, without being a fool, fo the other may be in all the buftle of the court, without knowing what is carrying on, and be a man of parts at the fame time. The envy, vy, strife, and all the feuds and jealousies of courts are so many safeguards to the liberty of the people, they never fail producing severe censors of those at helm, that watch over all their actions, magnify their failings, and heighten the least oversight into a capital crime; and the false steps of ministers are often not so much owing to the neglects of those who make them, as they are to the rubs and impediments which the malice of a crafty adversary has found means to fling in their way. Court intrigues are a perpetual warfare, where men are oblig'd to cut their trenches crooked, or be unavoidably expos'd to all the artillery of their enemies hatred.

WHEN parliaments are sitting, all the busy part of the year ministers have no great opportunities of doing any considerable damage to the nation, and seldom will attempt it. The laws and legislature are curbs which the boldest as well as the craftiest stand in awe of, and a better security for the people than all the virtues ministers can be possess'd of. See underneath

derneath ª the opinion of an anonymous author. The general complaints made against all miniftries are, that they abufe the king's ear and favour, and employ all their induftry in keeping others from him; that they enrich themfelves too faft, poftpone the publick to their private intereft, and engrofs all places of truft, of honour, and of profit among themfelves, their families and friends, with exclufion of all others, and no regard to merit or capacity.

THESE are all articles that men in power have ever been accus'd with by the malecontents, and whether there ever yet was a miniftry, that was altogether free from thofe faults, and every part of them or not, I leave others to determine. But where is the man who judges of them without prejudice? The courtiers,

---

ª *One good man may take another's word, if they fo agree, but a whole nation ought never to truft to any honefty, but what is built upon neceffity. For unhappy is the people, and their conftitution muft be ever precarious, whofe welfare muft depend upon the virtues and confciences of minifters and politicians.* Fable of the bees, *Pag.* 169.

L l

who

who are influenc'd by the warm beams of God's vicegerents, are by their panegyrists reprefented like angels; when that fun ceafes to fhine upon them, they fall; after which they are thought to meditate as much mifchief and revenge, to injure mankind, as thofe of old; at the fame time they become the patriots of thofe, who were their enemies before. A whole fet of ftatefmen of different tempers and capacities, virtues and vices, are extoll'd to the skies in one company,- in another they are damn'd to the pit of hell, and as often as thefe great men change fides, fo often fhall thofe companies change their language: a plain demonftration that we are far diftant from knowing the truth, and very infincere in our opinions.

As to be happy we ought on the one hand not to rely too much upon the virtue and probity of politicians, fo on the other we ought carefully to avoid mifconftruing their actions. How we have murmur'd at the war with *Spain!* and how unjuftly charg'd the king with being the firft aggreffor! The *Spaniards,* under the violent fway of an haughty prieft, would

im-

impoſe laws upon us; they render our trade with them precarious and impracticable, equip a great fleet, and make preparations for an invaſion, and provide all neceſſaries to raiſe a rebellion in the kingdom: they diſtreſs our allies, and treat the pretender to his majeſty's crown with all the marks of honour and eſteem that can be paid to a great monarch. King *George* ſees it, arms againſt them, beats their fleet, and, by the aſſiſtance of his allies, breaks and ruins all the meaſures of *Spain*, and makes them diſmiſs the great favourite, and ſue for peace. An *Engliſh* man who loves his country, and complains of this conduct, muſt be an arch politician.

WE ought likewiſe to forbear judging raſhly of miniſters and their actions, eſpecially when we are unacquainted with every circumſtance of an affair. Meaſures may be rightly concerted, and ſuch caſualties intervene, as may make the beſt deſign miſcarry. We ſhould not complain when the intentions of men are manifeſtly good, and they act for the intereſt of the

na-

nation, and fruftrate the defigns of the enemy.

I T is wrong alfo, when we differ in opinion, to charge men with having ill defigns, when the matter in debate may be varioufly interpreted, and admit of innumerable fpeculations. It is very difficult to judge what things, which we never had any experience of, would produce, if they were to be. I am neither for nor againft the peerage bill, becaufe it is above my capacity to judge of it; and I have often wonder'd to hear people with fmall knowledge fpeak confidently of what would be the confequences of it. From fuch fubjects I own the men of eloquence, of wit, and of learning of both fides, receive great opportunities of fetting themfelves off, and difplaying their parts, but thofe who are both fincere and impartial will hardly promife to affirm any thing about it with certainty. In the chapter of *Government,* I have hinted at the difference between our times and three or four hundred years ago, as to the property of the king, lords and commons. Had the lords never had the power of making their land alienable, and

and kings could not have parted with
what belong'd to the crown, the property
of the whole, except what the church is
poffefs'd of, muft ftill have been vefted in
the king and lords; and the vaft diminu-
tion in the property of the peers, is altogether owing to the liberty they have
fince receiv'd of felling their eftates. What
prudence or penetration could have forefeen,
this?

HUMAN underftanding is too fhal-
low to forefee the refult of what is fubject to many variations. A man may be
well vers'd in ftate affairs, have wit, penetration, a perfect knowledge of the world,
and every thing requifite to make a compleat politician, and yet not be able to
make any tolerable gueffes of what will
enfue from a thing which is new, and he
can get no infight into, either from hiftory, or his own experience. A man may
underftand one game at tables very well,
and be a great while endeavouring before
he is mafter of another that is nearly related to it; I fpeak of games of difficulty
and fpeculation: he can never judge with
any folidity which is the beft play, be-

I. l 3 fore

fore he has often feen it, and has an experience of the varieties in it, and is acquainted with the fudden changes it is fubject to, what contingencies are ufual in it, and which are counted extraordinary. I fhall make no other apology for the lownefs of this fimile, than the example of *Terence*, who has fo handfomely compar'd * human life to a game at tables, where it behoves every one, if he throws not what he ftands in need of, and could have wifh'd for, by his play to make the moft of what he has thrown, and by his skill fupply the deficiencies of his luck.

THAT we may not mifconftrue the intentions of princes and politicians, another caution is requifite, which is, to avoid launching out beyond the fphere of our underftanding: a man may be an induftrious trader, of fenfe and equity, and have good notions of the *Meum* and *Tuum* of private perfons, and yet not be able to

* Ita eft in vita hominum, quafi, cum ludas tefferis,
Si illud, quod maxume opus eft jactu, non cadit,
Illud, quod cecidit forte, id arte ut corrigas.
              Terent. Adelph. Act. iv. Scen. vii.

de-

determine any thing concerning the property of nations. There is no tribunal upon
earth, to which ſovereigns can appeal for
the deciſion of their differences, and therefore in all conferences and peaceable debates among the nations in *Europe*, the
ballance of power muſt ever be the ſtand-
ard, that all property and poſſeſſion, as
well as friendſhip and alliances are to be
weigh'd by. What elſe could have juſtify'd our demands for the demolition of
Dunkirk? Many who ſome time ago complain'd that the garriſon of *Gibraltar* was
an exceſſive charge to us, and that in
time of peace it was of no manner of uſe,
ſeem now highly concern'd at the very ſur-
miſe, that we are to part with a fortreſs
of that importance. I pretend to no fore-
ſight, but I ſhall wonder ſhould the reſt
of the powers of *Europe* let it remain in
our poſſeſſion.

T H I S I am ſure of, that it is inconſiſtent with the ſafety of our trade, that
it ever ſhould be in the hands of a nation
ſo powerful in ſhipping as either the *Dutch*
or the *French*, and I am afraid they will
think themſelves obliged to ſay the ſame

of

of us. There are artful people who, fore-
seeing this, make a handle of it, for murmurs and discontent, by insinuating that
whenever we part with *Gibraltar*, it must
be by the neglect or treachery of the ministry. If we consider how selfish and obstinate most people are, and how little
they would part with any thing they think
their own, it can be no difficult task to
make the multitude fall in with these notions, who can't make a difference between
the possessions of private persons, where
the same law governs all, and those of sovereign states and kingdoms, that are only accountable to GOD. *Gibraltar* is in
Spain, as much as *Portsmouth* is in *Great
Britain*, and whoever may prove a better
title to it than the *Spaniards*, none are fitter in the *Quadruple Alliance* to be possess'd
of it, and give less umbrage to the neigh-
bouring powers. If these criticks on the
publick management were in earnest, and
really animated by the love of their country, they would never publickly exagge-
rate the great moment that place is of,
and how vastly advantageous it would be
to *Great Britain* on many accounts, in case

of

of a rupture with her allies; but confider, that every article prov'd on this head is an argument put in the mouths of the allies for the unreafonablenefs of our keeping it.

GREAT caufes of difquiet may likewife be avoided, by forbearing to meddle with what is above, or at leaft foreign to us; it is ill manners for fubjects to pry into the family affairs of their kings; their paftimes, their pleafures and diverfions, have nothing to do with the ftate; but is it religion that awakens our care? then why are we infincere? We rail at concubines in one prince, who is very moderate in his amours; in him the want of chaftity is a heinous fin, it eclipfes all his good qualities, and is a fubject we can never have done with; when at the fame time we extol the good fenfe, the politenefs, the majefty, and are always lavifh in the praifes on the memory, without ever mentioning as a reproach the incontinency of another prince, whofe life was an entire fcene of unlawful love, and rambling lafcivioufnefs at a vaft expence, difplay'd on a multitude of objects.

WHEN

WHEN we have put the be/t con/tructi-
on on things, they will admit of, and /till
meet with grievances that are real, and
which every rea/onable man would wi/h
to have redre/s'd, there is a happine/s in
endeavouring to extenuate rather than aggravate them. Are we angry, that the
king is advis'd by /o many /trangers, that
his mini/try engro/s him to them/elves,
and that none of our friends can get into
places of tru/t or profit, let us examine
our /elves,   and con/ider how much we
/hould value /uch complaints in our ad-
ver/aries, if we were in favour, and the
king made u/e of us. We /hould not forget what we an/wered to them a con/ide-
rable part of the la/t reign: it is very
hard every private per/on may order
his family as he plea/es, without being controul'd, and the King of *Great
Britain* /hould not have the liberty of chu-
/ing his own /ervants. I will ea/ily grant,
that it is not plea/ant to a nation, to /ee
much wealth divided among foreigners,
but we have this comfort, that they can
only be /o for them/elves ; their po/terity
will be the /ame with ours. Mo/t of our
                                       fore-

forefathers were once ftrangers, but the firft children, they begot here, were *Engliſh*. When courtiers, that are foreigners, enrich themſelves with our money, their heirs ſpend it among us, and the ſons often with the ſame application, that the fathers ſcrap'd it together.

But ſhould this be a real cauſe of complaint, thoſe, who have no ambition to be great, honeſt men, who ſcorn to be beholden to any thing but their own induſtry for a livelihood, and all that can neither cringe, nor beg for a maintenance, having nothing to do with it. They are only courtiers, or ſuch as would be ſo, that can be affected by it. In behalf of them, let us caſt an eye on the remedy they preſcribe, and which ſo many of us hanker after in fear and ſilence, I mean the *Pretender*. It is manifeſt at firſt view, that this cannot eaſe us: for if we cannot bear the king's gratifying a few of his countrymen, how ſhould we have patience, or be able to diſcharge all the obligations the *Pretender* has made in ſo many countries? what papiſt in *Europe* is he not indebted to? I don't mean for their

pray-

prayers and hearty wifhes only: he has receiv'd fubftantial benefits from *French-men, Spaniards, Italians,* and others, and whenever he is able to beftow any favours, great part of *Poland* muft come in for a fhare.

THESE confiderations I know would be of little weight with many: what if our purfes pay for it they would fay, our confciences fhall be eas'd; indefeafible, hereditary right fhall take place: tell us but, what we fhall do to get him. Here indeed is the difficulty. To obtain this mighty bleffing, we muft in the firft place break the oath of allegiance, which we have taken to the king. But zealous people will not fcruple to forfwear themfelves for confcience fake, and if it be a fin, there are clergymen enough in *England,* that will abfolve them of it, even before it is committed. In the fecond we muft raife a rebellion and fight for him; the *Qua-druple Alliance* feems not very favourable for fuch attempts; and if the *Pretender* could find a foreign force to bring him hither, there is lefs doubt that king GEORGE on the other hand would have allies to

affift

affift him, who would always augment
their forces, as the friends of the *Pretender* encreas'd. What havock would this
make of the kingdom, and when would
our mifery be at an end? Can we imagine that either his majefty, or the prince,
on any difafter, would leave us as the *Pretender* left *Scotland?* They are neither of
them counted cowards as ever I heard of,
and we have no reafon to think either of
them very changeable, when they are fix'd
upon a thing.

MANY years might we fight for nothing but dry blows; for the probability
of conqueft is not on the *Pretender's* fide,
and if his friends were much more numerous, and their power greater than they
are, his cafe would be at beft but very
hazardous. But what fhall we venture all
this for? What is the end the malecontents propofe of their labours? and what
the mighty prize to be obtain'd? The
Pretender, whofe birth is at beft but dubious, a popifh bigot, who never was acquainted with men that underftood, or da-
red to fpeak of liberty, and has converfed
from his cradle with the groffeft flatterers,

and

and the moſt ſlaviſh aſſertors of arbitrary power. What a ſcope is here for declamation! but the cauſe I plead for ſtands in need of no rhetorick, or any other imbelliſhment. We want to be happy, and our felicity is to depend upon the wiſdom of our choice: the queſtion is, whether we ſhall be contented with the preſent eſtabliſhment, and the bleſſings, which it is in our power to enjoy under it in peace and tranquillity, or renounce both to go in queſt of an eutopia to be look'd for in a revolution, that in all human probability will never be brought about, and of which the very attempt, whether the thing it ſelf be compaſs'd or not, cannot coſt leſs, if made with any vigor or reſolution, than the ruin of at leaſt half the nation.

LET us compare all the petty grievances and apprehenſions, both real and imaginary, the ſevereſt ſtate-critick can pretend the nation to labour under, to the certain and ſubſtantial calamities, that ever muſt attend national diſcord and civil wars, and after that I leave any rational creature to judge, which of the two is moſt eligible.

I ſhall

I shall only exclude those of desperate fortunes and no principles, that have no substance, or any prospect of getting, but when every body loses, by publick troubles and intestine broils: for I have not patience to hear a bravo, who is ready to go upon the high way, complain of the church's danger; or a villain, who would be a false evidence for half a crown tell us on the least disaster, that the land can expect no blessing till the right heir is restor'd again.

WHEN we shall have carefully examin'd the state of our affairs, and so far conquer'd our prejudices as not to suffer our selves to be deluded any longer by false appearances, the prospect of happiness will be before us. To expect ministries without faults, and courts without vices, is grosly betraying our ignorance of human affairs. Nothing under the sun is perfect: human life it self is a mixture of good and evil: no mortal can be compleatly happy, and none are so miserable, but they might still be worse. There is happiness in knowing the narrow bounds of temporal felicity, and the surest way to content

is

is to moderate our desires. Where schism divides the people, the heats of parties must be troublesome, and the government will ever find it a difficult task to keep them quiet; but even schism [a] has its uses, and orthodoxy it self is not without inconveniencies: but what madness is it, that men should chuse to be wretched, because they cannot be compleatly happy!

THAT we cannot agree in one thing, ought not to be a reason to make us dif-

[a] *The clergy of* **England,** *by being severe upon the* **Schismaticks,** *and upbraiding them with want of learning, have rais'd themselves such formidable enemies as are not easily answer'd; and again, the dissenters by prying into the lives, and diligently watching all the actions of their powerful antagonists, render those of the established church more cautious of giving offence, than in all probability they would be, if they had no malicious overlookers to fear. It is very much owing to the great number of* **Hugonots,** *that have always been in* **France,** *till the late extirpation of them, that that kingdom has a less dissolute, and more learned clergy to boast of, than any* **Roman** *catholick country. The clergy of that church are no where more sovereign than in* **Italy,** *and therefore no where more debauch'd; nor any where more ignorant than they are in* **Spain,** *because their doctrine is no where less oppos'd.* **Fable of the Bees.** *p. 63.*

fer

fer in every thing elfe. Where the government is fteddy, the clergy of all communions kept in awe, and religious difputes are prohibited, many fects may live together in good harmony. When men who have perfecuted others come to labour under the fame affliction, they find it true what monfieur *Baile* [a] fays of arguments for perfecution, and in fome places in *Germany*, people of different religions make ufe of the fame churches without quarrelling; but where the magiftrate is remifs in curbing the licentioufnefs of divines, the leaft differences in religion may be the caufe of endlefs troubles. Of this *Hamburg*, the moft confiderable of all the *Hans* towns, is a deplorable inftance: that great and opulent city has been tore by divifions, and perplex'd with tumults and infurrections, for many years, fuftain'd vaft loffes

[a] *He compares them to the invention of bombs and carcaffes, and all kind of machines of war. Thofe that make ufe of them firft draw great advantages from them, and whilft they are the ftrongeft things go very well with them; but when they are the weakeft they are deftroy'd by their own inventions.* Dictionar. in the article Beza.

M m   and

and other calamities, and at this day labours ſtill under the miſery of civil diſcord, which are altogether owing to, and
never had any other cauſe than the un-
bridled zeal of furious preachers.

THERE will ever be perſecution whilſt
there are clergymen, and the laity will not
interpoſe, and take the means from them.
The ſword of juſtice, and the power of
puniſhing, ought never to be divided or
truſted into any other hands but the government's. I have hinted at this often,
but cannot help touching upon it again
in this place, ſince no nation can be happy,
where this maxim is not obſerv'd. All
magiſtrates in their ſuperiour wiſdom ſhould
be fathers to the publick, and the kindeſt
behaviour they can ſhew their ſubjects is,
what prudent perſons make uſe of to their
children. They never ſuffer them to handle any thing that might be hurtful to
themſelves or others : ſhould a child cry
for a knife, the father rather than indulg-
ing him would remove it farther out of
his way ; and ſhould he be more than ordinary froward, and by his bawling diſturb the family as well as himſelf, the o-
ther

ther would think it to be his duty to make him hold his tongue. Clergymen may be overcome by human paſſion, be violent, and rave, whilſt their zeal is hot, but as ſoon as they are cool again, if they have any goodneſs in them, they'll thank us, that we have hindred them from doing miſchief to others, and themſelves too.

THE laity ſhould be ever upon their guard againſt arguments for perſecution : the clergy look upon the bible as their own, and there is hardly a text in it, which moſt divines cannot diſcover a meaning in for their purpoſe. We find in *Geneſis,* that *Sarah* quarrell'd with *Hagar,* and made her leave the houſe, who would think, that this ever ſhould have been made a type of orthodoxy and ſchiſm, and be alledg'd as an apology for perſecution? yet the copious and imaginative mind of St. *Auguſtin* found this ſecret in it. He [a] maintain'd, by *Sarah*'s conduct towards *Hagar,* that the true church might inſlict chaſtiſements on the falſe one, exile it, torment it, *&c.* But what-

[a] *See* Baile's *Dictionary in the Article* Agar.

ever is quoted from the Old Teſtament, we may be aſſured from the New, that if it be capable of deſtroying charity and the publick peace, it can never be rightly apply'd; and the laity that have ſuffer'd by civil wars, on religious accounts, may meet with a better text for their purpoſe in the prophet [a] *Hoſea*, than any the clergy can alledge for diſcord or perſecution.

IF we are in love with true religion, let every one endeavour to ſubdue his paſſions for the love of GOD, and diligently labour at the amendment of his own life, and never attack others on that ſcore before he has made a conqueſt of himſelf. Whilſt we are neglectful of our own ſouls, we ought ever to ſuſpect our zeal to convert others. *Few men*, ſays a noble [b] author, *are ſo ignorant of human nature, and what they hold in common with their kind as not to comprehend, that where great vehemence is expreſs'd by any one in what relates ſolely to another, 'tis ſeldom without ſome private intereſt of his own.*

[a] Hoſea, *chap.* vi. v. 9.
[b] *Lord* Shaftsb. Charcteriſt.

BUT.

BUT when a man, neglecting all common civilities, shews himself on all accounts spiteful and vexatious to his neighbours, when he hires the mob to break his windows, and rejoice at every misfortune that befals him, how can we believe him sincere, when he pretends to have a very great concern, and nothing more at heart than his eternal welfare? What can be more impious to GOD, or base to men, than to profess religious motives for what we plainly feel our selves prompted to by envy, self-interest, hatred and aversion?

TO promote real goodness, and be a happy nation every subject ought to assist the magistrate in endeavouring to suppress vice and immorality, and be chiefly follicitous to discourage them by his own example; and as on the one hand the audaciousness of fiery pulpiteers should be restrain'd, so on the other, all scurrilous jests and witticisms, that can any ways tend to depreciate the holy function of divines, and render it less beneficial to us, should be prohibited under penalties; and here I would include all who dissent from us,

us, as well as the orthodox. First to tolerate, and afterwards to fcoff at a religion, is affronting GOD either the one way
or the other: religion, and whatever is
facred, can never become the proper objects of ridicule.

PROPHANENESS and irreligion above
all fhould be feverely punifhed, and the
moft fublime wit, if prophane, fhould never be preferr'd in the ftate, much lefs in
the church, in any part of the king's dominions. Thefe are the fureft ways to
promote peace and happinefs, at leaft a-
mong the laity; if divines will continue
their difputes, let us not fuffer our felves
to be drawn into their quarrels, with this
affurance, that whoever is guided by a
true chriftian fpirit, will ever prefer an
ounce of peace to a pound of victory.

WHEN we have left off all religious debates, and conquer'd the over-officious concern we have for other mens confciences,
it would be another happinefs, if we could
cure our felves of a piece of pride, which
is often the occafion of a vaft deal of
folly. Some men only belong to a party,
becaufe they would look upon themfelves

as

as inconfiderable without it; it furnifhes
them indeed with frequent opportunities
of fhewing their wit, honour, fteddinefs,
intelligence, and reading, which they know
not where to look for any where elfe;
but then often it caufes them a thoufand
difquiets for nothing: an argument begun
in jeft, if warmly maintain'd, becomes
earneft, and trifling difputes daily produce
fubftantial enmities. I could excufe a man,
who chufes a fide, and ftands up for it
with obftinacy to oblige his cuftomers, his
relations, or a friend, whom he has fome
expectation from; but it is unpardonable,
that a man fhould be ferious and vehe-
ment to maintain a caufe, which in the
firft place he is confcious he knows nothing of, in the fecond is fure he never
can, or fo much as propofes to get any
thing by, in behalf of others, whom he
never was acquainted with, and often never
faw or heard fpoke of, but with the utmoft partiality, and fuch as defpife him,
and would not dirty their fhoes to fave
him from hanging, unlefs they were paid
for it. Could we leave ftatefmen to fight
their own battles, and prove their own
vir-

virtues and good qualities, abundance of mifchief might be prevented. Men have had their heads broke for defending the honefty of a courtier, who at the fame time was a-bed with another man's wife, or bribing, over a bottle of *Champaign,* another minifter who was to audit his accompts.

THE laſt I ſhall ſpeak of, as a thing, defirable for our happineſs, is to have both the will and capacity of diſtinguiſhing between the evils that befal us from the faults of others, and thoſe we ſuffer on the ſcore of our own. Some are beggar'd by cards or dice ; ſome by cocks or horſes ; the ſubſtance of others is melted away in wine and debauchery: the ſpendthrift is undone at *Bath,* the miſer in *Change-Alley,* and many, not remarkably vicious, that yet for want of application to buſineſs, and following it with that induſtry and vigilance their callings require, can never thrive in the world, are ruin'd by ſloth, ſupineneſs or indolence. Theſe are generally the men who complain moſt of mifmanagements in publick affairs, and by their conſtant murmurs againſt miniſtries

ſtries and governments, keep off the cha-
green they would feel, ſhould they reflect
on the real cauſe of their misfortunes. If
theſe were ſet aſide, the nation would
be eas'd of a vaſt multitude of complaints.

From what has been ſaid, it is manifeſt, that on the one hand the greateſt
part of our complaints are frivolous and
unreaſonable ; that on the other, for grievances more real, we have remedies of
great efficacy, if we would make uſe of
them , and conſequently, that it is our
own faults, if, in the fruition of ſo many
native bleſſings, we enjoy not as much happineſs as the condition of mortals is ſuſ-
ceptible of.

N n   THE

THE
INDEX.

A.

Au-

Calvin

C.

When

P 4   *over-*

Mul-

Oro-

Plato,

O o 2   rea-

Re-

Will,

F I N I S.

CPSIA information can be obtained
at www.ICGtesting.com
Printed in the USA
BVHW010848290720
584937BV00014B/336